WITHDRAWAL

Fitness Information for Teens

TEEN HEALTH SERIES

First Edition

Fitness Information for Teens

Health Tips about Exercise, Physical Well-Being, and Health Maintenance

Including Facts about Aerobic and Anaerobic Conditioning, Stretching, Body Shape and Body Image, Sports Training, Nutrition, and Activities for Non-Athletes

Edited by Karen Bellenir

615 Griswold Street • Detroit, MI 48226

Bibliographic Note

Because this page cannot legibly accommodate all the copyright notices, the Bibliographic Note portion of the Preface constitutes an extension of the copyright notice.

Edited by Karen Bellenir

Teen Health Series

Karen Bellenir, Managing Editor
David A. Cooke, M.D., Medical Consultant
Elizabeth Barbour, Permissions Associate
Dawn Matthews, Verification Assistant
Laura Pleva Nielsen, Index Editor
EdIndex, Services for Publishers, Indexers

* * *

Omnigraphics, Inc.

Matthew P. Barbour, Senior Vice President
Kay Gill, Vice President—Directories
Kevin Hayes, Operations Manager
Leif Gruenberg, Development Manager
David P. Bianco, Marketing Director

* * *

Peter E. Ruffner, Publisher

Frederick G. Ruffner, Jr., Chairman

Copyright © 2004 Omnigraphics, Inc.

ISBN 0-7808-0679-4

Library of Congress Cataloging-in-Publication Data

Fitness information for teens : health tips about exercise, physical
well-being, and health maintenance including facts about aerobic and
anaerobic conditioning, stretching, body shape and body image, sports
training, nutrition, and activities for non-athletes / edited by Karen
Bellenir.
     p. cm. -- (Teen health series)
  Includes bibliographical references and index.
  ISBN 0-7808-0679-4 (hbk. : alk. paper)
  1. Teenagers--Health and hygiene. 2. Exercise. 3. Physical fitness for
children. I. Bellenir, Karen. II. Series.
  RA777.F55 2004
  613.7'043--dc22

                                                        2004005445

Printed in the United States

Table of Contents

Part III: Activities To Try

Part IV: Maintaining Health and Fitness

Part V: Avoiding Fitness Busters

Part VI: Resources for Additional Help and Information

Preface

About This Book

Fitness affects how a teen looks, feels, and performs—both physically and mentally. It impacts school work, job opportunities, and social activities. Fitness may also help prevent the development of disorders such as diabetes, high blood pressure, heart disease, osteoporosis, stroke, and some forms of cancer. Yet, according to the President's Council on Physical Fitness and Sports, adolescence itself is a risk factor for physical inactivity—a major contributor to poor fitness. During the teen years, opportunities for participation in organized sports decrease and fewer hours are spent in physical education classes. Additionally, teens walk less once they start driving, and activities like watching television, listening to music, playing video games, and online computing can lead to the development of a sedentary lifestyle. The habits teens adopt are likely to stay with them into adulthood.

Fitness Information For Teens helps teens understand the importance of fitness, discover ways to become more physically active, and take charge of health-related choices. It offers facts about the importance of fitness and explains how to start or continue a fitness program. Basic exercises are described, and essential information about a variety of fun activities to try—for both athletes and non-athletes—is included. The role of proper nutrition, mental health, and sleep habits in maintaining health and fitness is explained, and a special section provides tips for overcoming barriers to achieving fitness goals. A directory of resources and suggestions for additional reading provide guidance to students seeking more information.

How To Use This Book

This book is divided into parts and chapters. Parts focus on broad areas of interest; chapters are devoted to single topics within a part.

Part I: Before You Get Started provides information for teens thinking about starting a fitness program. It discusses the importance of fitness, outlines realistic expectations, and offers tips for evaluating fitness instructors, exercise equipment, and athletic shoes.

Part II: Fitness Fundamentals includes basic information about body mechanics, exercise requirements, and specific exercises for overall fitness. It provides guidelines for personal exercise programs, dispels common exercise myths, explains how to measure exercise intensity, and discusses the interrelationship between exercise and weight control.

Part III: Activities To Try features a wide sampling of individual hobbies, team sports, and recreational activities for both athletes and non-athletes. Individual chapters for each activity include basic information, such as how to participate, needed equipment, skills to be developed, and how the activity fits into a lifestyle focused on fitness.

Part IV: Maintaining Health and Fitness provides facts about how to stay healthy by paying attention to other essential components of overall fitness, including nutrition, hydration, mental health, sleep, and locker room hygiene.

Part V: Avoiding Fitness Busters discusses some of the most common physical and mental barriers to achieving fitness goals, including lack of motivation, boredom, weather, and substance abuse. Unexpected negative consequences of fitness efforts gone awry are also discussed, including inappropriate exercises, muscle soreness, injuries, compulsive exercise, and the female athlete triad (a life-threatening combination of amenorrhea, osteoporosis, and disordered eating).

Part VI: Resources for Additional Help and Information provides information about the President's Challenge Sports Awards, a directory of fitness organizations, and a list of suggested reading for further information.

Bibliographic Note

This volume contains documents and excerpts from publications issued by the following government agencies: BAM! (Body and Mind), a program of the Centers for Disease Control and Prevention (CDC); National Bone Health Campaign™; National Institute of Diabetes and Digestive and Kidney Diseases; National Women's Health Information Center; President's Council on Physical Fitness and Sports; U.S. Department of Agriculture; U.S. Department of Education; and the U.S. Department of Health and Human Services.

In addition, this volume contains copyrighted documents and articles produced by the following organizations: American Academy of Family Physicians; American Academy of Orthopaedic Surgeons; American Council on Exercise; American Heart Association; American Orthopaedic Foot and Ankle Society; American Podiatric Medical Association; American Psychological Association; Aquatic Exercise Association; Child and Youth Health (South Australia); B. Don Franks, PhD; Genesis Behavioral Health; George Mason University; Marjie Gilliam; IDEA Health and Fitness Association, Inc.; iEmily.com; International Food Informational Council Foundation; National Association for Fitness Certification; National Center for Drug Free Sport, Inc.; National Sleep Foundation; Nemours Center for Children's Health Media, a division of The Nemours Foundation; *Physician and Sportsmedicine* (McGraw-Hill Companies); President's Challenge; Shape Up America!; and the Women's Sports Foundation.

Full citation information is provided on the first page of each chapter. Every effort has been made to secure all necessary rights to reprint the copyrighted material. If any omissions have been made, please contact Omnigraphics to make corrections for future editions.

Acknowledgements

In addition to the organizations, agencies, and individuals listed above, special thanks go to many others who have worked hard to help bring this book to fruition. They include editorial assistants Michael Bellenir and Amanda Devitt, permissions associate Liz Barbour, and indexer Edward J. Prucha.

Note From The Editor

This book is part of Omnigraphics' *Teen Health Series*. The *Series* provides basic information about a broad range of medical concerns. It is not intended to serve as a tool for diagnosing illness, in prescribing treatments, or as a substitute for the physician/patient relationship. All persons concerned about medical symptoms or the possibility of disease are encouraged to seek professional care from an appropriate health care provider.

At the request of librarians serving today's young adults, the *Teen Health Series* was developed as a specially focused set of volumes within *Omnigraphics' Health Reference Series*. Each volume deals comprehensively with a topic selected according to the needs and interests of people in middle school and high school. If there is a topic you would like to see addressed in a future volume of the *Teen Health Series*, please write to:

Editor
Teen Health Series
Omnigraphics, Inc.
615 Griswold Street
Detroit, MI 48226

Our Advisory Board

The *Teen Health Series* is reviewed by an Advisory Board comprised of librarians from public, academic, and medical libraries. We would like to thank the following board members for providing guidance to the development of this *Series*:

Dr. Lynda Baker, Associate Professor of Library and Information Science, Wayne State University, Detroit, MI

Nancy Bulgarelli, William Beaumont Hospital Library, Royal Oak, MI

Karen Imarisio, Bloomfield Township Public Library, Bloomfield Township, MI

Karen Morgan, Mardigian Library, University of Michigan-Dearborn, Dearborn, MI

Rosemary Orlando, St. Clair Shores Public Library, St. Clair Shores, MI

Medical Consultant

Medical consultation services are provided to the *Teen Health Series* editors by David A. Cooke, M.D. Dr. Cooke is a graduate of Brandeis University, and he received his M.D. degree from the University of Michigan. He completed residency training at the University of Wisconsin Hospital and Clinics. He is board-certified in internal medicine. Dr. Cooke currently works as part of the University of Michigan Health System and practices in Brighton, MI. In his free time, he enjoys writing, science fiction, and spending time with his family.

Part 1

Before You Get Started

Chapter 1

A Teenager's Guide To Better Health

As a teenager, you are going through a lot of changes. Your body is changing and growing. Have you noticed that every year, you can't seem to fit into your old shoes anymore? Or that your favorite jeans are now tighter or 3 inches too short? Your body is on its way to becoming its adult size.

Along with your physical changes, you are also becoming more independent. You are starting to make more choices about your life. You are relying less on your parents and more on yourself and your friends when making decisions. Some of the biggest choices that you face are those about your health.

Why should you care about your health? Well, there are lots of reasons—like feeling good, looking good, and getting stronger. Doing well in school, work, or other activities (like sports) is another reason. Believe it or not, these can all be affected by your health.

Healthy eating and being active now may also help prevent diabetes, high blood pressure, heart disease, osteoporosis, stroke, and some forms of cancer when you are older.

Some teenagers are not very physically active and some do not get the foods that their growing bodies need.

About This Chapter: Text in this chapter is excerpted from "Take Charge of Your Health: A Teenager's Guide to Better Health," National Institute of Diabetes and Digestive and Kidney Diseases, NIH Pub. No. 01–4328, December 2001.

Now is the time to take charge of your health by eating better and being more physically active. Even small changes will help you look and feel your best.

Family Matters

Even if health problems run in your family, it doesn't mean that you will have the same problems.

To learn more about your health, start by looking at your family.

Are your parents, brothers, or sisters overweight? Do any of them have health problems related to their weight, such as type 2 diabetes? Your family's gene pool, eating habits, and activities can all play a role in your health and the way you look.

Type 2 diabetes is increasing in adolescents and teenagers who are overweight. Diabetes means that blood glucose (blood sugar) is too high. Diabetes is serious. It can hurt your eyes, kidneys, heart and blood vessels, gums, and teeth.

> **♣ It's A Fact!!**
>
> Exercise is good for your health—a lesson learned from the ancients—but the recommendations for achieving such benefits went through a significant transition in the closing decades of the twentieth century. Most particularly, there was a shift away from the importance of developing cardiovascular (aerobic) physical fitness and toward the promotion of life-long physical activity. This change resulted from an understanding that the biological mechanisms linking exercise to health are not simply related to achieving high cardiovascular function but also in increasing caloric expenditure, weight-bearing activities, and muscle strength.
>
> Source: Excerpted from "Adolescence: A 'Risk Factor' for Physical Inactivity, *Research Digest*, President's Council on Physical Fitness and Sports, June 1999.

Even if members of your family have type 2 diabetes or other health problems, it doesn't mean that you will have the same problems. To lower your chances of developing them, eat healthy foods, get moving, and talk to your family or health care provider if you are concerned about your weight or health.

So, Where Do I Start?

The road to better health starts with good eating and physical activity habits. Being aware of your habits will help you learn where you need to make changes.

Do you normally watch a lot of TV or play a lot of video games? These activities can be relaxing, but you don't need to move much to do them. Spending too much time not moving around can make you feel tired and lazy, and lead to poor muscle tone. You can be active every day and still have time to do other things you enjoy, like playing video games.

Physical Activity—It Doesn't Have To Be A Chore

Being active means moving more every day. You can choose activities that are fun and do them on your own or with your friends.

Being more active will make you feel better and give you more energy. It can also help you think and concentrate better, which will help you in school or at work. Activity can help you feel less bored and depressed, and help you handle stress.

So don't wait—start today. Begin slowly and make small changes in your daily routine, like

- spending less time in front of the TV

- taking the stairs instead of the elevator

- walking to school instead of taking the bus (or if you drive, parking further away on the school parking lot).

What you choose to do is up to you. Just pick something that you like to do and keep it up. Have fun while being active each day to stay healthy and fit. Remember, you don't have to give up the video games—just make sure that you also fit activity into your day.

Get Moving

- Walk—to school, to work, to your friend's house, to the mall

- Ride your bike

♣ It's A Fact!!

The daily caloric expenditure (relative to body size) of an 18-year old is approximately half that of when he/she was 6 years old. During the school-age years, daily physical activity decreases at a rate of about 2.7% per year in males and 7.4% per year in females.

Source: Excerpted from "Adolescence: A 'Risk Factor' for Physical Inactivity, *Research Digest*, President's Council on Physical Fitness and Sports, June 1999.

- Skateboard

- Rollerblade

- Walk with a friend or family member—make it "quality time"

- Play basketball

- Join a school sports team or club

- Walk the family dog. If you don't have one, find a neighbor who does

- Go dancing

- Go for a hike

- Go for a swim

- Wash the car

- Clean the house

- Mow the lawn

(OK, the last three aren't fun, but your parents will appreciate you doing them.)

You Are What You Eat

Take a look at your eating habits. What you eat, where you eat, and why you eat are important to your health. As a teen, you need to eat a variety of foods that give you the nutrients your growing body needs. Eating better and being more active can make you feel better and think more clearly.

♣ **It's A Fact!!**

The motivation for physical activity for the typical adolescent, no longer a biological issue, is shaped by factors that involve peer acceptance, physical capabilities, sexual attractiveness, and self-concept. For the talented high school athlete, sports play satisfies these issues. But for the non-athletic teenager, physical activity may be the antithesis of these goals, which are met by "hanging out", rebelling from adult forms, and adopting strange dress or hair styles. For many teenagers, vigorous physical activity is simply not "cool."

These social barriers to regular physical activity are compounded by the growing need for independence with rejection of adult-oriented health goals. The adolescent becomes old enough to drive, has more money and access to fast foods, and increases exposure to cigarette smoking and drugs. All these factors combine to make regular physical activity and other healthy lifestyles unattractive options for many adolescents.

Source: Excerpted from "Adolescence: A 'Risk Factor' for Physical Inactivity, *Research Digest*, President's Council on Physical Fitness and Sports, June 1999.

What Do You Eat?

If you eat a lot of burgers and fries or pizza loaded with toppings—plus an extra helping of dessert—your diet is probably not balanced.

There's nothing wrong with eating these foods—you just need to eat smaller amounts and balance them with other foods.

Where Do You Usually Eat?

If you eat in places such as your room or in front of the TV, you may want to change that habit. Eating while doing other things makes it easy to lose track of how much you've already eaten.

By eating meals and snacks at a table, you can pay more attention to what you're eating so that you don't overeat.

(If you want to snack while watching TV, take a small amount of food with you—such as a handful of pretzels or a couple of cookies—not the whole bag.)

Why Do You Eat?

To see if you need to change your eating habits, let's look at why you eat. For most people, reasons to eat are: time of day; hunger; food looks tempting; everyone else is eating; and boredom, frustration, nervousness, or sadness.

The best reason to eat is because your body tells you that you are hungry. If you are eating when you are not hungry, try doing something else to get food off of your mind. Call a friend, exercise, read, or work on a craft. These activities can help you to cut back on eating when you are feeling bored, upset, or stressed. (For more information about the relationship between nutrition and fitness, see Chapters 36 and 37.)

Tips For Keeping Weight Under Control

- Get moving. Activity can make you stronger and more flexible.

- Eat healthy every day. Choose fruits, vegetables, breads, cereals, lean meat, poultry, fish, dry beans, and lowfat or nonfat milk and cheeses.

- Eat slowly. You will be able to tell when you are full before you eat too much.

- Eat less fats, oils, and sweets. Butter, margarine, oils, candy, high-fat salad dressings, and soft drinks offer little or no protein, vitamins, or minerals.

- Eat when you are hungry. Your body will tell you when it's hungry. Snacking is OK, but try to go for a variety of nutritious snacks.

Staying Healthy And Happy

Being a teenager can be tough, and sometimes teens who are healthy try to lose weight even though they don't need to. You may feel a lot of pressure to look a certain way. Acting on this pressure may lead to eating disorders like anorexia nervosa or bulimia nervosa.

Anorexia nervosa is a form of self-starvation where a person does not eat enough food to keep healthy and does not maintain a healthy weight.

Bulimia nervosa is when a person eats a lot of food and then vomits or uses other methods, such as fasting or over-exercising, to avoid gaining weight after overeating.

If you are concerned about your eating habits or the way you look, it's important to talk to someone you trust. Try talking to a parent, friend, doctor, teacher, or counselor at your school.

Being happy with who you are and what you look like is important for a healthy body and mind. You don't have to be an athlete, supermodel, or movie star to like who you are and to stay fit and healthy.

☞ **Remember!!**

You can take charge of your health by making small changes in your eating and physical activity habits. These changes will help you feel and look better now and be healthier for the rest of your life.

Chapter 2

Why Get Fit?

You've probably heard about how fitness can help you live longer and prevent diseases like heart disease in your future. But what can physical fitness do for you right now? A whole lot! Most of all, getting fit can and should be fun. Physical fitness involves 3 main components: strength, stamina, and flexibility. If you train properly, you'll get all the benefits including:

Increased Strength

When you are fit, you are more able to generate force with your body—whether that force is needed to lift weights or your book bag or your little brother. Being strong is useful for all sports as well as for life in general. Life is full of effort. Being strong all around makes everything a little easier, and it is a critical component of team and individual exercise activities.

Increased Stamina And More Energy Overall

Physical fitness training increases your stamina—your ability to keep going during moderate or strenuous activity. Stamina is also known as endurance.

About This Chapter: This chapter includes excerpts from "Fit for Life," prepared by the National Women's Health Information Center, a project of the Office on Women's Health in the U.S. Department of Health and Human Services, updated July 2002, and excerpts from "Promoting Better Health for Young People through Physical Activity and Sports," a report to the President from the Secretary of Health and Human Services and the Secretary of Education, 2000.

Your heart and lungs are able to work longer the more fit you are. You can run farther, dance longer, and keep on playing well past sundown when you have good stamina. Exercise gives you more energy in general to do things you want to do.

Increased Flexibility

Flexibility refers to your range of motion around a joint. Touching your toes, reaching a high shelf, and arching your back gracefully are all examples of flexibility. Flexibility is very important to daily life, as well as to mastering the techniques of most sports activities. Many adults lose their flexibility as they grow older. Being flexible when you are young and maintaining it through the years can help you prevent that decline.

Psychological Benefits, Including Better Sleep

Exercise is a fabulous way to feel better any day of the week. Is family or school stressing you out? A moderate workout can ease the tension and leave you with an all-over good feeling. That's because exercise releases endorphins, special chemicals in the brain that make you feel peaceful and relaxed. When you are fit, you are generally bet-

♣ **It's A Fact!!**
Despite the health problems associated with physical inactivity, only 25% of Americans are physically active at the recommended levels.

Source: President's Council on Physical Fitness and Sports, *Research Digest*, March 2003.

ter able to handle life's ups and downs too. You feel more self-confident and strong on the inside when you are strong on the outside. Regular exercise also helps you sleep better, which can really brighten your whole outlook each day.

Social Benefits

Participating in sports clubs, group exercise classes, or team sports can be a great way to meet new people and make friends with people with similar interests. If you're fit, your self-confidence will make you less shy.

Muscle-To-Fat Balance

Regular, moderate exercise is one of the healthiest ways to keep your muscle-to-fat ratio where it should be. While each person has their own unique shape and size, everyone benefits from having a good balance of muscle and fat. It is important to remember that too little or too much fat can be a serious problem, so it is important to maintain a moderate exercise program and a healthy diet to ensure you get all of the nutrients, vitamins, minerals, and fat that you need.

Promoting Better Health For Young People Through Physical Activity And Sports

America loves to think of itself as a youthful nation focused on fitness. But behind the vivid media images of robust runners, Olympic Dream Teams, and rugged mountain bikers is the troubling reality of a generation of young people that is, in large measure, inactive, unfit, and increasingly overweight.

The consequences of the sedentary lifestyles lived by so many of our young people are grave. In the long run, physical inactivity threatens to reverse the decades-long progress we have made in reducing death and suffering from cardiovascular diseases. A physically inactive population is at increased risk for many chronic diseases, including heart disease, stroke, colon cancer, diabetes, and osteoporosis. In addition to the toll taken by human suffering, surges in the prevalence of these diseases could lead to crippling increases in our national health care expenditures.

In the short run, physical inactivity has contributed to an unprecedented epidemic of childhood obesity that is currently plaguing the United States. The percentage of young people who are overweight has doubled since 1980. Of children aged 5 to 15 who are overweight, 61% have one or more cardiovascular disease risk factors, and 27% have two or more. The negative health consequences linked to the childhood obesity epidemic include the appearance in the past two decades of a new and frightening public health problem: type 2 diabetes among adolescents. Type 2 diabetes was previously so rarely seen in children or adolescents that it came to be called "adult-onset diabetes." Now, an increasing number of teenagers and preteens must be treated for diabetes and strive to ward off the life-threatening health complications that it can cause.

Obesity in adolescence also has been associated with poorer self-esteem and with obesity in adulthood. Among adults today, 25% of women and 20%

✔ Quick Tip
Are You Ready To Get Started?

If you are not already active, the process of getting fit means making changes in your lifestyle. Making changes requires motivation. Where you are in terms of motivational readiness can help point you toward where you should begin. Which of the following stages describes you?

Precontemplation. Individuals in the Precontemplation Stage are currently not active and are not thinking about becoming active. The goal for individuals in this stage is to help them begin thinking about becoming physically active and the role physical activity could have in their lives. At this stage, it is important to assess an individual's perception of the pros and cons of becoming physically active.

Contemplation. Individuals in the Contemplation Stage are not currently physically activity but are thinking about becoming active. The goal of this stage is to increase the individuals' likelihood that they will take steps to become physically active. Similar to individuals in the Precontemplation Stage, individuals in this stage should consider the pros and cons of physical activity. Additionally, individuals need specific information about starting a physical activity program and advice as to how to make physical activity a part of their daily lives.

Specific physical activity goals can next be made based on the physical activity plan. It is important that the goals be realistic given that unrealistic goals can lead to disappointment and frustration. The individual may discontinue a physical activity program if goals are set too high. The individuals should be reminded that it is important to start slowly and gradually increase physical activity over time.

Preparation. Individuals in the Preparation Stage are engaging in physical activity but not at the recommended levels. The goal for individuals in this stage is to increase their physical activity participation to the recommended levels. Individuals in this stage should develop a physical activity plan in which they engage in physical activity at the recommended levels.

of men are obese. The total costs of diseases associated with obesity have been estimated at almost $100 billion per year, or approximately 8% of the national health care budget.

The key to the Preparation Stage is overcoming the barriers that prevent the individual from progressing from some activity to physical activity participation at the recommended levels. For example, individuals may report that inclement weather interferes with their physical activity program. Individuals may participate in physical activity sporadically due to changes in weather conditions. This barrier can be overcome by developing a list of activities for when the weather prohibits physical activity outdoors (e.g., walking in the mall, exercise videos, walking stairs). Another factor that may influence regular physical activity is fatigue in that individuals may be less likely to engage in physical activity on days they feel fatigued. Individuals should be educated that physical activity may actually improve fatigue by increasing energy levels and improving quality of sleep. Similarly, mood variations may lead to irregular activity patterns. Research indicates that physical activity can improve mood and it is important that individuals consider this when skipping a physical activity session.

Goal setting can play an instrumental role in progressing the individual to the next stage of change. Individuals should be encouraged to set specific goals that are daily, weekly, and/or monthly goals and that gradually increase their physical activity to the recommended levels.

Action and Maintenance. Individuals in the Action Stage are physically active at the recommended levels but have been regularly active for less than six months. Individuals in the Maintenance Stage are physically active at the recommended levels and have been for six or more months. The goal for individuals in the Action and Maintenance Stages is to maintain their physical activity participation.

Source: Excerpted and adapted from "Physical Activity and The Stages of Motivational Readiness for Change Model," by Bess H. Marcus and Beth A. Lewis in *Research Digest*, President's Council on Fitness and Sports, March 2003.

Benefits Of Physical Activity

The landmark 1996 Surgeon General's report, *Physical Activity and Health*, identified substantial health benefits of regular participation in physical activity, including reducing the risks of dying prematurely; dying prematurely from heart disease; and developing diabetes, high blood pressure, or colon cancer. When physical inactivity is combined with poor diet, the impact on health is devastating, accounting for an estimated 300,000 deaths per year. Tobacco use is the only behavior that kills more people.

The Surgeon General's report made clear that the health benefits of physical activity are not limited to adults. Regular participation in physical activity during childhood and adolescence

- Helps build and maintain healthy bones, muscles, and joints.

- Helps control weight, build lean muscle, and reduce fat.

♣ **It's A Fact!!**

Because weight-bearing activity stimulates bone growth, regular exercise during the teen years should be expected to be important in decreasing the incidence and severity of adult osteoporosis.

Source: Excerpted from "Adolescence: A 'Risk Factor' for Physical Inactivity, *Research Digest*, President's Council on Physical Fitness and Sports, June 1999.

- Prevents or delays the development of high blood pressure and helps reduce blood pressure in some adolescents with hypertension.

- Reduces feelings of depression and anxiety.

Although research has not been conducted to conclusively demonstrate a direct link between physical activity and improved academic performance, such a link might be expected. Studies have found participation in physical activity increases adolescents' self-esteem and reduces anxiety and stress. Through its effects on mental health, physical activity may help increase students' capacity for learning. One study found that spending more time in physical education did not have harmful effects on the standardized academic achievement test scores of elementary school students; in fact, there was some evidence that participation in a 2-year health-related physical education program had several significant favorable effects on academic achievement.

Participation in physical activity and sports can promote social well-being, as well as physical and mental health, among young people. Research has shown that students who participate in interscholastic sports are less likely to be regular and heavy smokers or use drugs, and are more likely to stay in school and have good conduct and high academic achievement. Sports and physical activity programs can introduce young people to skills such as teamwork, self-discipline, sportsmanship, leadership, and socialization. Lack of recreational activity, on the other hand, may contribute to making young people more vulnerable to gangs, drugs, or violence.

Promoting Better Health For Young People

One of the major benefits of physical activity is that it helps people improve their physical fitness. Fitness is a state of well-being that allows people to perform daily activities with vigor, participate in a variety of physical activities, and reduce their risks for health problems. Five basic components of fitness are important for good health: cardiorespiratory endurance, muscular strength, muscular endurance, flexibility, and body composition (percentage of body fat). A second set of attributes, referred to as sport- or skill-related physical fitness, includes power, speed, agility, balance, and reaction time. Although skill-related fitness attributes are not essential for maintaining physical health, they are important for athletic performance or physically demanding jobs such as military service and emergency and rescue service.

How Much Physical Activity And Fitness Do Young People Need?

The Surgeon General's report on physical activity and health concluded that:

- People who are usually inactive can improve their health and well being by becoming even moderately active on a regular basis.

- Physical activity need not be strenuous to achieve health benefits.

- Greater health benefits can be achieved by increasing the amount (duration, frequency, or intensity) of physical activity.

Rigorous scientific reviews have led to two widely accepted sets of developmentally appropriate recommendations—one for adolescents, the other for elementary school-aged children—for how much and what kinds of physical activity young people need. The International Consensus Conference on Physical Activity Guidelines for Adolescents issued the following recommendations:

- All adolescents should be physically active daily, or nearly every day, as part of play, games, sports, work, transportation, recreation, physical education, or planned exercise, in the context of family, school, and community activities.

- Adolescents should engage in three or more sessions per week of activities that last 20 minutes or more at a time and that require moderate to vigorous levels of exertion.

The developmental needs and abilities of younger children differ from those of adolescents and adults. The National Association for Sport and Physical Education (NASPE) has issued physical activity guidelines for elementary school-aged children that recommend the following:

- Elementary school-aged children should accumulate at least 30 to 60 minutes of age-appropriate and developmentally appropriate physical activity from a variety of activities on all, or most, days of the week.

- An accumulation of more than 60 minutes, and up to several hours per day, of age-appropriate and developmentally appropriate activity is encouraged.

- Some of the child's activity each day should be in periods lasting 10 to 15 minutes or more and include moderate to vigorous activity. This activity will typically be intermittent in nature, involving alternating moderate to vigorous activity with brief periods of rest and recovery.

- Children should not have extended periods of inactivity.

Chapter 3

Why You Need A Sports Physical

You already know that playing sports helps keep you fit. You also know that sports are a fun way to socialize with your friends and meet people. But you might not know why the physical you may have to take at the beginning of your sports season is so important.

In the sports medicine field, the sports physical exam is known as a pre-participation physical examination (PPE). The exam helps determine whether it's safe for you to participate in a particular sport. Many states actually require that kids and teens have a sports physical before they can start a new sport or begin a new competitive season. But even if a PPE isn't required, doctors still highly recommend them.

What Is A Sports Physical?

There are two main parts to a sports physical: the medical history and the physical exam.

About This Chapter: "Sports Physicals," reviewed by Joseph A. Congeni, MD, FAAP, and Peter G. Gabos, MD, July 2003. This information was provided by TeensHealth, one of the largest resources online for medically reviewed health information written for parents, kids, and teens. For more articles like this one, visit www.TeensHealth.org, or www.KidsHealth.org. © 2003 The Nemours Center for Children's Health Media, a division of The Nemours Foundation.

Medical History

This part of the exam includes questions about:

- serious illnesses among other family members
- illnesses that you had when you were younger or may have now, such as asthma, diabetes, or epilepsy
- previous hospitalizations or surgeries
- allergies (to insect bites, for example)
- past injuries (including concussions, sprains, or bone fractures)
- whether you've ever passed out, felt dizzy, had chest pain, or had trouble breathing during exercise

> ### ✎ Weird Words
>
> Female Athlete Triad: A disorder that can afflict extremely active girls; it consists of three-parts: disordered eating, amenorrhea (an absence of menstrual periods), and osteoporosis (a weakening of the bones).
>
> Pre-Participation Physical Examination (PPE): A medical exam that helps determine whether it's safe for you to participate in a particular sport.

The medical history questions are usually on a form that you can bring home, so ask your parents to help you fill in the answers. If possible, ask both parents about family medical history.

Looking at patterns of illness in your family is a very good indicator of any potential conditions you may have. It's important that you answer any questions about medical history accurately and honestly—don't try to guess the answers. Most sports medicine doctors believe the medical history is the most important part of the sports physical exam, so you should take time to answer the questions carefully.

Physical Examination

During the physical part of the exam, the doctor will usually:

- record your height and weight
- take a blood pressure and pulse (heart rate and rhythm) reading
- test your vision

- check your heart, lungs, abdomen, ears, nose, and throat

- evaluate your posture, joints, strength, and flexibility

Although most aspects of the exam will be the same for males and females, if a person has started or already gone through puberty, the doctor may ask girls and guys different questions. For example, if a girl is heavily involved in a lot of active sports, the doctor may ask her about her period and diet to help her avoid such conditions as female athlete triad.

A doctor will also ask questions about a person's use of drugs, alcohol, or dietary supplements, including steroids or other "performance enhancers" and weight-loss supplements, because these can affect a person's health.

Some schools may require that a sports physical include an electrocardiogram, or EKG, for all kids. An EKG, which takes about 10 minutes, measures the electrical activity of a person's heart. EKGs don't hurt—electrodes that measure a person's heart rate and rhythm are placed on the chest, arms, and legs, and a specialist reads the results.

At the end of your exam, the doctor will either fill out and sign a form if everything checks out OK or, in some cases, recommend a follow-up exam, additional tests, or specific treatment for medical problems.

> ✔ **Quick Tip**
> Even if you have a sports physical at school, it's a good idea to see your regular doctor for an exam as well.

Why Is A Sports Physical Important?

A sports physical can help you find out about and deal with health problems that might interfere with your participation in a sport. For example, if you have frequent asthma attacks but are a starting forward in soccer, a doctor might be able to prescribe a different type of inhaler or adjust the dosage so that you can breathe more easily when you run.

Your doctor may even have some good training tips and be able to give you some ideas for avoiding injuries. For example, he or she may recommend specific exercises, like certain stretching or strengthening activities, that help prevent injuries. A doctor can also identify risk factors that are linked to specific sports. Advice like this will make you a better, stronger athlete.

When And Where Should I Go For A Sports Physical?

Some people go to their own doctor for a sports physical; others have one at school. During school physicals, you may go to half a dozen or so "stations" set up in the gym; each one is staffed by a medical professional who gives you a specific part of the physical exam.

It's convenient to get the exam done at school. But even if you have a sports physical at school, it's a good idea to see your regular doctor for an exam as well. Your doctor knows you—and your health history—better than anyone you talk to briefly in a gym.

If your state requires sports physicals, you'll probably have to start getting them when you're in ninth grade. Even if sports physicals aren't required by your school or state, it's still a good idea to begin these exams if you participate in school sports. If you will be competing regularly in a sport before ninth grade, however, you should begin getting these exams even earlier.

Getting a sports physical once a year is usually adequate. If you're healing from a major injury, like a broken wrist or ankle, however, get checked out after it's healed before you start practicing or playing again. You should have your physical about 6 weeks before your sports season begins so there's enough time to follow up on something, if necessary. Neither you nor your doctor will be very happy if you come into his or her office the day before baseball practice starts and then find out there's something that needs to be taken of care before you can suit up.

What If There's A Problem?

What happens if you don't get the OK from your own doctor and have to see a specialist? Does that mean you won't ever be able to letter in softball or hockey? Don't worry if your doctor asks you to have other tests or go for a follow-up exam—it could be something as simple as rechecking your blood pressure a week or two after the physical.

Your doctor's referral to a specialist may help your athletic performance. For example, if you want to try out for your school's track team but get a slight pain in your knee every time you run, an orthopedist or sports medicine specialist can help you figure out what's going on. Perhaps the pain comes from previous overtraining or poor running technique. Maybe you injured the knee a long time ago and it never totally healed. Or perhaps the problem is as simple as running shoes that don't offer enough support. Chances are, a doctor will be able to help you run without the risk of further injuring the knee by giving you suggestions or treatment before the sports season begins.

It's very unlikely that you'll be disqualified from playing sports. The ultimate goal of the sports physical is to ensure safe participation in sports, not to disqualify the participants. Most of the time, a specialist won't find anything serious enough to prevent you from playing your sport. In fact, fewer than 1% of kids have conditions that might limit sports participation, and most of these conditions are known before the examination takes place.

♣ **It's A Fact!!**
Fewer than 1% of kids have conditions that might limit sports participation.

Do I Still Have To Get A Regular Physical?

In a word, yes. It may seem like overkill, but a sports physical is different from a standard physical.

The sports physical focuses on your well-being as it relates to playing a sport. It's more limited than a regular physical, but it's a lot more specific about athletic issues. During a regular physical, however, your doctor will address your overall well-being, which may include things that are unrelated to sports. You can ask your doctor to give you both types of exams during one visit; just be aware that you'll need to set aside more time.

Even if your sports physical exam doesn't reveal any problems, it's always a good idea to monitor yourself when you play sports. If you notice changes in your physical condition—even if you think they're small, such as muscle pain or shortness of breath—be sure to mention them to a parent or coach. You should also inform your physical education teacher or coach if your health needs have changed in any way or if you're taking a new medication.

☞ **Remember!!**

Just as professional sports stars need medical care to keep them playing their best, so do teenage athletes. You can give yourself the same edge as the pros by making sure you have your sports physical.

Chapter 4

Heredity And Your Body Shape

When I was young, my dream was to become a dancer. I pictured myself on point, gracefully dancing with the Joffrey Ballet. Harsh reality set in when my body (and shoe size) continued growing past the acceptable height and weight for a prima ballerina whose partner could easily lift her into any amazing position. My dreams and goals were matched up with my body makeup when I discovered the sportier movement of group fitness and aerobics.

People decide to exercise for many reasons, but a common one is a desire to change the way they look. And although many factors contribute to how much exercise can change a person's looks, heredity is one of the most influential.

Everyone is born with a basic body type that cannot be changed. Body type is defined by fat distribution, muscle definition, fat-to-muscle ratio, limb length, and body shape. There are three "classic" body types: endomorph, mesomorph, and ectomorph.

Most people are a blend of these body types, but resemble one more than the others. Exercise will not change one type to another, but is will enhance the potential of each body type.

About This Chapter: "Heredity and Your Body Image," by Pam Germain. Reprinted with permission from The National Association for Fitness Certification (NAFC), Pam Germain, Director. © 2003 NAFC. All rights reserved. For additional information, visit www.body-basics.com.

Another genetic factor that affects what exercise will do for a particular body is the length of the muscle belly between the tendons. If the muscle belly is long and the tendons are short, a person looks more muscular than if the muscle is short and the attaching tendons are long. This in an important factor in the sport of body building. However, any person's muscles can become stronger and leaner with exercise.

Heredity also dictates the ratio of slow-twitch and fast-twitch fibers that make up muscles. Slow-twitch fibers are used for endurance activities. Slow-twitch muscle fibers don't fatigue fast and don't grow large. Marathon athletes have a larger percentage of the slow-twitch fibers.

Fast-twitch fibers, which are powerful and can grow very large, work best during short, intense effort. Strength and short distance athletes have muscles with a high percentage of fast-twitch fibers.

Since you have inherited your basic look, it is important to know your body before you try to change it. Analyze what your body type is, the length of your muscle belly, and whether you seem to have a higher percentage of fast-twitch or slow-twitch muscle fibers. A few questions that may help you decide:

• What is the basic shape of your silhouette?

✎ Weird Words

There are three "classic" body types:

Ectomorph: The ectomorph's body looks slender and frail, due to small bones, long arms and legs, a short trunk and small hips.

Endomorph: The endomorph has a round, soft, pear shaped body supported by small bones. The legs, arms and neck are short and heavy, the hips are broad, and the shoulders are narrow.

Mesomorph: Mesomorphs have a muscular, rectangular, or V-shaped outline, large bones, broad shoulders, and a long neck. They build muscle easily and look very athletic.

- Is it pear shaped (endomorph), V-shaped (mesomorph), or straight and narrow (ectomorph)?

- When you flex your biceps or calf muscles, do they bulge readily or is there a lot of room between your joints with a slight curve to the muscle?

- What activities are you better at—short, powerful bursts of energy or long extended duration activities?

☞ **Remember!!**

Sometimes it is difficult to accept oneself as less than that "ideal" of perfection, but by doing so exercise can become the healthy, anti-stress activity it should be. Concentrate on how good you feel because of exercise and it will be a reward for a special person, YOU!

Once you understand your body type, you will be able to set reasonable fitness goals and avoid the stress caused by unrealistic expectations. For example, many people have a mental image of the "ideal" body weight and size. Women tend to feel a social pressure to conform to a commercially encouraged look without giving any thought to their genetic makeup.

Twenty-two percent body fat is the recommended average for healthy, fit women. A woman who is already below 30 percent body fat and sticks to a low fat food plan and regular exercise for a year or more but just can't get down to 22 percent body fat may have to accept a genetic predisposition to a higher body fat percentage.

Likewise, someone who wants to build bigger muscles and trains vigorously and eats a very nutritious diet may find after a year of exercise that heredity didn't give him or her the muscle types for large mass.

One way to deal with a necessary change in an unrealistic goal is to really think about the weight you feel best at; the weight at which you feel energetic and productive, and which you can maintain for a long time (more than 6 months). Women especially should accept a range that allows for natural fluctuations.

Chapter 5

Body Image And Self-Esteem

I'm fat. I'm too skinny. I'd be happy if I were taller, shorter, had curly hair, straight hair, a smaller nose, bigger muscles, longer legs.

Is there something wrong with me?

Do any of these statements sound familiar? Are you used to putting yourself down? If so, you're not alone. As a teen, you're going through a ton of changes in your body, and as your body changes, so does your image of yourself. Read on to learn more about how your body image affects your self-esteem and how you can develop a healthy body image.

Why Are Self-Esteem And Body Image Important?

You may have heard the term self-esteem on talk shows or seen it in your favorite magazine. But what does it mean? Self-esteem involves how much a person values herself, and appreciates her own worth. Self-esteem is important because when you feel good about yourself, you enjoy life more.

About This Chapter: "Body Image and Self-Esteem," updated and reviewed by Kim Rutherford, MD. This information was provided by TeensHealth, one of the largest resources online for medically reviewed health information written for parents, kids, and teens. For more articles like this one, visit www.TeensHealth.org, or www.KidsHealth.org. © 2001 The Nemours Center for Children's Health Media, a division of The Nemours Foundation.

Although self-esteem applies to every aspect of how you see yourself, it is often mentioned in terms of appearance or body image. Body image is how you see and feel about your physical appearance. We tend to relate self-esteem to body image for several reasons. First of all, most people care about how other people see them. Unfortunately, many people judge others by things like the clothes they wear, the shape of their body, or the way they wear their hair. If a person feels like he or she looks different than others, then body image and self-esteem may be affected negatively.

Teens with a poor body image may think negative thoughts like, "I'm fat, I'm not pretty enough, I'm not strong enough."

What Shapes Self-Esteem?

The Effects Of Puberty

Some teens struggle with their self-esteem when they begin puberty. That's because the body undergoes many changes when puberty starts. These rapid changes and the desire for acceptance make it difficult for teens to judge whether they are "normal" when they look at other teens around them. And many people worry about what's normal during puberty. But puberty doesn't proceed at the same pace for everyone.

Puberty usually begins with a growth spurt. Usually, this happens to girls first but guys tend to catch up with their own spurts around the ages of 13 or 14. In general, puberty for both sexes takes between 2 to 5 years to complete but every teen has her own genetic timetable for the changes of puberty.

The sexual development of girls typically starts around age 9 to 10 with the appearance of budding breasts, pubic hair, and later the start of menstruation. Other changes include wider hips, buttocks and thighs, and a greater proportion of body fat. These changes can make a girl feel self-conscious about her body. She may feel like her maturing body

> **♣ It's A Fact!!**
> The effects of different things combine to shape self-esteem. These include:
> - puberty
> - culture
> - home
> - school
> - body image

draws attention to her, and feel uncomfortable or embarrassed. Or she may feel as though her body is weird and different than her friends' bodies. Unhealthy "crash" dieting or eating disorders can result.

Meanwhile, guys will begin to notice their shoulders getting wider, muscles developing, voices deepening, testicles getting larger, and penises growing longer and wider. Guys who are dissatisfied with their development may become obsessed with weight training and may take steroids or other drugs to help boost their physiques and athletic performance.

The Effects Of Culture

Media images from TV, movies, and advertising may affect self-esteem. Girls may struggle with media images of teen girls and women who are unrealistically thin. Many women and teen girls in magazines, the news, or on TV are unusually thin, which may lead girls who are not thin to believe that something is wrong with them. It's important to realize that self-worth should not be determined by body size. It's more important to lead a healthy lifestyle by exercising regularly and eating nutritiously than to try to change your body to fit an unrealistic ideal.

Guys can also have body image problems. Although girls may feel pressured to be smaller, guys may feel pressured to become larger and look stronger. Sports and other guys may put pressure on guys to gain muscle mass quickly, which can lead them to feel unhappy or dissatisfied with their bodies.

Sometimes low self-esteem is too much to bear. Instead of getting help, some teens may drink or do drugs to help themselves feel better, especially in social situations.

The Effects Of Home And School

Your home or school life may also affect your self-esteem. Some parents spend more time criticizing than praising their children. Sometimes this criticism reduces a teen's ability to have a positive body image—the teen may model her own "inner voice" after that of a parent, and learn to think negative thoughts about herself.

It's hard to succeed at school when the situation at home is tense, so sometimes teens who suffer from abuse at home may have problems in school, both of which contribute to poor self-esteem.

Teens may also experience negative comments and hurtful teasing or bullying from classmates and peers. This can definitely affect a person's self-esteem, but it's important to remember that the people who are being hurtful probably have low self-esteem as well, and putting others down may make them feel better about themselves.

Sometimes racial and ethnic prejudice is the source of hurtful comments. These comments come from ignorance on the part of the person who makes them, but sometimes they can negatively affect a person's body image and self-esteem.

Checking Your Own Self-Esteem And Body Image

If you have a positive body image, you probably like the way you look and accept yourself the way you are. This is a healthy attitude that allows you to explore other aspects of growing up, such as increasing independence from your parents, enhanced intellectual and physical abilities, and an interest in dating.

When you believe in yourself, you're much less likely to let your own mistakes get you down. You are better able to recognize your errors, learn your lessons, and move on. The same goes for the way you treat others. Teens who feel good about themselves and have good self-esteem are less likely to use putdowns to hurt themselves or anyone else.

A positive, optimistic attitude can help you develop better self-esteem. For example, saying, "Hey, I'm human," instead of "Wow, I'm such a loser," when you've made a mistake. Or avoiding blaming others when things don't go as expected.

Knowing what makes you happy and how to meet your goals can make you feel capable, strong, and in control of your life. A positive attitude and a healthy lifestyle are a great combination for developing good self-esteem.

Tips For Boosting Your Self-Esteem

Some teens think they need to change how they look or act to feel good about themselves. But if you can train yourself to reprogram the way you look at your body, you can defend yourself from negative comments—both those that come from others and those that come from you.

The first thing to do is recognize that your body is your own, no matter what shape, size, or color it comes in. If you are very worried about your weight or size, you can check with your doctor to verify that things are OK. But remember that it is no one's business but your own what your body is like—ultimately, you have to be happy with yourself.

Remember, too, that there are things about yourself you can't change—such as your height and shoe size—and you should accept and love these things about yourself. But if there are things about yourself that you do want to change, make goals for yourself. For example, if you want to lose weight, commit yourself to exercising three to four times a week and eating nutritiously. Accomplishing the goals you set for yourself can help to improve your self-esteem.

When you hear negative comments coming from within, tell yourself to stop. Your inner critic can be retrained. Try exercises like giving yourself three compliments every day. While you're at it, every evening list three things in your day that really gave you pleasure. It can be anything from the way the sun felt on your face, the sound of your favorite band, or the way someone laughed at your jokes. By focusing on the good things you do and the positive aspects of your life, you can change how you feel about yourself.

☞ **Remember!!**

When others criticize your body, it's usually because they are insecure about the changes happening to themselves.

✔ Quick Tip

Where Can I Go If I Need Help?

Sometimes low self-esteem and body image problems are too much to handle alone. Some teens may become depressed, and lose interest in activities or friends. Talk to a parent, coach, religious leader, guidance counselor, therapist, or an adult friend. An adult can help you put your body image in perspective and give you positive feedback about your body, your skills, and your abilities.

If you can't turn to anyone you know, call a teen crisis hotline (check the yellow pages under social services). The most important thing is to get help if you feel like your body image and low self-esteem are affecting your life.

Chapter 6

Don't Let Asthma Keep You Out Of The Game

Who Has Asthma?

Asthma—which makes it hard to breathe, and causes coughing and wheezing—affects about five million American kids and teens. That's almost 1 in 10.

Famous people like rapper Coolio have asthma, although he's better known for his hit songs like "Gangsta's Paradise" than for his fight against the illness. Olympians like Misty Hyman and Amy VanDyken, Tom Dolan and Karen Furneaux, and Kurt Grote also have asthma.

Physical Activity And Asthma

Things like cold or dry air, dust, pollen, pollution, cigarette smoke, or stress can "trigger" asthma. This can make your body pump out chemicals that close off your airways, making it hard for air to get into to your lungs, and causing an asthma attack.

Physical activity can trigger asthma attacks too. Experts don't know for sure why physical activity sometimes brings one on, but they suspect that

About This Chapter: "Meeting the Challenge: Don't Let Asthma Keep You Out of the Game," BAM! (Body And Mind), Centers for Disease Control and Prevention (CDC), reviewed April 30, 2002.

fast breathing through the mouth (like happens when you get winded) can irritate the airways. In addition, when air pollution levels are high, physical activity in the afternoon is harder on the lungs than morning activity—pollution levels raise later in the day.

Get Fit

So, should you get a doctor's note and skip gym class? Sorry, no. Doctors want their asthma patients to get active, especially in asthma-friendly activities like these: swimming, bicycling, golf, inline skating, and weightlifting.

♣ It's A Fact!!

Today, more than ever, asthma is not a barrier to physical activity. In fact, if you keep your asthma under control, you can do it all. Need proof? Well, did you know that:

- At the 1984 summer Olympics, 67 of the 597 American athletes had asthma. Among them, they won 41 medals.

- Twenty percent of the athletes at the 1996 summer Olympics had asthma brought on by physical activity.

- Almost 30% of the American swimmers on the 2000 summer Olympic team had asthma and used inhalers.

Asthma didn't hold them back, and it shouldn't hold you back, either.

Weird Words

Trigger: A term describing a system in which a relatively small input turns on a relatively large output, the magnitude of which is unrelated to the magnitude of the input.

Source: From *Stedman's Medical Dictionary, 27th Edition,* Copyright © 2000 Lippincott Williams & Wilkins. All rights reserved.

Why are these good choices if you want to be physically active?

- They let you control how hard and fast you breathe

- They let you breathe through your nose at all times

- They don't dry out your airways

- They mix short, intense activities with long endurance workouts

- You can do them in a controlled environment (for example, a gym with air that's not too cold or dry)

- Usually you do them with other people, who can help you if an attack comes on

Feel Good

To feel your best, do the right stuff to control your asthma. And listen to your doctors—they're on your team.

According to Dr. Stephen Redd, an asthma expert at the Centers for Disease Control and Prevention (CDC), people with asthma, "should expect to live a life that really isn't affected by asthma, except for having to follow the directions." He also says to speak up if you are having symptoms, and remember to "keep a good attitude and keep working to control the disease."

So, get out there and get moving. With good habits and today's medicines, you can go for the gold—or just join your friends on the basketball court, in the pool, on the dance floor.

✔ **Quick Tip**

Getting regular physical activity can improve your breathing, and lead to fewer asthma attacks. Just remember to follow these tips. (In fact, this is good advice for everyone, not just those with asthma.)

- **Ease into it.** Start your workout with a warm-up, and don't overdo it by running five miles on your first day if you get winded walking around the block. Finish up with a cool-down.

- **Take a buddy.** It's more fun and a friend can help if you get into trouble.

- **Respect your body.** Stay away from the things that trigger your asthma. Help out your airways by breathing through your nose instead of your mouth. Take it easy on days when your asthma symptoms are really bugging you. And stick to the medicine routine that your doctor has set up.

- **Take breaks.** Treat yourself to rest and drink plenty of water.

- **Mix it up.** For example, try going inline skating one day and taking a long walk the next.

Chapter 7

How To Choose A Quality Fitness Instructor

What makes an exercise class enjoyable and effective? Is it the music, the movements, or the feeling of camaraderie among the students? The factor underlying all these aspects is the instructor. A knowledgeable fitness instructor, who's able to engage and motivate the students, determines the quality of the class. Remember, a good instructor realizes the focus of the class should be on exercising to improve or maintain your health, not just on working out to look better.

So if you're considering taking—or already participate in—a cycling, step, rowing, strength training, in-line skating, boxing-based, or other type of fitness class, the following questions will assist you in evaluating an instructor's credentials and help you make the most of your exercise class.

Points To Help You Select A High-Quality Instructor

Is the instructor certified by a nationally recognized organization or a recognized equivalent? Is the instructor trained in anatomy, exercise physiology, injury prevention, first aid, and monitoring of exercise?

To conduct a class that gives you a safe and effective workout, an instructor needs a good grounding in exercise science and exercise technique. An exercise certification indicates that the instructor has at least basic knowledge in areas necessary to teach a quality class. You can check with the instructor, fitness director, or facility owner/manager to verify what kind of education, training and certification the instructor has.

Does the instructor belong to a professional fitness association such as IDEA or IHRSA (International Health, Racquet, and Sportsclub Association) to keep current with the latest exercise science and techniques?

The fitness industry is changing all the time so it is crucial that an instructor know the latest research and trends so they conduct a safe and effective class. Membership in a professional fitness association is one way you can tell that an instructor is staying current.

Does the instructor ask about medical conditions and previous injuries that may affect your exercise program?

Many medical conditions can affect your participation in a fitness program and a good instructor will help you make the most of class without compromising your health.

Is the instructor certified in cardiopulmonary resuscitation (CPR)?

Exercisers of all ages and ranges of medical backgrounds take group exercise classes. CPR training enables an instructor know what to do in case of a medical emergency.

Does the instructor ask about your current level of fitness? Does the instructor provide modifications of exercises or alternatives for students of varying fitness levels or with special limitations?

An instructor should be able to show moves that are suitable for beginning, intermediate, and advanced participants and those with a variety of health concerns. An instructor should encourage you to go at your own pace and to stop and rest if you feel pain or fatigue.

Does the instructor explain the benefits of each exercise and demonstrate how to do each one correctly and in a controlled manner?

Your instructor should let your know which muscles you are working and how to exercise using proper technique. The instructor shouldn't set a pace faster than a majority of the class can keep up with.

Does the instructor explain the importance of heart rate monitoring and perceived exertion and have students check levels during class?

For an effective cardiovascular workout, participants need to exercise at a certain intensity during class. The instructor should either have you take your pulse rate or teach you the perceived exertion scale and ask you to rate your exertion during class.

Does the instructor move around the room to give individual instruction?

A good instructor will move throughout the class at different points to check for proper technique and to get to know participants.

Can the instructor be heard clearly above the music?

The music used in class should be exciting and motivate you to exercise. But the movement directions and the safety reminders the instructor gives are important so you should be able to hear these above the music.

Does the class move smoothly from one type of activity to the next?

A fitness class should be well organized and an instructor shouldn't need to stop and think between sections. The class should also start with warm up exercises and end with cool-down and stretching exercises.

Does the instructor encourage a noncompetitive atmosphere that allows all participants to work out at their own level?

A good instructor will make all students feel like winners. You should never feel you have to keep up with more advanced exercisers. All shapes and sizes of exercisers should feel welcome in the class and all students should be encouraged.

Is the instructor friendly and interested in you as a person?

Does the instructor make an attempt to learn your name? Do you feel like the instructor really cares about you and your well-being? A good instructor will make an effort to build a one-on-one relationship with regular students.

Does the instructor interact with the students most of the time or does he or she look into the mirror more frequently?

An instructor should never focus on his or her own workout before helping you have an effective, safe and enjoyable class. A good instructor will be interested in what you are doing not in his or her own movements.

Will the instructor answer questions before or after class?

A qualified instructor will be happy to explain moves you don't understand. He or she should be eager to share health and fitness knowledge with you and provide advice on how you can improve your fitness level in class.

☞ Remember!!

Does the instructor create a fun atmosphere?

You may be able to answer "yes" to all of the questions in this chapter but if you don't have fun in class, you probably won't stick with it for long. An instructor's enthusiastic personality and manner should help you enjoy the class.

Chapter 8

Tips For Buying Exercise Equipment

Selecting Home Exercise Equipment

The current economic reports show that home fitness products are a booming business and this is reflected in the many new home exercise products flooding the market. Exercising at home is convenient and even 63% of people who belong to fitness clubs also use home equipment.

Perhaps you are considering setting up a home workout areas in your home. There is a wide selection of equipment out there; some excellent and some very poorly made. Home fitness equipment can be one of the most enjoyable purchases you will every make, or it can be an unused dust collector. Exercise equipment is a major investment that should be researched and planned to make sure you get the best value.

Try to buy your exercise equipment from a specialty fitness retailer or exercise equipment dealer, not a department store or general sporting goods store. Fitness equipment stores are more likely to have sales staff who understand exercise and can answer questions and demonstrate the proper use of equipment. Equipment stores will also offer the home versions of brand equipment found in fitness clubs, which is better quality than department store brands. Also, in an exercise-based store, the equipment will be displayed on the floor, not on shelves, making it easier to try out the equipment.

An additional suggestion for individuals who like to look for great prices with online shopping: Go try out the exercise equipment first, decide what you like, and then hunt for that great price online.

Many people face a challenge when deciding which fitness product is the right one for them. Because there is so much exercise equipment on the market you need to assess your priorities. Personal home fitness areas should include a cardiovascular and a strength component. The specific pieces chosen must be based on the anatomy, interests, and fitness level of the user.

Preparing To Purchase Exercise Equipment

When preparing to make an exercise equipment purchase, take the time to try out a variety of pieces, ask a lot of questions, expect correct answers, and choose the machine that suits you best.

✔ Quick Tip

In general you should know the following about yourself and each machine you examine before your buy:

- Your fitness needs
- Your budget
- Your available space
- The product features, including safety
- Warranty and serviceability
- The comparison with similar products.
- What fitness activities do you enjoy?
- What are your fitness goals?
- Who else will use the equipment?

The equipment you buy should be compatible with activities you and other users enjoy and the level of fitness you want to achieve.

How much space is available? Is it a separate room or shared space. Measure the size of the exercise area, including ceiling height, before you shop for equipment.

Choose exercise equipment that will fit in the space your home can provide, so that your workouts will be safe and effective.

Dress comfortably in loose clothes and sneakers so you can really use the equipment. Try the equipment out—play with it. Make sure you understand how to use it and what it will and won't do before deciding on a purchase. Compare different models of the item. Assess the fit, feel and features of the equipment. Always try it out before you buy it. This is the big advantage to the exercise equipment specialty store over the department stores. If the store won't let you try out the machines for as long as you need to, go somewhere else.

With cardiovascular equipment, test it for the kind of resistance it provides. Resistance is built into the equipment to make exercise harder or easier. Belts, chains, wind resistance, hydraulic pistons, and computers are the most common forms of resistance, and each kind has a different feel. Try out several kinds to see which you like best.

When testing exercise equipment check it for smooth movement, comfort, stability, safety, and funny noises or vibrations. The machine should not wiggle, sway or rock when used. Make sure that the bodily movements are correct and safe. Check to see if the equipment is adjustable, comfortable, easy to learn and designed in a user friendly way. Find out if advertising claims are backed up by research or objective consumer publications. Select equipment that enhances user safety, and avoid any piece with obvious flaws or weaknesses that increase the chances of injury.

When deciding if a piece of exercise equipment is a good price, consider what may involve a lower pricing. Is it manufactured off shore or domestic? Are the components cheaper with a less rigorous design and assembly, or is it better engineering that allows less costly assembly. For the higher priced products, are the features better, providing longer durability, better performance, and less service? What is the warranty and can it be repaired locally?

Cardiovascular Equipment

Here is some information about the most common types of cardiovascular equipment:

Treadmills are the most popular piece of aerobic equipment for the home exerciser. Treadmills take the aerobic conditioning of walking, jogging, or running activities indoors, providing a safe place to exercise and avoid bad weather and pollution. Look for a treadmill with smooth action, a steady pace, monitoring systems, and incline settings. Make sure the treadmill is motorized, not manual. Check out any electronic display, emergency stop, railings, side runners, and elevation adjustment. Quality models range from $1,500 and up. Make sure any treadmill you consider is built to withstand a load many times your body weight and that local customer service is available.

✔ Quick Tip
Buying Exercise Equipment

Buying fitness equipment for home workouts can represent a sizable financial commitment as well as a lifestyle change. Exercise good judgment when evaluating advertising claims for fitness products. Before you buy, ask yourself the following questions:

What Are Your Goals?

Remember that the best route to overall fitness and health is one that incorporates a variety of physical activities as part of a daily routine.

Will You Really Use Exercise Equipment?

Before you buy, prove to yourself that you're ready to stick to an ongoing fitness program. Set aside some time in your day for physical activity—and then do it.

Can Exercise Equipment Help You Spot Reduce?

No. No exercise device can burn fat off a particular part of your body. To lose the proverbial spare tire or trim your hips, you must combine sensible eating with regular exercise that works the whole body.

Can You See Through Outrageous Claims?

Exercising regularly can help you shape up. But some companies claim that you can get results by using their equipment for three or four minutes a day, three times a week. Sounds fabulous, right? But realistic? Not really. Here's how you can spot the fantasies when you're sizing up claims by equipment manufacturers:

- Any ads that promise "easy" or "effortless" results are false. Many ads that make big promises about the number of calories you'll burn also may be

Elliptical trainers offer a comfortable, non-impact exercise activity that almost anyone can do. The movement is horizontally oval. You can adjust the intensity or keep the movement easy for the very sedentary. It is currently popular second to the treadmill.

Stationary bikes are widely used home exercise equipment. They offer a non-impact cardiovascular workout and are great for the overweight or

deceptive. Indeed, some of the claims are true only for athletes who already are in top physical condition; others may not be true for anyone.

- Claims that one machine can help you burn more calories or lose weight faster than others can be tough to evaluate —especially when you can't read the "scientific studies" mentioned in the ads. For these claims, apply two rules:

- Equipment that works the whole body, or major portions of it, probably will burn more calories than devices that work one part of the body.

- The more you use your equipment, the more calories you'll burn. That's why it's important to select equipment that suits you and your lifestyle. A study might show that a different device burns more calories an hour, but if it's uncomfortable or difficult to use, chances are it will gather dust rather than help you burn calories.

Have You Checked The Fine Print?

Look for tip-offs that getting the advertised results requires more than just using the machine. Sometimes the fine print mentions a diet or "program" that must be used in conjunction with the equipment. Even if it doesn't, remember that diet and exercise together are much more effective for weight loss than either diet or exercise alone.

Many ads also feature dramatic testimonials or before-and-after pictures from satisfied customers. These stories may not be typical. Just because one person has had success doesn't mean you'll get the same results. And endorsements—whether they're from consumers, celebrities, or star athletes—don't mean the equipment is right for you.

Quick Tip continued on next page

sedentary person just starting to exercise. The legs and hips are the major muscles used. When riding it, a good stationary bike should perform smoothly and feel solid. Many bikes come with monitors that record elapsed time, speed, distance covered, a calorie counter, and pulse meter. A basic, high quality exercise bike costs $500–1,000, while the electronic or computer controlled bikes cost from $1,200–4,000.

Quick Tip continued from previous page

Can You Try The Equipment Before You Buy?

A few minutes at a sporting goods store while you're wearing street clothes isn't very helpful. Test different types of equipment at a local gym or recreation center. Better still, go to the store dressed for exercise and give the equipment a full work-out.

Have You Shopped Around?

Before you buy, check out articles in consumer or fitness magazines that rate the exercise equipment on the market. Much of the equipment advertised on television or in magazines also is available at local sporting goods, department, or discount stores. That makes it easier to shop for the best price. Don't be fooled by companies that advertise "three easy payments of…" or "just $49.95 a month." Before you buy any product, find out the total cost, including shipping and handling, sales tax, delivery, and set-up fees. Get the details on warranties, guarantees, and return policies: A "30-day money back guarantee" may not sound so good if you have to ante up a hefty fee to return a bulky piece of equipment you've bought through the mail. Check out the company's customer service and support, too. Who can you call if the machine breaks down or you need replacement parts? Try any toll-free numbers to see whether help really is accessible.

Occasionally, you can get a great deal on a piece of fitness equipment from a second-hand store, a consignment shop, a yard sale, or the classifieds in your local newspaper. But buy wisely. Items bought second-hand usually aren't returnable and don't have the warranties of new equipment.

Source: Excerpted from "Tips for Buying Exercise Equipment," FirstGov for Seniors, available online at www.seniors.gov/articles/0401/exercise-equipment.html.

Recumbent cycles have their pedals in front, rather than underneath the rider. They have some advantages over conventional exercise bikes with a chair-style seat that gives a lot of back support and minimizes the stress on the knees. Recumbent cycles work the buttocks and upper hamstrings, as well as the abdominal muscles.

Step machines were very popular in the past and exercisers who enjoy intense workouts still like them. Steppers give a good workout aerobically, strengthen and build the lower body muscles, and are low impact. The step machine works the buttocks more than other machines. It must be used properly or back injury could result. You must have the strength and stamina to stand upright while climbing because bending and leaning on the railing causes undue stress on the back.

Cross country ski machines can provide a full body workout for cardio-vascular and muscle endurance, however, they are the hardest machine to learn to use. They use nearly all the major muscles in the arms, legs, abdominal muscles, chest and shoulders, and can give an intense workout. These take some practice to use well and are best for people who already exercise and want a challenge. The model you choose should feel smooth with a gliding motion.

People with limited spaces may like owning a rower, because it can fold and be stored in a corner. It uses the upper and lower body, and is an aerobic exercise, not a muscle builder. It is important to learn proper form and technique to avoid back strain.

Resistance Equipment

Many people want to supplement their home aerobic fitness equipment with resistance equipment, so that they can get a balanced fitness program. Careful selection of the right equipment will help make exercise successful. There are more than a few types of home resistance equipment on the market. The two most widely recognized kinds of weight equipment are home gyms or multi-stations and free weights. Free weights require greater instruction and supervision for proper use, and are more likely to cause injury. The multi-station machines with captured weight stacks are easier to learn and safer to use.

An exerciser who enjoys working with free weights can purchase an adjustable weight set for under $150, and a good stable adjustable bench can be had for under $300. The inexpensive home benches with lots of extras may not be good buys due to lack of quality construction.

Home gyms or multi-stations are a major purchase, and the quality of the machine has a direct correlation to its durability. A quality unit with a single weight stack and no cable changes needed between exercises costs between $1,000 and $2,000. Top brands look and feel like quality units, with clean welds, smooth movement, and tight upholstery. These weight stack machines are nearly maintenance free.

The multi-function home strength units with lots of parts and low prices often require bothersome changes of the pieces between exercises. Many cheap machines are anatomically incorrect and can cause injury.

Just as with cardiovascular equipment, take the time to try out various weight training equipment before you purchase it. Spend enough time trying the piece to know if you would really be comfortable and enjoy using the equipment before you buy it.

Once you have made your purchases, protect your investment and follow the manufacturers' maintenance suggestions.

☞ **Remember!!**

The most important consideration in buying exercise equipment is your personal preference. The quality of your commitment to training will provide the best results and you must enjoy the equipment you buy enough to use it regularly.

Chapter 9

Tips For Buying Athletic Shoes

The athletic shoe industry continues to offer new features and technologies, but the basic criteria for choosing athletic shoes remain the same as ever—comfort and safety. New developments such as unique designs for women and new lacing systems have improved shoe fit. Beyond the fit, knowledge of foot types and of the demands of each sport helps physicians guide patients toward shoes that will help them avoid injuries.

The abundant marketing glitz and hoopla may suggest that athletic shoes have undergone a revolution in recent years. They haven't. Rather, the trend has been a steady evolution in design and materials as manufacturers have sought to improve safety and performance.

"Even if [the shoe industry] had something that was earth-shattering, it would be evolved into place, not thrown into place," says Tom Brunick, director of the Athlete's Foot Stores Research and Development Center in Naperville, Illinois, and footwear editor of *Walking* magazine.

About This Chapter: Text in this chapter is reproduced with permission from Martin, DR: How to steer patients toward the right sport shoe. *Physician and Sportsmedicine* 1997, 25 (9), 138-144. © 1997. The McGraw-Hill Companies. All Rights Reserved. Reviewed in June 2003 by Dr. David A. Cooke, MD Diplomate, American Board of Internal Medicine.

What's New?

Improvements within the last 4 or 5 years cover a broad range of design details, from the shape of the shoe to new lacing systems.

Options for women. Perhaps the most significant recent advance in athletic footwear is the acknowledgment that women's feet are usually anatomically different from men's and that they therefore benefit from specially designed shoes. A woman's foot is typically narrower than a man's and has a narrower heel relative to the forefoot.

"There are more and more women's shoes that aren't based on downsized or graded men's shoes," says Carol Frey, MD, director of the Orthopedic Foot and Ankle Center in Manhattan Beach, California. "More of them are now being developed based on the shape and function of a female foot. Companies are developing entire female divisions, developing [women's] lasts, the form over which a shoe is made." Shoes built from women's lasts reduce the heel slippage that can occur in downsized men's shoes.

> ✔ **Quick Tip**
>
> Companies that have used women's lasts [the form over which a shoe is made], according to Frey, include Nike, Asics, and Reebok.

More women than men now buy athletic footwear, and their demands have influenced the athletic shoe market. Though general fitness footwear remains important, competitive female athletes want performance shoes, just like their male counterparts. For example, Nike offers a line of basketball shoes designed specifically for women—11 different styles. Adidas has seven different women's soccer shoes. Brunick says, "You wouldn't have had that 4 years ago."

Midsole changes. The cushioning midsole of athletic shoes has been the Achilles heel of shoe design; the ethyl vinyl acetate (EVA) or polyurethane foam used in them breaks down relatively quickly. To improve durability, shoe manufacturers have devised midsoles that encapsulate air or gel; some running-shoe midsoles are cushioned entirely with air. Though midsoles with encapsulated air or gel have never been wear tested. Frey says they do improve durability. "A good guess would be 25% to 50%," she says.

Another recent improvement is better support at the midsole; many companies are inserting support devices, according to *Runner's World* magazine.[1] Older split-sole shoe designs tended to flex incorrectly at the midfoot rather than the forefoot, contributing to problems such as plantar fasciitis.

Laces and loops. Round laceroni shoelaces—similar to those used in hiking boots—are starting to show up in athletic shoes. Though the new laces untie more readily during use (without double-knotting or lace locks), when used with the new loop or web eyelets, they slide more easily through a shoe's loops and distribute the pressure across the top of the foot more evenly than flat laces.

Glenn Pfeffer, MD, an orthopedic surgeon and assistant clinical professor at the University of California, San Francisco, says the new laces allow a better fit than flat laces do. "They don't kink, they don't cause pressure points, and they glide easily," he says.

Neoprene sleeves. New shoe technology usually appears first in running shoes, and the latest development is the neoprene sleeve—an elasticized, padded cuff around the opening of the shoe. Neoprene sleeves "keep the shoe from pistoning up and down as you run," says Frey. "It gives you a better fit and grips the foot."

Thinner midsoles. In court shoes, the trend is to bring athletes closer to the court by reducing the thickness of the midsole, yet still provide good cushioning. Thinner midsoles lower the athlete's center of gravity and reduce side-to-side ankle motion.

Good Fit, Bad Fit

If female-specific shoes, laceroni, and neoprene sleeves were merely marketing gambits, they would merit little notice. However, they are providing active people and athletes with improvements that augment the fit and therefore the safety of athletic footwear. Poorly fitted shoes, after all, can cause many difficulties that don't happen when shoes fit well.

"Even the smallest [fit] problem can prevent athletes from performing to the best of their capabilities," writes Tom Clanton, MD, chair of the department of orthopedic surgery at the University of Texas Medical School at Houston.[2] Medical conditions that can arise from improper shoe fit, according to Clanton, include new-onset bunion pain (from narrow shoes or those with rigid material covering the forefoot), metatarsalgia or Morton's neuroma (shoes that are too tight across the forefoot), and black toe (a shallow toe box). Toe deformities such as hammer toe, claw toe, and overlapping fifth toe may become symptomatic in athletes whose shoes have toe boxes that are either too narrow or too shallow. Though calluses and blisters are more or less expected in many sports, they are more common with a shoe that rubs the skin excessively or allows the foot to move or slide around.

Physicians and other health professionals can help point patients who ask about shoes in the right direction. The physician can start by showing the patient the type of arch he or she has: high (pes cavus), medium, or low (pes valgus).

About 25% of the population needs some type of specialized shoe, says Pfeffer: patients who are flat-footed, are pronators, or have very high arches. "What should come to the doctor's mind are the two Cs—cushioning or control," says Pfeffer. "Patients who have very high-arched feet have very stiff feet, and they need cushioning. Patients who have flat feet and are prone to a lot of motion need a shoe that can control that motion," he says.

The average foot needs a middle style of shoe—one that's not too hard or too soft, says Michael Lowe, DPM, a podiatrist in Salt Lake City and president of the American Academy of Podiatric Sports Medicine. "That midrange is going to give you a nice, stable, functional kind of shoe," he says.

A patient's arch determines which type of last, or shape, the shoe should have. Patients who have low arches do best in a shoe that has a straight shape and a board last; those who have high arches require a shoe with a curved shape and slip-lasted construction; and those who have a medium arch benefit from one that has a semi-curved shape with a combination last.

Obviously, active people are wise to try a shoe on before buying it. That usually means buying at a retail store rather than by mail order or on the

Internet. Physicians can help pick a good store. Clanton, for example, recommends that physicians develop a relationship with a local shoe store. "I've gone to several different shoe stores and tried on shoes myself and talked with some of the salesmen," he says. "I've gotten an idea of stores where I feel like my patients could benefit from the knowledge of the people there. That's where I make referrals."

Also, to help patients select correctly sized shoes, Clanton provides them with shoe-fit cards. He traces the patient's foot on a piece of paper, cuts an index card to match the tracing of the widest part of the foot, and then cuts out a half-inch notch where the card is the widest. The patient can place the card against the ball area of shoes being considered. Shoes narrower than the card may cause problems; shoes narrower than the notched width are almost certain to.

A Role In Injury Prevention

Besides comfort, injury prevention is what athletic shoes are all about. Shoes for running and other foot-strike activities are designed to prevent stress fractures, and shoes for court sports are designed to prevent ankle sprains.

✔ **Quick Tip**

Patients should be reminded to consider their past foot problems when selecting new athletic shoes, says Pierce Scranton, MD, an associate clinical professor at the University of Washington. For example, if the patient has a history of repeated ankle sprains, perhaps he or she should select high-topped rather than low-topped aerobic shoes or cross-trainers.

"If you look at overall injuries and problems created by shoes, fit is the number one consideration," says Clanton. However, he says researchers focus not on how well shoes fit, but on how cushioning and control features prevent injuries. One study[3] put Israeli military recruits into modified basketball shoes, substantially reducing the incidence of metatarsal stress fractures that related to regular military boots. Other research has produced similar findings.[4] It's also been suggested that inadequate cushioning in shoes can cause injuries to runners.[5]

✔ Quick Tip

Athletic Shoes

Proper-fitting sports shoes can enhance performance and prevent injuries. Follow these specially-designed fitting facts when purchasing a new pair of athletic shoes.

- Try on athletic shoes after a workout or run and at the end of the day. Your feet will be at their largest.

- Wear the same type of sock that you will wear for that sport.

- When the shoe is on your foot, you should be able to freely wiggle all of your toes.

- The shoes should be comfortable as soon as you try them on. There is no break-in period.

- Walk or run a few steps in your shoes. They should be comfortable.

- Always relace the shoes you are trying on. You should begin at the farthest eyelets and apply even pressure as you a crisscross lacing pattern to the top of the shoe.

- There should be a firm grip of the shoe to your heel. Your heel should not slip as you walk or run.

- If you participate in a sport three or more times a week, you need a sports specific shoe.

It can be hard to choose from the many different types of athletic shoes available. There are differences in design and variations in material and weight. These differences have been developed to protect the areas of the feet that encounter the most stress in a particular athletic activity.

Athletic shoes are grouped into seven categories:

- **Running, training, and walking.** Includes shoes for hiking, jogging, and exercise walking. Look for a good walking shoe to have a comfortable soft upper, good shock absorption, smooth tread, and a rocker sole design that encourages the natural roll of the foot during the walking motion. The features of a good jogging shoe include cushioning, flexibility, control and stability in the heel counter area, lightness, and good traction.

- **Court sports.** Includes shoes for tennis, basketball, and volleyball. Most court sports require the body to move forward, backward, and side-to-side. As a result, most athletic shoes used for court sports are subjected to heavy abuse. The key to finding a good court shoe is its sole. Ask a coach or shoes salesman to help you select the best type of sole for the sport you plan on participating in.

- **Field sports.** Includes shoes for soccer, football, and baseball. These shoes are cleated, studded, or spiked. The spike and stud formations vary from sport to sport, but generally are replaceable or detachable cleats, spikes, or studs affixed into nylon soles.

- **Winter sports.** Includes footwear for figure skating, ice hockey, alpine skiing, and cross-country skiing. The key to a good winter sports shoe is its ability to provide ample ankle support.

- **Track and field sport shoes.** Because of the specific needs of individual runners, athletic shoe companies produce many models for various foot types, gait patterns, and training styles. It is always best to ask your coach about the type of shoe that should be selected for the event you are participating in.

- **Specialty sports.** Includes shoes for golf, aerobic dancing, and bicycling.

- **Outdoor sports.** Includes shoes used for recreational activities such as hunting, fishing, and boating.

Source: Reprinted with permission from "Athletic Shoes," a patient information fact sheet co-developed by the American Orthopaedic Foot & Ankle Society (AOFAS) and the American Academy of Orthopaedic Surgeons (AAOS) © 2001. For additional information, visit www.aofas.org or http://ortho info.aaos.org.

Shoe traction plays a role in preventing knee injuries such as noncontact anterior cruciate ligament ruptures. Traction is a particular issue with court and cleated sports shoes in regards to their interface with the playing surface. Frey explains that proper traction depends on the specific sport; too little traction may impair athletic performance, while too much traction increases the risk of injury.

Clanton says that while collegiate and professional athletes are apt to take the risk of higher-traction footwear for performance's sake, it makes little sense for people at the high school or less competitive levels to chance serious knee injuries.

Shorter cleats on football shoes or use of soccer shoes, for example, have been shown to reduce knee and ankle injuries in high school football players.[6,7] Clanton recommends that cleats on a shoe for younger people be no longer than one-half inch.

Scranton, team physician for the Seattle Seahawks of the National Football League, recalls a football shoe that was designed for play on snow and ice that could generate incredible torque. "My concern is that some starstruck kid, on a hot summer day, remembers seeing the Green Bay Packers slug it out on an ice-covered field wearing [this shoe]," he says, "and he goes down to the store and orders them."

Traction concerns can also apply to court shoes, since the friction produced by the outer sole depends on the material used and its interaction with the playing surface. "Different surfaces have different characteristics related to the shoes, and while the human body can adapt to a great degree, there are different exposure rates to injury based on traction," Scranton says.

Clanton says understanding of the shoe-surface interface hasn't advanced enough to warrant specific recommendations to athletes. "But it has become clear that friction is a critical factor in injury rates," he says. One study[8] has suggested that shoe manufacturers provide indications and suggested playing surface conditions for their shoes.

Scranton says that what's needed is "the development of a shoe that has good frictional characteristics but that will not 'Velcro' to a surface—whether it be a cleated shoe getting stuck in natural grass or a turf shoe getting stuck on a dry, hot field on a summer day."

Pairing Shoes With Sports

In general, patients who participate in a certain sport or type of exercise three or more times a week should wear shoes designed for that activity. This will avoid problems such as the higher midsoles that cushion running shoes creating instability during the lateral movements of aerobics and court sports like tennis or basketball, and court shoes lacking the cushioning that running requires.

Cross-training shoes combine some elements of both running and court shoes, says Lowe. "For low mileage in either activity they're moderately successful, and they function well as a walking shoe," he says. "We're very comfortable placing our couch-potato patients in a cross-training shoe and letting them do multiple activities."

Patients whose main activity is walking should be advised to consider a shoe designed for walking, says Pfeffer. "It has a much more cushioned heel and a stiffer midsole [than joggers], and more spring in the toe to encourage the follow-through when toeing off."

Health And Comfort

The human foot is a remarkable structure that comes in many shapes and sizes. It's asked to bear extraordinary loads and strain. A 200-lb. man, for example, lands with up to 600 lb. of force on each foot several thousand times in a few miles of running. But with appropriate footwear, athletes and duffers alike can help keep pain and injuries at bay and enjoy the physical activities they choose.

"I would bet that if we were allowed to wear athletic shoes to work we could save the healthcare system in excess of a billion dollars a year," says Pfeffer. "These shoes are comfortable, and what's comfortable is probably what's healthy."

References

1. Wischina B, Brunick T: Spring 1997 shoe buyer's guide. *Runner's World* 1997;32(4):50.

2. Clanton TO: Sport shoes, insoles, and orthoses, in DeLee J, Drez D, Stanitski CL (eds), *Orthopaedic Sports Medicine: Principles and Practice.* Philadelphia, WB Saunders, 1994, pp 1982-2021.

3. Milgrom C, Giladi M, Kashtan H, et al: A prospective study of the effect of a shock-absorbing orthotic device on the incidence of stress fractures in military recruits. *Foot Ankle* 1985;6(2):101-104.

4. Frey C: Footwear and stress structures. *Clin Sports Med* 1997;16(2):249-256.

5. Gardner LI Jr, Dziados JE, Jones BH, et al; Prevention of lower extremity stress fracture: a controlled trial of a shock absorbent insole. *Am J Public Health* 1988;78(12):1563-1567.

6. Torg JS, Quedenfeld T: Knee and ankle injuries traced to shoes and cleats. *Phys Sportsmed* 1973;1(2):39-43.

7. Torg JS, Quedenfeld TC, Landau S: Football shoes and playing surfaces: from safe to unsafe. *Phys Sportsmed* 1973;1(3):51-54.

8. Heidt RS Jr, Dormer SG, Cawley PW, et al: Differences in friction and torsional resistance in athletic shoe-turf surface interfaces. *Am J Sports Med* 1996;24(6):834-842.

☞ Remember!!

The right sport shoe will be comfortable and will help you to avoid injury.

Special Issues Guide Hiking Boot Choice

Hiking boots are perhaps the most costly off-the-shelf sport footwear, with $250 price tags not uncommon for high-end models. But for serious hikers and backpackers, there's no more vital piece of gear. The wrong boot can lead to a sprained ankle or broken leg miles from help. It can even mean the difference between life and death.

Hiking boot selection is guided by the wearer's hiking level, says Steven Zell, MD, associate professor of medicine at the University of Nevada School of Medicine in Reno and an experienced back-country hiker. He co-wrote the chapter on medical equipment and supplies in *Wilderness Medicine: Management of Wilderness and Environmental Emergencies.*[c]

Zell says an ideal hiking boot for serious hikers should support an adult and a pack of up to 100 lb. with a high center of gravity. The upper should be full-grain leather reaching above the ankle, and the boot should have a shank running through a thick sole for torsional rigidity. For good breathability, patients should seek a good-quality boot made from leather at critical support areas and a breathable waterproof material such as Gore-Tex.

A casual hiker probably won't be carrying much more than a small day pack or fanny pack. His or her center of gravity is lower, so there's less torsion on the ankle. In case of a misstep, the day hiker can more easily maintain an upright posture. Such a hiker, says Zell, can wear a day boot that's light and breathable. Michael Lowe, DPM, a podiatrist in Salt Lake City and past president of the American Academy of Podiatric Sports Medicine, suggests at least a three-quarter top for day boots.

Patients should be aware that some shoes on the market look like hiking boots, but lack a steel, carbon resin, or fiberboard shank that provides the necessary support and torsional stability. Lowe teaches patients to grab the heel and forefoot and bend the boot or shoe upward. "The boot they buy should bend across the toes, not across the midfoot," he says.

Socks are also an important part of the hiking boot equation, says Lowe. Acrylic socks are preferred because they don't compress and they wick moisture away from the foot. "They're warmer in the winter, cooler in the summer, and virtually don't wear out," he says. "We significantly decrease blister formation with them."

In no other athletic shoe is break-in more important than in hiking boots, since they're so much stiffer. Break-in allows hikers to know what to expect on the trail, says Tom Clanton, MD, chair of the department of orthopedic surgery at the University of Texas Medical School at Houston. To break in the boots, patients should wear them at home for a couple weeks and during a few short day hikes. Clanton says, "The fit and relationship of the boot to the foot is probably more critical than in just about any other situation."

Reference

9. Zell S, Goodman P: Wilderness equipment and medical supplies, in Auerbach PS: *Wilderness Medicine: Management of Wilderness and Environmental Emergencies*, ed 3. St Louis, CV Mosby, 1995, pp 413-445.

—D.R. Martin

D.R. Martin is a medical journalist and copywriter in Minneapolis.

Part 2

Fitness Fundamentals

Chapter 10

Meet Your Muscles

Flex Appeal: Biceps

Where are my biceps?

Your biceps are the two muscles on the front of your upper arm between your shoulder and elbow. You can see your biceps when you flex your arms out to your sides like a bodybuilder. The size of your biceps doesn't determine how strong they are. A girl with small biceps could be stronger than another girl who has big biceps. What's important is that your biceps be able to do their job for you.

What do biceps do?

Biceps are very busy muscles. They're responsible for everything from helping you bend your elbows to turning the pages of a book. Your biceps also help your back muscles when you pull on things like a door or a dog's leash. If you like playing sports, biceps help you do things like throw a ball, swing a tennis racket, shoot baskets, or row.

Your biceps get exercise throughout the day because they're used for so many different tasks. But this doesn't mean that they're as strong as they should be. You tone your biceps by challenging them with resistance training, like weight lifting. Any exercise that bends and straightens your arm will do the trick.

Weak Triceps Tripping You Up?

Where are my triceps?

Have you heard of batwings? That's what some people call those flabby flaps that hang off untoned arms when you wave good-bye. And that's where you'll find your tricep muscles—at the back of the upper arm. Strong triceps keep your arms looking good and they can make your life a lot easier, too.

What do triceps do?

The triceps work opposite your biceps. Together, they are in charge of straightening your arm. They help you do everything from picking up your keys to reaching up to catch a Frisbee. If you like playing sports, triceps help you do things like throw a ball, swing a tennis racket, shoot baskets, or row.

> ♣ **It's A Fact!!**
> Information about specific exercises to work each of the muscle groups described in this chapter is available online at www.iemily.com.

Your tricep muscles are small and hard to isolate. That means you have to concentrate and use proper form to strengthen them. To keep your triceps toned, you'll need to include exercises that involve straightening and bending your arms and resistance training.

Super Shoulders

Where are my delts?

Delts (short for deltoids) refers to a group of muscles around your shoulder joint. You have front, middle, and back deltoid muscles. They all work together to support and move your shoulders and arms. Most people refer to the whole group of muscles as the delts.

What do my delts do?

Your shoulders come into play every time you move your arm. That's because the deltoid muscles help connect your arms to your upper body. Delts are essential for everyday stuff, too. Without them, you couldn't wave to your friends across the cafeteria or slam your locker shut before everything inside comes pouring out. If you like sports, your delts help you do everything from spiking a volleyball to swimming laps.

Most exercises that involve your arms will help strengthen your shoulders. Upper body exercises, such as push-ups and pull-ups, also work the shoulders.

Pectoral Muscles

Where are my pecs?

Your pectorals (called pecs) are the chest muscles under your breasts. The pecs run from your breastbone to the shoulder on each side. Maybe that's why so many marketing gimmicks promise you'll increase the size of your breasts if you buy their chest-toning gadgets. The truth is that working your pecs will only firm your pecs. Chest exercises won't make your breasts bigger or smaller.

What do my pecs do?

Strong pecs help you push and hug, as well as add oomph to any movements that involve your arms and shoulders. Powerful pecs help you maneuver your bike up a steep hill when your legs are giving out. They help you mow the lawn quickly and give your friend a hug when she finds the earring you lost when you slept over her house. Pecs give gymnasts the strength to perform those powerful vaults and bar routines and give cross-country skiers speed and control.

Any movement that involves pushing or pressing a weight (or your own body weight) will strengthen your pectoral muscles. While you're working your pecs, you'll be strengthening your shoulder muscles and triceps too.

The Geometry Of Your Upper Back

Where are my rhomboids, traps, and lats?

Rhomboids, trapezius, and latissimus dorsi sound like shapes you study in geometry class. But, unlike geometric shapes, you can't see them. These upper back muscles are right behind you.

The latissimus dorsi muscles (called lats) run in a fan-shape fashion from your armpit to your spine. They help you lift your arms up overhead. You use your trapezius muscles (called traps) when you shrug your shoulder. These muscles cross your shoulders and run down along your spine in something like a diamond shape. The rhomboids, which pull your shoulder blades together, sit between your spine and those blades.

> ✔ **Quick Tip**
> After you finish your strength training routine, be sure to stretch your muscles. Stretching helps your muscles get rid of the lactic acid that builds up and makes you feel sore a day or two after your workout.

What do my upper back muscles do?

You may not give these muscles much thought, but every time you pull something—a tug of war rope, an oar, a car door—your upper back is working. Swimmers, who spend so much time pulling water out of their way, have well-developed upper backs and shoulders.

Any exercise that involves a pulling motion will strengthen your upper back muscles. Since there are a lot of muscles involved, there are a lot of exercises to choose from.

The Abdominal Muscles

What are abdominal muscles?

Abdominals are more than just the muscles that wrap around your middle. Strong abs provide the balance that keeps a ballerina on her toes. They protect a kickboxer's internal organs. Abs help yogis do breathing exercises. And they support your lower back when you lift weights or lug books around in your backpack. Your abs are actually three different muscles with three different jobs.

What do I use my abdominal muscles for?

The rectus abdominis muscles are found in the outermost part of your abdomen. They run down the front of your body from your rib cage to your pelvis. They help stabilize your body, support your spine, help you keep your balance and your back straight, and allow you to bend at the waist. You use them when you walk and run, and even when you breathe.

Your external and internal oblique muscles are found on the sides of your stomach. They define your waist. Your obliques are your "twister" muscles. They allow you to twist and turn at the waist. You use them when you pivot, play basketball, or swing a golf club.

To tone your abdominal muscles, basic crunches are the place to start, especially if you haven't been working out. Unless you already have very strong abs, you don't need to use weights. Remember to gaze up toward the ceiling to avoid straining your neck. Also, because your abs are really three different muscles, doing a variety of exercises helps target them all.

Building Lower Back Muscles

What do my lower back muscles do?

Together with your stomach muscles (abdominals, or "abs"), your lower back muscles act like a girdle supporting your torso. Strong lower back muscles give you the support you need to help a friend re-arrange her bedroom furniture. They also keep you comfortable when you're stuck at a desk doing homework for hours on end. Those lower back muscles are also the key to safety when you lift weights (or the kid you are babysitting). And gymnasts know a strong lower back puts the spring in back handsprings.

You've heard at least one adult—your mother or father, a teacher, or friend—grumble about his or her aching back. Chances are the problem stemmed from the tailbone or lower back. You can avoid this misery by strengthening the muscles that run along both sides of your spine.

Some lower back exercises require no equipment. You can do them any-where you have enough space to lie down. You can also strengthen your lower back—along with your abs and the rest of your torso—using a medi-cine ball, or weighted workout ball.

Get Your Rear In Gear

Where are my glutes and quads?

The muscles that you sit on have an important sounding name, gluteus maximus (called glutes). Your glutes are some of the biggest muscles you've got, covering all of each cheek in your butt and extending down the back of your outer thigh. Four big muscles called the quadriceps (or quads) run down the front of your thigh.

What do my glutes and quads do?

Your glutes are in charge of straightening your leg from the hip. Every time you pedal a bike, climb stairs, or get up from a chair, you have your glutes to thank. Your quads straighten your leg from the knee. Strong glutes and quads boost your power, speed, and stamina for most activities and sports. Cyclists need them to crank up big hills. Speed skaters couldn't hold that low crouch without strong glutes and quads. Soccer players need them to sprint and boot the ball. Glutes and quads give figure skaters the lift they need to get airborne for double axels and triple toe loops. And kickboxers get their kick from strong glutes and quads. Strong glutes and quads help protect your hips and knees. And toning these muscles will help you walk those endless halls at school or dance 'til dawn.

Thigh Master

Where are my adductors and abductors?

In addition to the hamstrings on the back of your thighs and the quadri-ceps on the front of your thighs, you have outer and inner thigh muscles. The muscles that run down the outside of your thigh are called abductors. Your inner thigh muscles are called adductors.

What do my inner and outer thigh muscles do?

Your adductors and abductors help you move from side to side. Strong thigh muscles help you sidestep a brigade of charging snowballers and help you step aside just before your dog plows you over with an enthusiastic greeting. Basketball players need them to dodge a player on the way to the hoop. Kickboxers count on them for all those sidekicks. Tennis players need them to leap across the court for a wide ball. And girls who do aerobics use the inner and outer thigh muscles to do step patterns like the grapevine.

Your Hamstring Muscles

Where are my hamstrings?

Your hamstrings are the muscles behind the thigh. This big muscle stretches all the way from your butt to the back of your knee.

What do my hamstrings do?

In a never-ending tug of war, the hamstrings straighten the knee, while the quadriceps (on the front of your thighs) bend it. You couldn't even walk if you didn't have hamstring muscles. Runners and other athletes tend to develop very strong hamstrings. But most of us forget about those muscles on the back of our thighs and end up with weak hamstrings. Strong quads and weak hams is a recipe for injury—that's why athletes spend a lot of time strengthening and stretching their hamstrings.

How do I get strong hamstrings?

The hamstrings, quads, and the muscles of your buttocks (glutes) work as a team. Quad and glute exercises such as lunges and squats also target the hamstrings. If you want to focus on the hamstrings alone, add an exercise that involves bending only the knee, not the hip and the knee. The most common one is called a hamstring curl. These can be done on a machine at the gym. If you who don't have access to weight-training machines can get great results with elastic rubber tubing (sold at sporting goods stores). It doesn't take up any space and comes in cool, neon colors.

Calf Muscles

Where are my calf muscles?

Their official names are gastrocnemius and soleus, but calf muscle is a lot easier to say. You'll find these muscles at the back of your lower leg. The gastrocnemius is the bulkier one, just below your knee. The soleus sits underneath the gastrocnemius and reaches down towards your ankle.

What do my calf muscles do?

The big gastrocnemius does the heavy lifting when you go up on tiptoes. That comes in handy for ballet but also when you're stuck in a crowd and you want to see over some guy's head. The smaller soleus gets in on the action whenever you bend your knees. In other words, your calf muscles are working almost all the time.

Any aerobic activity that involves pushing off with your toes works your calves can help you develop strong calves. That includes pushing a skateboard uphill with one foot, walking, running, doing step aerobics, dancing, and kickboxing.

About iEmily

iEmily.com is a health website that provides teen girls with respectful, in-depth information about physical health and emotional well-being. The site includes articles reviewed by physicians, psychologists, and educators on nutrition, physical fitness, sexual health, emotional and psychological concerns, and other topics. iEmily.com also offers links to websites for additional information, as well as a list of hotlines for immediate help.

Chapter 11

Bones Need Weight-Bearing Activity And Calcium

Bone Up: How To Make Strong Bones

From the day you're born, your bones are being built with calcium to make them stronger.

So you've got the message that you need to eat and drink plenty of foods with calcium and do lots of weight-bearing physical activity. But I bet you're wondering why these things give you powerful bones.

Calcium Makes Bones As Strong As Steel

When your body makes new bone tissue, it first lays down a framework of collagen. Then, tiny crystals of calcium from your blood spread throughout the collagen framework. The hard crystals fill in all the nooks and crannies. Calcium and collagen work together to make bones strong and flexible.

Too Little Calcium Makes Bones Weak

Your body needs calcium to do lots of things. Calcium helps your muscles work so you can throw a softball. It helps send out nerve impulses. If you

About This Chapter: Text in this chapter is from "Bone Up: How to Make Strong Bones," and "Staying Strong: Fitness Fun," Division of Nutrition and Physical Activity, National Center for Chronic Disease Prevention and Health Promotion, Centers for Disease Control and Prevention (CDC), September 2001.

touch something hot, for instance, your brain quickly gets the message to say, "Ouch!" and move your hand away. It also helps your body heal cuts and scrapes.

Every cell in your body needs calcium. Your bones store calcium for your blood and cells. If your body doesn't get enough calcium, which can be found in some foods and drinks, it takes it from your bones. And that can make your bones weak.

From the day you're born, your bones are built and strengthened with calcium. In fact, when you're in your 20s (like, forever from now), your bones will be their strongest ever.

To make sure your bones are still powerful, even after you're 30, 40, or even 50, you need to get enough calcium now and keep getting it.

Run, Jump, And Dance To Make Bones Strong

Are you saying, "I get the whole calcium thing, but why is weight-bearing physical

✎ Weird Words

Bone Density: How solid and how strong your bones are on the inside. Bone density is a measure of bone strength.

Calcium: The mineral in your body that makes your bones and keeps them hard and strong. In fact, most of the calcium in your body is stored in your bones and teeth.

Milligram (mg): A unit of measure. A milligram is a little itty-bit of a gram (there are 1,000 milligrams in a gram). Nutrition labels use milligrams to show the amount of calcium and other minerals in foods. One 8-ounce glass of milk contains 300 milligrams of calcium.

Osteoporosis: A bone disease that adults sometimes get. People with osteoporosis have bones that are weak and that can easily break.

Peak Bone Mass: The highest level of bone density you can achieve (which probably happens in your 20s). Girls in the teenage years are building to their peak.

Vitamin D: The vitamin that helps your body absorb calcium. You can get vitamin D from milk, tuna fish, or eggs. Fifteen minutes of sunshine gives you plenty of vitamin D. Remember the sunblock if you're outside longer, though.

Source: Excerpted from "Dictionary," National Bone Health Campaign, Centers for Disease Control and Prevention.

activity so important?" Here's why: activities like walking and soccer make your bones work against gravity (the force that keeps us from floating out to space). Bones are living tissue. Weight-bearing physical activity stimulates new bone tissue to form, making them stronger. Also, weight-bearing physical activity makes muscles stronger, and muscles push and tug against bones, making them even stronger.

Swimming, which is good for your heart and other muscles, isn't the #1 choice for building bones. Ever notice how you feel a lot lighter in a pool? Water cuts down on how much you feel the pull of gravity, so your bones really don't get a good workout.

It Takes Two

Strong bones need both calcium and weight-bearing physical activity. It's not enough to just eat right or just do lots of weight-bearing physical activity. It takes both to make bones strong.

Staying Strong: Fitness Fun

You know how important it is to have strong, healthy bones now and when you grow up, right? Here are some ideas of weight-bearing physical activities to get you started. Weight-bearing means your muscles (and bones) are working against gravity—think jumping, running, lifting weights. Do some of these bone-healthy activities every day.

- Soccer is a sport of U.S. champions and great for you, too.
- Try out your moves. Dancing is fun and good for your bones.
- Ask a friend to sign up for karate or tae kwon do classes with you.
- You can be the next tennis superstar. Grab a racket and hit the court.
- A couple sets of push-ups will make for a stronger body and stronger bones.
- Chalk + Sidewalk = Hopscotch, a super workout for your bones.
- Jog around the neighborhood—feel good about your bones and yourself.

- Challenge some friends to a jump rope contest—it helps your heart as well as your bones.

- Views, nature, and lots of fun. Hiking is good for your bones and your mind.

- Want to be the next WNBA star? Then hit the court and practice those intense basketball moves.

Riding a bike, scooter, or skateboard doesn't really count as a bone-building physical activity. Neither does swimming. But these are all still terrific because they help your heart and other muscles. Just be sure to mix them with weight-bearing physical activity. So swimming and playing tennis would be a perfect body workout.

Chapter 12

How Much Exercise Do You Need?

How Much Exercise I Need?

U.S. Government experts recommend 60 minutes of moderate exercise most days of the week for kids and teens. In addition, you should do some sort of strength training at least twice a week.

What Do You Mean By 'Moderate'?

Moderate exercise means you do an activity vigorously enough to significantly increase your heart rate and breathing for an hour, which is called "aerobic exercise." This kind of exercise trains your heart and lungs to become stronger. How hard should you exercise? Some people like to follow the talk/sing rule, which says that you should be able to talk to someone while you exercise, but you should not be working so lightly that you can sing.

Another way to know if you are exercising hard enough is to calculate your Target Heart Rate range. By keeping your heart rate within the correct training range for your age, you can be sure you're getting all the benefits of aerobic exercise.

About This Chapter: Excerpted from "Fit For Life," updated February 2003, produced by The National Women's Health Information Center, a project of the Office on Women's Health in the U.S. Department of Health and Human Services. For more information visit www.4girls.gov.

Make A Fitness Plan

Decide what your fitness goals are and make a plan for achieving them (for example, I want to jog three miles without stopping; I want to be able to do 10 pushups). You are much more likely to achieve your goals if you actually write them down somewhere, and share them with friends or family.

Be sure to set reasonable goals. If you've never exercised much until now, it's not realistic to expect that you'll start exercising every day for an hour. Start with 30 minutes of moderate exercise a few times a week, letting your

---

✔ Quick Tip

Calculating Your Target Heart Rate

It is important to know if you're exercising hard enough and at a safe level! You'll need to figure out your target heart rate. Your target heart rate can depend on the type of exercise you're doing.

Moderate exercise includes activities like brisk walking, swimming, dancing, or water aerobics. For moderate-intensity physical activity, a person's target heart rate should be 50 to 70% of his or her maximum heart rate. This maximum rate is based on the person's age. An estimate of a person's maximum age-related heart rate can be obtained by subtracting the person's age from 220. If you are 14 years old your target heart rate for moderate exercise will be between 103 and 144 beats per minute.

Vigorous exercise includes activities like jogging, aerobics, basketball, fast swimming, or fast dancing. For vigorous-intensity physical activity, a person's target heart rate should be 70 to 85% of his or her maximum heart rate. To calculate this range, follow the same formula as used above, except change "50 and 70%" to "70 and 85%." If you are 14 years old, your target heart rate for vigorous exercise will be between 144 and 175 beats per minute.

Make It Simple

When you're on your computer, you can use the target heart rate calculator at www.4girls.gov/fit/thr_calc.cfm to figure out your target heart rate. The calculator

body recover for a day between exercise sessions. Then, as you get fit, you can add more time and/or more days to your routine. If you're already fit but want to train more, write down your current schedule and see where you can reasonably add more time or days to your workout routine.

It is important to plan ahead for dealing with potential obstacles to your exercise plan. For example, if your parents suddenly ask you to help with something around the house during your exercise time, when and where will you make it up? If you will need assistance getting somewhere or buying equipment for your workouts, make those arrangements in advance. Remember

will give your maximum and minimum heart rate. This is called your target zone. Try to exercise in this zone.

To Measure Your Heart Rate

Stop exercising briefly to take your heart rate (pulse). We recommend taking your pulse at the wrist. You can feel your pulse on your wrist in line with the thumb. Place the tips of the index and middle fingers over the artery and press lightly. Do not use the thumb. Take a full 60-second count of the heartbeats, or take for 30 seconds and multiply by 2. Start the count on a beat, which is counted as "zero."

Your Target Heart Rate Is Only A General Guide

Remember that your target heart rate and zone is only a general guide to help you know how hard to exercise. You should listen to your body when you're exercising. If you feel sick or get injured, you should slow down or stop.

Keep in mind that if you just started exercising, keep your heart rate at the lower end of the zone while you exercise. After 6 months, you should start reading the higher end of the zone.

Source: Adapted from "Target Heart Rate Calculator," Office on Women's Health, U.S. Department of Health and Human Services, and "Target Heart Rate and Estimated Maximum Heart Rate," National Center for Chronic Disease Prevention and Health Promotion, Centers for Disease Control and Prevention, updated February 2003.

that missing one day or one exercise session won't ruin your training; just get back on schedule as soon as possible.

♣ **It's A Fact!!**

What is the current physical activity recommendation to reduce your risk of chronic disease?

For adults, 6–7 days a week, 30 minutes or more of moderate intensity activity; for teens, 6–7 days a week, 60 minutes or more.

An example of a moderate intensity exercise is walking at a 12-minute mile pace. You can measure exercise intensity by determining your heart rate (the number of beats of your heart per minute) or your own perception of how hard you are working.

Source: Reprinted with permission from Shape up America! © 2003. All rights reserved. Shape Up America! is a national initiative to promote healthy weight and physical activity. For additional information about weight management, nutrition, and fitness, visit the Shape Up America! website at www.shapeup.org.

Chapter 13

Guidelines For Personal Exercise Programs

Making A Commitment

You have taken the important first step on the path to physical fitness by seeking information. The next step is to decide that you are going to be physically fit. This chapter is designed to help you reach that decision and your goal.

The decision to carry out a physical fitness program cannot be taken lightly. It requires a lifelong commitment of time and effort. Exercise must become one of those things that you do without question, like bathing and brushing your teeth. Unless you are convinced of the benefits of fitness and the risks of unfitness, you will not succeed.

Patience is essential. Don't try to do too much too soon and don't quit before you have a chance to experience the rewards of improved fitness. You can't regain in a few days or weeks what you have lost in years of sedentary living, but you can get it back if your persevere. And the prize is worth the price.

In the following pages you will find the basic information you need to begin and maintain a personal physical fitness program. These guidelines are intended for the average healthy adult. They tell you what your goals should

About This Chapter: "Fitness Fundamentals: Guidelines for Personal Exercise Programs," the President's Council on Physical Fitness and Sports. For additional information visit www.fitness.gov.

be and how often, how long and how hard you must exercise to achieve them. It also includes information that will make your workouts easier, safer, and more satisfying. The rest is up to you.

Checking Your Health

Teens generally don't need to see a doctor before beginning an exercise program. Some conditions that indicate a need for medical clearance are:

- High blood pressure

- Heart trouble

- Family history of early stroke or heart attack deaths

- Frequent dizzy spells

- Extreme breathlessness after mild exertion

- Arthritis or other bone problems

- Severe muscular, ligament, or tendon problems

- Other known or suspected disease

> **♣ It's A Fact!!**
> Vigorous exercise involves minimal health risks for persons in good health or those following a doctor's advice. Far greater risks are presented by habitual inactivity and obesity.

Defining Fitness

Physical fitness is to the human body what fine tuning is to an engine. It enables us to perform up to our potential. Fitness can be described as a condition that helps us look, feel, and do our best. More specifically, it is:

> "The ability to perform daily tasks vigorously and alertly, with energy left over for enjoying leisure-time activities and meeting emergency demands. It is the ability to endure, to bear up, to withstand stress, to carry on in circumstances where an unfit person could not continue, and is a major basis for good health and well-being."

Physical fitness involves the performance of the heart and lungs, and the muscles of the body. And, since what we do with our bodies also affects what we can do with our minds, fitness influences, to some degree, qualities such as mental alertness and emotional stability.

As you undertake your fitness program, it's important to remember that fitness is an individual quality that varies from person to person. It is influenced by age, sex, heredity, personal habits, exercise, and eating practices. You can't do anything about the first three factors. However, it is within your power to change and improve the others where needed.

Knowing The Basics

Physical fitness is most easily understood by examining its components, or "parts." There is widespread agreement that these four components are basic: cardiorespiratory endurance, muscular strength, muscular endurance, and flexibility. Body composition is also often considered a component of fitness. It refers to the makeup of the body in terms of lean mass (muscle, bone, vital tissue, and organs) and fat mass. An optimal ratio of fat to lean mass is an indication of fitness, and the right types of exercises will help you decrease body fat and increase or maintain muscle mass.

A Workout Schedule

How often, how long, and how hard you exercise, and what kinds of exercises you do should be determined by what you are trying to accomplish.

✎ Weird Words

Cardiorespiratory Endurance: The ability to deliver oxygen and nutrients to tissues, and to remove wastes, over sustained periods of time. Long runs and swims are among the methods employed in measuring this component.

Muscular Strength: The ability of a muscle to exert force for a brief period of time. Upper-body strength, for example, can be measured by various weight-lifting exercises.

Muscular Endurance: The ability of a muscle, or a group of muscles, to sustain repeated contractions or to continue applying force against a fixed object. Pushups are often used to test endurance of arm and shoulder muscles.

Flexibility: The ability to move joints and use muscles through their full range of motion. The sit-and-reach test is a good measure of flexibility of the lower back and backs of the upper legs.

Your goals, your present fitness level, age, health, skills, interest, and convenience are among the factors you should consider. For example, an athlete training for high-level competition would follow a different program than a person whose goals are good health and the ability to meet work and recreational needs.

Here are the amounts of activity necessary for the average healthy person to maintain a minimum level of overall fitness. Included are some of the popular exercises for each category.

Warm-up: 5–10 minutes of exercise such as walking, slow jogging, knee lifts, arm circles, or trunk rotations. Low intensity movements that simulate movements to be used in the activity can also be included in the warm-up.

Muscular Strength: A minimum of two 20-minute sessions per week that include exercises for all the major muscle groups. Lifting weights is the most effective way to increase strength.

Muscular Endurance: At least three 30-minute sessions each week that include exercises such as calisthenics, pushups, sit-ups, pull-ups, and weight training for all the major muscle groups.

Cardiorespiratory Endurance: At least three 20-minute bouts of continuous aerobic (activity requiring oxygen) rhythmic exercise each week. Popular aerobic conditioning activities include brisk walking, jogging, swimming, cycling, rope-jumping, rowing, cross-country skiing, and some continuous action games like racquetball and handball.

Flexibility: 10–12 minutes of daily stretching exercises performed slowly, without a bouncing motion. This can be included after a warm-up or during a cool-down.

Cool Down: A minimum of 5–10 minutes of slow walking, low-level exercise, combined with stretching.

> ✔ **Quick Tip**
>
> Your exercise program should include something from each of the four basic fitness components described previously. Each workout should begin with a warm-up and end with a cool-down. As a general rule, space your workouts throughout the week and avoid consecutive days of hard exercise.

A Matter Of Principle

The keys to selecting the right kinds of exercises for developing and maintaining each of the basic components of fitness are found in these principles:

Specificity: Pick the right kind of activities to affect each component. Strength training results in specific strength changes. Also, train for the specific activity you're interested in. For example, optimal swimming performance is best achieved when the muscles involved in swimming are trained for the movements required. It does not necessarily follow that a good runner is a good swimmer.

Overload: Work hard enough, at levels that are vigorous and long enough to overload your body above its resting level, to bring about improvement.

Regularity: You can't hoard physical fitness. At least three balanced workouts a week are necessary to maintain a desirable level of fitness.

Progression: Increase the intensity, frequency, and/or duration of activity over periods of time in order to improve.

Some activities can be used to fulfill more than one of your basic exercise requirements. For example, in addition to increasing cardiorespiratory endurance, running builds muscular endurance in the legs, and swimming develops the arm, shoulder, and chest muscles. If you select the proper activities, it is possible to fit parts of your muscular endurance workout into your cardiorespiratory workout and save time.

Measuring Your Heart Rate

Heart rate is widely accepted as a good method for measuring intensity during running, swimming, cycling, and other aerobic activities. Exercise that doesn't raise your heart rate to a certain level and keep it there for 20 minutes won't contribute significantly to cardiovascular fitness.

The heart rate you should maintain is called your target heart rate. There are several ways of arriving at this figure. One of the simplest is: maximum heart rate (220 minus age) multiplied by 70%.

Some methods for figuring the target rate take individual differences into consideration. Here is one of them:

- Subtract age from 220 to find maximum heart rate.

- Subtract resting heart rate (see below) from maximum heart rate to determine heart rate reserve.

- Take 70% of heart rate reserve to determine heart rate raise.

- Add heart rate raise to resting heart rate to find target rate.

Resting heart rate should be determined by taking your pulse after sitting quietly for five minutes. When checking heart rate during a workout, take your pulse within five seconds after interrupting exercise because it starts to

---

✔ Quick Tip
Dress Right For Exercise

All exercise clothing should be loose-fitting to permit freedom of movement, and should make the wearer feel comfortable and self-assured.

As a general rule, you should wear lighter clothes than temperatures might indicate. Exercise generates great amounts of body heat. Light-colored clothing that reflects the sun's rays is cooler in the summer, and dark clothes are warmer in winter. When the weather is very cold, it's better to wear several layers of light clothing than one or two heavy layers. The extra layers help trap heat, and it's easy to shed one of them if you become too warm.

In cold weather, and in hot, sunny weather, it's a good idea to wear something on your head. Wool watch or ski caps are recommended for winter wear, and some form of tennis or sailor's hat that provides shade and can be soaked in water is good for summer.

Never wear rubberized or plastic clothing, such garments interfere with the evaporation of perspiration and can cause body temperature to rise to dangerous levels.

The most important item of equipment for the runner is a pair of sturdy, properly fitting running shoes. Training shoes with heavy, cushioned soles and arch supports are preferable to flimsy sneakers and light racing flats.

go down once you stop moving. Count pulse for 10 seconds and multiply by six to get the per-minute rate.

Controlling Your Weight

The key to weight control is keeping energy intake (food) and energy output (physical activity) in balance. When you consume only as many calories as your body needs, your weight will usually remain constant. If you take in more calories than your body needs, you will put on excess fat. If you expend more energy than you take in you will burn excess fat.

Exercise plays an important role in weight control by increasing energy output, calling on stored calories for extra fuel. Recent studies show that not only does exercise increase metabolism during a workout, but it causes your metabolism to stay increased for a period of time after exercising, allowing you to burn more calories.

How much exercise is needed to make a difference in your weight depends on the amount and type of activity, and on how much you eat. Aerobic exercise burns body fat. A medium-sized adult would have to walk more than 30 miles to burn up 3,500 calories, the equivalent of one pound of fat. Although that may seem like a lot, you don't have to walk the 30 miles all at once. Walking a mile a day for 30 days will achieve the same result, providing you don't increase your food intake to negate the effects of walking.

If you consume 100 calories a day more than your body needs, you will gain approximately 10 pounds in a year. You could take that weight off, or keep it off, by doing 30 minutes of moderate exercise daily. The combination of exercise and diet offers the most flexible and effective approach to weight control.

Since muscle tissue weighs more than fat tissue, and exercise develops muscle to a certain degree, your bathroom scale won't necessarily tell you whether or not you are "fat." Well-muscled individuals, with relatively little body fat, invariably are "overweight" according to standard weight charts. If you are doing a regular program of strength training, your muscles will increase in weight, and possibly your overall weight will increase. Body composition is a better indicator of your condition than body weight.

Lack of physical activity causes muscles to get soft, and if food intake is not decreased, added body weight is almost always fat. Once-active people, who continue to eat as they always have after settling into sedentary lifestyles, tend to suffer from "creeping obesity."

When To Exercise

The hour just before the evening meal is a popular time for exercise. The late afternoon workout provides a welcome change of pace at the end of the work day and helps dissolve the day's worries and tensions.

Another popular time to work out is early morning, before the day's activities begin. Advocates of the early start say it makes them more alert and energetic during the day.

Among the factors you should consider in developing your workout schedule are personal preference and responsibilities, availability of exercise facilities, and weather. It's important to schedule your workouts for a time when there is little chance that you will have to cancel or interrupt them because of other demands on your time.

You should not exercise strenuously during extremely hot, humid weather or within two hours after eating. Heat and/or digestion both make heavy demands on the circulatory system, and in combination with exercise can be an overtaxing double load.

Chapter 14

The Fitness Formula

The Formula

Whether you're interested in training for a sport, losing weight, or just trying to get in shape, the following fitness formula covers the bases, promoting cardiorespiratory fitness, muscle strength, and flexibility. Integrate each component into your program for a balanced workout.

Cardiorespiratory Fitness

Of all the things you can do in your quest for fitness, aerobic activities are the most important. Aerobic activities like brisk walking, running, cycling, swimming, rowing, or skating are all examples of activities that get you breathing harder while keeping you constantly on the move.

Developing the heart and lungs to efficiently transport oxygen through the bloodstream will make for a more endurable you. But there's a difference between filling your lungs with oxygen-rich blood and buffing and puffing your way to exhaustion. To get it right, we'll address the most frequently asked questions in regards to aerobic activity: How often? How hard? How long?

About This Chapter: "The Fitness Formula," by Sharon Barbano, M.Ed., is reprinted with permission from the Women's Sports Foundation, www.womenssports foundation.org. © 1996. All rights reserved. Despite the date of this document, the information is still pertinent.

How Often?

To improve your aerobic fitness level, the American College of Sports Medicine recommends exercising three to five days a week. If you are just beginning, give yourself a day or two in-between workouts to let your body recover. This is especially true if you choose high impact activities that include lots of running and jumping, or if you are overweight.

How Hard?

We all want to know how fast we should run; how hard we should pedal; how high we should climb. The answer is simple. Listen to your body If you feel comfortable doing what you're doing, at an effort that's between fairly light and somewhat hard, you're on target. You can also use the "talk test:" If you can carry on a conversation during your activity, you're in the appropriate effort zone.

If you prefer a more scientific approach, find your "target heart rate zone," and stay within it. To find the zone, determine your maximum heart rate (MHR) by subtracting your age from 220. Next, multiply your MHR by .65 to determine your minimum aerobic

---

✔ Quick Tip

Your fitness plan should include:

Exercise for aerobic fitness: Aerobic-type activities improve the function and efficiency of your heart, lungs, and blood vessels. Start out with short workouts, and then gradually progress to 20 or 30 minutes three to five times a week. Try a variety of activities such as walking, jobbing, swimming, biking and tennis.

Exercise for muscle strength and endurance: Using resistance builds muscle tone and strength, helps improve posture, and makes muscles and bones more resistant to injury. Keep your movements slow and controlled, and train only every other day or twice a week. Calisthenics, such as push-ups, sit-ups, or moderate weight lifting build strength and muscle endurance.

Exercise for flexibility: Proper stretching every day reduces the chance of muscle strain and injury. Move body joints through a full range of motion, gently and slowly stretching each muscle group. Hold each stretch until you feel a slight pulling sensation, but not pain. Breathe comfortably, holding the stretch for 15 to 20 seconds. Repeat several times.

Source: Excerpted from "Introducing the Physician's Rx: Exercise," President's Council on Physical Fitness and Sports, undated. Available at www.fitness.gov.

training rate. Then, multiply your MHR by .80 for your maximum training rate. Following this formula, the target heart rate of a 40-year-old is between 117 and 144 beats per minute. Sports physiologists have determined that exercising at 65 to 80 percent of your maximum heart rate is enough for basic fitness.

How Long?

According to the American College of Sports Medicine, aerobic activity should last between 20 to 60 minutes per session in order to gain the cardiorespiratory benefits. Beginners should stick to a shorter duration, and build up gradually. Moderate activities such as walking or dancing, done in five-to-ten-minute increments for a total of 30 minutes a day are effective as well.

Getting Strong

All workout regimens must include some form of strength training. Whether your goal is better sports performance, weight loss, or toning, strength training will deliver the results.

Aim for exercises that target all the major muscle groups, including: arms; shoulders; chest; back; abdomen; and upper and lower legs. If strength training is new to you, consult with a professional who can get you started safely.

Begin with a weight you can lift comfortably for 8 to 12 repetitions. Once 12 reps become easy, you can increase the weight slightly or increase the number of repetitions. Beginners should aim for one set of each exercise. As you become stronger, you can increase the number of sets to two or three. Be sure to give yourself one to three minutes of rest between sets. Try to include at least two strength workouts a week, and allow at least one day between strength training sessions.

Always include a few minutes of light to moderate aerobic activity and easy stretching before and after your strength workout.

Stretch It Out

Flexibility is probably the most overlooked component of the fitness formula. It's easy to leave out, especially when time is short. But its inclusion offers many benefits for those who take the time. Five to 10 minutes a day of easy stretching will reduce potential injuries and increase range of motion. Additionally, stretching will reduce muscle soreness after a hard game or workout, improve posture, decrease stress, increase performance, and generally make you feel good all over.

♣ It's A Fact!!
Stretching Facts

- Never stretch a cold muscle. Do a few minutes of light aerobic activity like walking or stationary biking as part of your warm-up before you stretch.

- Avoid bouncing when you stretch. It won't help you stretch farther and it might even cause injury.

- Stretch the major muscle groups and the muscles used most in the activity. For example, if you're playing racquetball, be sure to focus on your forearm and shoulder muscles.

- During your cool-down, slow your pace for a few minutes before you stop. This will relax your body and mind, ensuring a safer, gentler stretching session.

- Stretching should always be part of your warm-up and cool-down.

- Stretch slowly, to the point where you feel a little bit of tension. Hold that position for 10 to 20 seconds, keeping your breathing relaxed.

Chapter 15

Exercise: How To Get Started

Why Should I Exercise?

Increased physical activity can lead to a longer life and improved health. Exercise helps prevent heart disease and many other problems. Exercise builds strength, gives you more energy, and can help you reduce stress. It is also a good way to curb your appetite and burn calories.

Who Should Exercise?

Increased physical activity can benefit almost everyone. Most people can begin gradual, moderate exercise on their own. If you think there is a reason you may not be able to exercise safely, talk with your doctor before beginning a new exercise program. In particular, your doctor needs to know if you have heart trouble, high blood pressure, or arthritis, or if you often feel dizzy or have chest pains.

What Kind Of Exercise Should I Do?

Exercises that increase your heart rate and move large muscles (such as the muscles in your legs and arms) are best. Choose an activity that you enjoy and that you can start slowly and increase gradually as you become

About This Chapter: Text in this chapter is reprinted with permission from "Exercise: How To Get Started," http://familydoctor.org/015.xml. © 1995 American Academy of Family Physicians; reviewed/updated December 2000. All rights reserved.

Five Fun Ways To Get Physical

Who says you have to play sports to have fun and be fit? There are lots of great ways to put more action in your life. Being active helps you build strong bones and muscles. It also helps you look and feel your best. And it helps give you more energy to do other things.

Pick and choose some of these fun ways to get fit. Or think of your own ways to get moving. Your body will thank you.

1. *Use your feet.* Your feet were made for walking, so use them every chance you get. Walk to a friend's house, to the store, around the mall or wherever it's safe to walk. While you're at it, walk your dog. Or offer to walk your neighbor's dog.

2. *Move to the beat.* Turn up the music and dance! Dance with your friends or on your own. And who says you can't do two things at once? Dance while you talk on the phone. Dance while you watch TV. You can even dance while you clean your room!

3. *Roll around town.* Make your muscles do the work on your bike, skates, or scooter as you enjoy the cool breeze. Don't forget to wear the gear: a helmet, and knee, wrist, and elbow pads for skating.

4. *Get your friends moving.* Gather a few friends to shoot hoops, kick around a soccer ball, play street hockey, or throw around a football or baseball. You don't need to be on a team to enjoy sports. Check out the recreation center in your neighborhood for open gym times and other fun activities like tennis, swimming, or dance classes.

5. *Be a buddy.* Stuck babysitting or playing with younger brothers or sisters? Make it play time. Young kids love games like hopscotch, tag, hide-and-seek, Hula-Hoops, jump rope, squirt guns, T-ball, kickball, or flying a kite—especially when they're doing it with a "cool" older friend like you.

used to it. Walking is very popular and does not require special equipment. Other good exercises include swimming, biking, jogging, and dancing. Taking the stairs instead of the elevator or walking instead of driving may also be a good way to start being more active.

How Long Should I Exercise?

Start off exercising 3 or more times a week for 20 minutes or more, and work up to at least 30 minutes, 4 to 6 times a week. This can include several short bouts of activity in a day. Exercising during a lunch break or on your way to do errands may help you add physical activity to a busy schedule. Exercising with a friend or a family member can help make it fun, and having a partner to encourage you can help you stick to it.

Is There Anything I Should Do Before And After I Exercise?

You should start an exercise session with a gradual warm-up period. During this time (about 5 to 10 minutes), you should slowly stretch your muscles first, and then gradually increase your level of activity. For example, begin walking slowly and then pick up the pace.

After you are finished exercising, cool down for about 5 to 10 minutes. Again, stretch your muscles and let your heart rate slow down gradually. You can use the same stretches as in the warm-up period.

A number of warm-up and cool-down stretching exercises for your legs are shown at the end of this handout. If you are going to exercise your upper body, be sure to use stretching exercises for your arms, shoulders, chest, and back.

How Hard Do I Have To Exercise?

Even small amounts of exercise are better than none at all. Start with an activity you can do comfortably. As you become more used to exercising, try to keep your heart rate at about 60 to 85% of your "maximum heart rate." To figure out your target heart rate, subtract your age in years from 220 (which gives your maximum heart rate), and then multiply that number by 0.60 or 0.85. For example, if you are 16 years old, you would subtract 16 from 220, which would give you 204 (220 - 16 = 204). Then you would multiply this number by either 0.60 or 0.85, which would give you 122 or 173 (204 x 0.60 = 122 and 204 x 0.85 = 173).

When you first start your exercise program, you may want to use the lower number (0.60) to calculate your target heart rate. Then, as your conditioning gradually increases, you may want to use the higher number (0.85) to calculate your target heart rate. Check your pulse by gently resting 2 fingers on the side of your neck and counting the beats for 1 minute. Use a watch with a second hand to time the minute.

✔ Quick Tip

How To Get Moving And Have Fun When It's Just You

You don't have to be a couch potato just because you have some time by yourself. It's fun to go solo, too.

Hop on your bike (don't forget your helmet!). Take a ride around the neighborhood and see what's going on. Bike to the store and see if there are any new comics or magazines you want to buy.

If you have skates or blades, give them a spin (don't forget your helmet and pads!). If you skateboard, grab your board, helmet, and pads, and try some new moves. Try jumping rope and counting how many times you can jump before you miss—jumping rope is a really great way to get aerobic exercise (the kind that makes your muscles use oxygen and your heart stronger).

Sometimes being by yourself lets you practice things over and over, which you usually can't do when you're playing with somebody else. Plus, you can work on your technique so that you'll amaze your friends when you play with them again!

How Do I Avoid Injuring Myself?

The safest way to keep from injuring yourself during exercise is to avoid trying to do too much too soon. Start with an activity that is fairly easy for you, such as walking. Do it for a few minutes a day or several times a day. Then slowly increase the time and level of activity. For example, increase how fast you walk over several weeks. If you feel tired or sore, ease up somewhat on the level of exercise, or take a day off to rest. Try not to give up entirely even if you don't feel great right away. Talk with your doctor if you have questions or think you have injured yourself seriously.

If you play tennis, try hitting a tennis ball against a brick wall. Count how many times in a row you can hit the ball without missing—then try to beat your own record. If basketball's your thing, try shooting hoops and seeing how many foul shots you can sink. Or if you're into soccer, grab a ball and see how long you can keep it in the air using your feet, knees, and head.

More Things To Do When It's Just You

- Jump rope (try jumping backwards or while moving forward).

- Try to hop on one foot all the way through your favorite song.

- Do jumping jacks to music. See if you can jump all the way through a short song, then a longer song.

- Invent some dance moves.

- See how fast you can run for one block.

- Practice martial arts.

- Try a yoga video.

Source: Reprinted with permission from www.kidnetic.com, a website of the International Food Informational Council Foundation. © 2003 IFIC Foundation. All rights reserved.

✔ Quick Tip
Get In The Groove With The 10-Minute Move

Moving your body by running, jumping, walking, and playing gives you energy, makes your muscles stronger, and helps you feel good about yourself. Moving for 60 minutes every day is a great goal. But don't worry if that seems like too much to do at one time. Try doing your moves for just 10 minutes, but do them at least a few times each day.

See how many 10-minute moves you can do each day, like during a homework break or while you're watching TV. Do your favorite thing or try one of the ideas below. If you want to do more than 10 minutes at a time, you'll feel even better!

- Turn on your favorite music and dance.
- Walk to a friend's house that's a few blocks away.
- Go outside and rake leaves, pull weeds or sweep the sidewalk.
- Do inside chores like vacuuming, dusting or emptying the garbage.
- Do jumping jacks for one minute, march in place for one minute and step up and down a stair for one minute. Repeat until 10 minutes are up.
- Play tag with your younger brother or sister.
- Skip rope.
- Walk the dog.
- In-line skate.
- Do part of an exercise tape.
- Shoot baskets in the driveway or at the rec center.
- Practice the Hula-Hoop.
- Kick a soccer ball.
- Ride an exercise bike.
- Jog around the block.

What About Strength Training?

Most kinds of exercise will help both your heart and your other muscles. Resistance training is exercise that develops the strength and endurance of large muscle groups. Weight lifting is an example of this type of exercise. Exercise machines can also provide resistance training. Your doctor or a trainer at a gym can give you more information about exercising safely with weights or machines.

Warm-Up And Cool-Down Stretches

Calf Stretch

Face a wall, standing about 2 feet away from it. Keeping your heels flat and your back straight, lean forward slowly and press your hands and forehead to the wall. You should feel stretching in the area above your heels (this area is shaded in the picture). Hold the stretch for 20 seconds and then relax. Repeat.

Quad Stretch

Face a wall, standing about 1 foot away from it. Support yourself by placing your right hand against the wall. Raise your right leg behind you and grab your foot with your left hand. Gently pull your heel up toward your buttock, stretching the muscles in the front of your right leg for 20 seconds. Repeat the stretch with your left leg.

Groin Stretch

Squat down and put both hands on the floor in front of you. Stretch your left leg straight out behind you. Keep your right foot flat on the floor and lean forward with your chest into your right knee, then gradually shift weight back to your left leg, keeping it as straight as possible. Hold the stretch for 20 seconds. Repeat the stretch with your right leg behind you.

Hamstring Stretch

Lie down with your back flat on the floor and both knees bent. Your feet should be flat on the floor, about 6 inches apart. Bend your right knee up to your chest and grab your right thigh with both hands behind your knee. Gradually straighten your right leg, feeling gentle stretching in the back of your leg. Hold the stretch for 20 seconds. Repeat the stretch with your left leg.

This chapter provides a general overview on this topic and may not apply to everyone. To find out if this chapter applies to you and to get more information on this subject, talk to your family doctor.

Chapter 16

Ten Exercise Myths

Although some old fitness fictions, such as "no pain, no gain" and "spot reducing" are fading fast, plenty of popular exercise misconceptions still exist. Here are some of the most common myths as well as the not-so-common facts based on current exercise research.

Myth: You will burn more fat if you exercise longer at a lower intensity.

Fact: The most important focus in exercise and fat weight control is not the percentage of exercise energy coming from fat but the total energy cost, or how many calories are burned during the activity. The faster you walk, step, or run, for example, the more calories you use per minute. However, high-intensity exercise is difficult to sustain if you are just beginning or returning to exercise, so you may not exercise very long at this level. It is safer, and more practical, to start out at a lower intensity and work your way up gradually.

Myth: If you're not going to work out hard and often, exercise is a waste of time.

Fact: This kind of thinking keeps a lot of people from maintaining or even starting an exercise program. Research continues to show that any exercise is better than none. For example, regular walking or gardening for as little as an hour a week has been shown to reduce the risk of heart disease.

Myth: Yoga is a completely gentle and safe exercise.

Fact: Yoga is an excellent form of exercise, but some styles are quite rigorous and demanding both physically and mentally. As with any form of exercise, qualified, careful instruction is necessary for a safe, effective workout.

Myth: If you exercise long and hard enough, you will always get the results you want.

Fact: In reality, genetics plays an important role in how people respond to exercise. Studies have shown a wide variation in how different exercisers respond to the same training program. Your development of strength, speed, and endurance may be very different from that of other people you know.

> ✔ **Quick Tip**
>
> **Get FITT**
>
> - **Frequency:** Get active at least five times a week.
>
> - **Intensity:** Get your body revved up and your heart pumping.
>
> - **Time:** Spend at least 60 minutes doing a variety of activities.
>
> - **Type:** Do a variety of different types of activities that work your body and fit your style; AND, have some fun while you're at it.
>
> Source: Excerpted from "Motion Commotion," BAM! (Body And Mind), Centers for Disease Control and Prevention, April 30, 2002.

Myth: Exercise is one sure way to lose all the weight you desire.

Fact: As with all responses to exercise, weight gain or loss is impacted by many factors, including dietary intake and genetics. All individuals will not lose the same amount of weight on the same exercise program. It is possible to be active and overweight. However, although exercise alone cannot guarantee your ideal weight, regular physical activity is one of the most important factors for successful long-term weight management.

Myth: If you want to lose weight, stay away from strength training because you will bulk up.

Fact: Most exercise experts believe that cardiovascular exercise and strength training are both valuable for maintaining a healthy weight. Strength training helps maintain muscle mass and decrease body fat percentage.

Myth: Water fitness programs are primarily for older people or exercisers with injuries.

Fact: Recent research has shown that water fitness programs can be highly challenging and effective for both improving fitness and losing weight. Even top athletes integrate water fitness workouts into their training programs.

Myth: The health and fitness benefits of mind-body exercise like Tai chi and Yoga are questionable.

Fact: In fact, research showing the benefits of these exercises continues to grow. Tai chi, for example, has been shown to help treat low-back pain and fibromyalgia. Improved flexibility, balance, coordination, posture, strength, and stress management are just some of the potential results of mind-body exercise.

Myth: Overweight people are unlikely to benefit much from exercise.

Fact: Studies show that obese people who participate in regular exercise programs have a lower risk of all-cause mortality than sedentary individuals, regardless of weight. Both men and women of all sizes and fitness levels can improve their health with modest increases in activity.

Myth: Home workouts are fine, but going to a gym is the best way to get fit.

Fact: Research has shown that some people find it easier to stick to a home-based fitness program. In spite of all the hype on trendy exercise programs and facilities, the "best" program for you is the one you will participate in consistently.

✔ Quick Tip

- Start slow and learn the right techniques for the activity you're doing. It's a good idea to take a lesson or get some tips from an expert.

- Warm it up, stretch it out, and cool it down—your muscles that is! It's important to warm up before and cool down after each workout.

- If the activity you're doing requires protective gear, make sure you wear it at all times—and check it regularly to make sure it fits or works right.

Source: Excerpted from "Survival for the Fittest," BAM! (Body And Mind), Centers for Disease Control and Prevention, April 30, 2002.

Chapter 17

Measuring Exercise Intensity

For years, many fitness experts believed that using a certain formula could determine proper exercise intensity, one challenging but not so hard that it endangers your health. Some experts still believe that this formula is the best measurement, but others have doubts.

Understand The Standard Maximum Heart Rate Formula

Traditionally, exercise experts have used this formula to determine maximum heart rate: 220 minus age (plus or minus 10%). This number predicts the heart rate that you would attain by exercising at an all-out effort. According to the Karvonen formula, your goal should be to attain 50 to 90 percent of this number when exercising.

Know Why This Formula Isn't Perfect

Of course, the standard heart rate formula may not always work. "We are all on a bell-shaped curve," says Jeffrey Potteiger, PhD, director of the Health and Human Performance Laboratory at Virginia Commonwealth University in Richmond, Virginia. "So many factors influence heart rate: caffeine, stress, lack of sleep, etc. We want to measure intensity to get a training effect and to make it safe, but it's not a hard and fast rule."

Learn About A New Formula

Hirofumi Tanaka, PhD, researcher at the University of Colorado, Boulder, proposes a new formula for determining maximum heart rate: 208 minus 70 percent of age. In research published in *the Journal of the American College of Cardiology*, Tanaka and colleagues analyzed 351 studies and tested 514 subjects; their findings show that the original formula overestimates maximum heart rate in young adults and underestimates it in older adults. Tanaka believes that the new formula would determine a more appropriate maximum heart rate for everyone. However, he adds that your actual maximum

Table 17.1. Rating of Perceived Exertion Scales (Borg)

Category Scale		Category-Ratio Scale	
6	No exertion at all	0	Nothing at all
7	Extremely light	0.5	Extremely weak (just noticeable)
8		1	Very weak
9	Very light	2	Weak (light)
10		3	Moderate
11	Light	4	
12		5	Strong (heavy)
13	Somewhat hard	6	
14		7	Very strong
15	Hard	8	
16		9	
17	Very hard	10	Extremely strong (almost max)
18			
19	Extremely hard		
20	Maximal exertion		

heart rate may vary by as many as 10 beats per minute (above or below), so this new equation isn't a perfect prediction, either.

Consider RPE

Experts such as Richard Stein, MD, chief of cardiology at Brooklyn Hospital Center in New York, advise using RPE (Rating of Perceived Exertion) instead. RPE is a self-assessment scale that rates symptoms of breathlessness and fatigue during your workout to determine how hard you are exercising. You can use either the original RPE scale of 6 to 20 or the modified scale of 0 to 10. (See Table 17.1 for more details.) Most exercisers should aim for a perceived exertion of "somewhat hard," about 13 on the original scale or 4 on the modified scale.

Get Support And Listen To Your Body

Stein cautions that a learning curve is involved in using RPE. A personal trainer can help you understand how to match what your body feels to the RPE scale. Ultimately, you are the expert on your body. By paying attention to how it feels at different exercise intensities, you can learn to challenge yourself safely.

Chapter 18

Exercise And Weight Control

Physical activity helps you control your weight by using excess calories that would otherwise be stored as fat. Most foods you eat contain calories, and everything you do uses calories, including sleeping, breathing, and digesting food. Balancing the calories you eat with the calories you use through physical activity will help you reach and maintain a healthy weight.

Becoming Physically Active

Experts recommend at least 30 minutes (60 minutes for children and teens) of moderate-intensity physical activity on most, if not all, days of the week. To achieve and maintain a healthy weight, particularly after you have lost a large amount of weight, you may need to do 60 minutes or more of moderate-intensity physical activity each day.

Physical activity may include structured activities such as walking, running, basketball, or other sports. It may also include daily activities such as household chores, yard work, or walking the dog. Pick a combination of structured and daily activities that fit your schedule.

If you have been inactive for a while, start slowly and work up to 30 minutes a day at a pace that is comfortable for you. If you are unable to be

About This Chapter: This chapter includes text from "Physical Activity and Weight Control," National Institute of Diabetes and Digestive and Kidney Diseases (NIDDK), NIH Pub. No. 03-4031, March 2003.

♣ It's A Fact!!

Counting Calories

Each pound of fat your body stores represents 3,500 calories of unused energy. In order to lose one pound, you would have to create a calorie deficit of 3,500 calories by either taking in 3,500 less calories over a period of time than you need or doing 3,500 calories worth of exercise. It is recommended that no more than two pounds (7,000 calories) be lost per week for lasting weight loss.

Adding 15 minutes of moderate exercise, say walking one mile, to your daily schedule will use up 100 extra calories per day. (Your body uses approximately 100 calories of energy to walk one mile, depending on your body weight.) Maintaining this schedule would result in an extra 700 calories per week used up, or a loss of about 10 pounds in one year, assuming your food intake stays the same. To look at energy balance another way, just one extra slice of bread or one extra soft drink a day—or any other food that contains approximately 100 calories—can add up to ten extra pounds in a year if the amount of physical activity you do does not increase.

If you already have a lean figure and want to keep it you should exercise regularly and eat a balanced diet that provides enough calories to make up for the energy you expend. If you wish to gain weight you should exercise regularly and increase the number of calories you consume until you reach your desired weight. Exercise will help ensure that the weight you gain will be lean muscle mass, not extra fat.

Source: Excerpted from "Exercise and Weight Control," President's Council on Physical Fitness and Sports. The full text is available online at http://fitness .gov/exerciseweight.html.

active for 30 minutes at one time, accumulate activity over the course of the day in 10–15 minute sessions.

Health Benefits Of Physical Activity

Regular physical activity helps control your weight and may help:

• Reduce your risk of or manage chronic diseases such as type 2 diabetes, high blood pressure and cholesterol, heart disease, osteoporosis, arthritis, and some cancers;

- Build strong muscles, bones, and joints;

- Improve flexibility and balance;

- Ward off depression; and

- Improve mood and sense of well-being.

Aerobic Activity

You can meet your goal of at least 30 minutes of moderate-intensity physical activity by participating in aerobic activities. Aerobic exercise includes any activity that makes you breathe harder than when you are resting and increases your heart rate.

Experts recommend moderate-intensity exercise. At this pace, you may breathe harder and find it more difficult to talk, but you should still be able to carry on a conversation. If you are just beginning, slowly work up to moving at a moderate-intensity pace.

Get Started!

To add more physical activity to your daily life try:

- Taking a brisk walk around the block with family, friends, or coworkers.

- Raking the leaves.

- Walking up the stairs instead of taking the elevator when it is safe to do so.

- Mowing the lawn.

☞ **Remember!!**

Regular physical activity can help you reach and maintain a healthy weight. Being physically active can also make you more energetic, improve your mood, and reduce the risk of developing some chronic diseases.

- Taking an activity break at work or home. Get up and stretch or walk around.

- Parking your car further away from entrances of stores, movie theatres, or your home and walk the extra distance when it is safe to do so.

✦ It's A Fact!!

The Benefits Of Exercise In A Weight Control Program

The benefits of exercise are many, from producing physically fit bodies to providing an outlet for fun and socialization. When added to a weight control program these benefits take on increased significance.

Proper exercise can help control weight by burning excess body fat. It also has two other body-trimming advantages 1) exercise builds muscle tissue and muscle uses calories up at a faster rate than body fat; and 2) exercise helps reduce inches and a firm, lean body looks slimmer even if your weight remains the same.

Remember, fat does not "turn into" muscle, as is often believed. Fat and muscle are two entirely different substances and one cannot become the other. However, muscle does use calories at a faster rate than fat, which directly affects your body's metabolic rate or energy requirement. Your basal metabolic rate (BMR) is the amount of energy required to sustain the body's functions at rest and it depends on your age, sex, body size, genes, and body composition. People with high levels of muscle tend to have higher BMRs and use more calories in the resting stage.

Some studies have even shown that your metabolic rate stays elevated for some time after vigorous exercise, causing you to use even more calories throughout your day. Additional benefits may be seen in how exercise affects appetite. A lean person in good shape may eat more following increased activity, but the regular exercise will burn up the extra calories consumed. On the other hand, vigorous exercise has been reported to suppress appetite. And, physical activity can be used as a positive substitute for between meal snacking.

Source: Excerpted from "Exercise and Weight Control," President's Council on Physical Fitness and Sports. The full text is available online at http://fitness.gov/exerciseweight.html.

Strength Training

Strength training is another way for you to meet the recommended minimum of 30 minutes of moderate-intensity physical activity each day. Strength training will also help you burn extra calories and build strong muscles, bones, and joints.

Experts recommend strength training 2 to 3 days each week, with 1 full day of rest between workouts to allow your muscles to recover. If you are new to strength training, or physical activity in general, consider hiring a certified personal trainer who can plan an individualized program to help you work out safely and effectively. A personal trainer who has a degree in exercise physiology or is certified through a national certification program such as the American College of Sports Medicine or National Strength and Conditioning Association may be able to help you reach your physical activity goals.

Get Strong!

Build strong muscles and bones with strengthening exercise. Try:

- Lifting weights
- Using resistance bands
- Using stability or medicine balls
- Doing push-ups and abdominal crunches

Mind And Body Exercise

In addition to aerobic activity and strength training, you may wish to include other forms of exercise in your physical activity program. Alternatives to traditional exercise provide variety and fun. They may also help reduce stress, increase muscular strength and flexibility, and increase energy levels. Examples of these exercises include yoga, Pilates, and tai chi.

Keep Moving!

Move at your own pace while you enjoy some of these activities:

- Brisk walking

- Jogging

- Bicycling

- Swimming

- Aerobic exercise classes (step aerobics, kick boxing, high/low)

- Dancing (square dancing, salsa, African dance, swing)

- Playing sports (basketball, soccer)

♣ It's A Fact!!

Calories in Food > Calories Used = Weight Gain

Calories in Food < Calories Used = Weight Loss

Calories in Food = Calories Used = Weight Control

Tips To A Safe And Successful Physical Activity Program

- Check with your health care provider. If you have a chronic health problem such as obesity, diabetes, heart disease, or high blood pressure, ask your health care provider about what type and amount of physical activity is right for you.

- Start slowly. Incorporate more physical activity into your daily routine and gradually work up to the 30-minute goal to improve health and manage your weight.

- Set goals. Set short-term and long-term goals and celebrate every success.

- Track progress. Keep an activity log to track your progress. Note when you worked out, what activity you did, how long you did the activity, and how you felt during your workout.

- Think variety. Choose a variety of physical activities to help you meet your goals, prevent boredom, and keep your mind and body challenged.

- Be comfortable. Wear comfortable shoes and clothes, and ones that are appropriate to the activity you will be doing.

- Listen to your body. Stop exercising and consult your health care provider if you experience chest discomfort or pain, dizziness, severe headache, or other unusual symptoms while you work out. If pain does not go away, get medical help right away. If you are feeling fatigued or sick, take time off from your routine to rest. You can ease back into your program when you start feeling better.

- Eat nutritious foods. Choose a variety of nutritious foods every day. Remember that your health and weight depend on both your eating plan and physical activity level.

- Get support. Encourage your family and friends to support you and join you in your activity. Form walking groups with coworkers, play with your children outside, or take a dance class with friends.

☞ Remember!!

If you are overweight, loss of 5 to 15 percent of your body weight may improve your health, ability to function, and quality of life. Aim to lose about 10 percent of your weight over about 6 months. This would be 20 pounds of weight loss for someone who weighs 200 pounds. Loss of ½ to 2 pounds per week is usually save. Even if you have regained weight in the past, it's worthwhile to try again.

Source: Excerpted from "Dietary Guidelines: Aim for Fitness," U.S. Department of Health and Human Services (www.health .gov), 2000.

Chapter 19

Basic Exercises For Getting Into Shape

Motivational Tips

Every person can be active and improve physical fitness. By following the instructions in this chapter you can gain fitness and improve your physical capabilities. With determination, work, and commitment you will improve your physical abilities. All of you can improve your fitness, even those of you who are already active.

When beginning a fitness program it is important to do the correct amount of work. If you try to do too much work too soon you might hurt or injure yourself. Getting in shape requires time and the right amount of effort. When exercising, your effort should be challenging, but not painful. If you feel too much pain or exhaustion you should ease off and talk to your parents or teachers. As you get in better shape your effort will improve.

Being fit and healthy means performing exercises that will improve endurance, flexibility, and strength. There are many advantages to trying to be

About This Chapter: Text in this chapter is excerpted from "Get Fit!" August 2001; reprinted with permission from The President's Challenge, the physical activity and fitness awards program of the President's Council of Physical Fitness and Sports. For additional information visit www.presidentschallenge.org. Photographs and text of exercises on pages 124–132 of this chapter reprinted by permission from, B.D. Franks, E.T. Howley, and Y. Iyriboz, 1999, The Health Fitness Handbook (Champaign, IL: Human Kinetics).

active in ways that improve these elements of fitness. People who are active are healthier, feel better, and perform better in school and in daily activities.

When you make exercise an important part of your day you will begin to see the benefits. Keep a daily log of your activity. This should include time spent walking, biking, swimming, or running. Many times it is fun and rewarding to include your friends and family members in your physical activities. You can try skating, playing active games, or other fun activities with friends or family members. Oftentimes you will help each other to continue to be active and you can now earn an award for doing just that.

Frequently people say that they do not have enough time to be active. Try to set aside a specific time of day to be active; if you can not do this try to be active by watching less television, limiting your time spent on a computer, or playing fewer video games. The most important aspect is making the commitment to being active and healthy. Try your best to be active every day and after a period of time you will begin to see the benefits.

Principles Of Exercise

To improve your fitness level and improve at completing the President's Challenge physical fitness test items you should follow certain principles of exercise: regularity, overload, specificity, and progression.

Regularity

Set up a regular schedule for exercising. You should accumulate at least 1 hour of activity daily with more vigorous workouts 3 to 4 days a week. You are more likely to see improvements when you exercise regularly and have a regular schedule for exercise. Additionally, you are more likely to continue to exercise when you have a regular exercise schedule.

Overload

For your muscles to get stronger, or your body to get fit, you must work harder when exercising than when you are at rest. Your heart should beat faster and your breathing should increase when you are performing aerobic exercise and when you are lifting weights. Make sure you work harder when you are exercising but do not overdo it. Lifting too much weight or working out too hard can cause you to be injured.

Specificity

You need to exercise your body the same way that you are going to use it. For example, aerobic exercise will not build flexibility and lifting weights will not increase your aerobic endurance. To be flexible you must stretch, to be aerobically fit you must do aerobic activities and to become stronger you must work your muscles. To be good at a certain sport or activity you must practice that activity and exercise in ways that are similar to the sport or activity.

Progression

Gradually increase the number of times you do an exercise, the length of time that you perform an exercise, and how hard you exercise. It generally takes 6 to 8 weeks to be able to see physical improvements, but you will feel better shortly after starting to exercise. For example, do not increase the number of curl-ups you perform from 5 to 35 in just a few days. You should begin to do a few more curl-ups each week until you have reached your goals.

Following is an outline of how you should exercise:

Warm-up: Before you exercise you should always warm up your body. When you warm up your body you increase your blood flow and get your muscles and joints ready to exercise. Most people are warmed up when they begin to sweat and breathe heavier. Warming up makes your muscles more limber and decreases your chance of being injured during exercise.

Stretching: Once you have warmed up you can complete stretching exercises that will prepare your whole body and specifically, the muscles that will be used while you are actively exercising.

Exercise: Complete the exercise activities in which you choose to participate. Always make sure to take appropriate safety precautions when participating (e.g., wear protective gear) and to exercise for a duration and at an intensity that is appropriate for your fitness level.

Cooling Down: Once you have completed exercising you are ready to cool down. It is just as important to cool down after exercise as it is to warm up before exercise. When you cool down you should let your breathing return to normal. It is best to walk around for a few minutes to make sure your breathing is normal and let your heartbeat slow down. After you have walked around for a few minutes following vigorous exercise you are ready to begin your cool down stretches.

The stretching exercises you do after exercise can be the same exercises you did for your warm-up or you can add other stretches. Most importantly you should stretch all major muscle groups, especially those that you used during exercise.

Physical Activity

Physical activity is a general term that encompasses most movements that are produced by skeletal muscles and result in an increase in energy expenditure. Being physically active leads to many lifestyle improvements, including physical and mental health benefits. Activities that would generally result in a change in energy expenditure include tumbling, walking to school, and playing games that require movement.

You should try to be as active as possible at an early age. Building active habits now will result in keeping these habits into adulthood.

Physical Fitness

Physical fitness is made up of many parts. When you are physically fit you have the energy and strength to perform daily activities without getting tired. Also, you have the energy to participate in leisure and recreation activities. When you are fit you have a strong heart, lungs, and muscles. Being fit benefits your daily activities and makes it easier to meet daily demands. Fitness also improves your mental health and your ability to cope with stressful events or occurrences. Being fit will help you be successful at recreational activities, school, sports, and work. The time to begin being fit is now. Children who are physically active and eat correctly become healthier and more active adults.

Measuring Physical Fitness

Each of the four components of physical fitness can be measured. Additionally, specific exercises can be done to improve each of these areas. The four components of physical fitness are: aerobic capacity, muscular strength and endurance, flexibility, and body composition.

Aerobic Capacity

Aerobic capacity, or the ability of your heart and lungs to supply the muscles of your body with oxygen, is an indicator of aerobic fitness. Exercises like cycling, running, swimming, and walking build this type of endurance. How quickly you can run a mile (or shorter distances for younger children) is a test of cardiorespiratory endurance.

Muscular Strength And Endurance

Muscular strength is the amount of force you can exert with a muscle. There are many muscles in the body and you should exercise all of them to help make all of them strong. The amount of weight you can move can be your body weight or additional weights like a barbell or the weight that is on special weight training machines.

You should do exercises to improve your strength because people who are strong are less likely to get injured when working or playing. Being strong is also good for your posture and helps to strengthen your bones.

Muscular endurance, or the ability of your muscles to move for long periods of time, is an indicator of a muscle's ability to do work. Exercises like curl-ups and push-ups are good for building muscular endurance. The number of repetitions you can do at these exercises is an indicator of muscle strength and endurance.

You need to build endurance so you have more energy and are able to play or work harder for longer periods of time. When you have good endurance you will not be "out of breath" as easily. When your heart and lungs are in good shape you will be healthier and will be less likely to develop some diseases.

Flexibility

Flexibility, or the ability to move your muscles and joints through their full range of motion, is beneficial in injury prevention and relaxation. Stretching exercises help you increase your flexibility. When stretching you should reach easily in the direction and hold the stretch, do not bounce.

Flexible people are able to reach, bend and stretch more easily. When you are flexible you are less likely to injure your muscles and joints. Stretching also helps to relieve stress and will help you relax.

Many other factors can help you be fit. Some factors that can help you do well in completing the physical fitness portion of the President's Challenge are agility, coordination, and speed. When you do exercises to improve these factors your performance in daily and sport activities will improve.

Body Composition

Body composition is the amount of lean body mass, including bones, muscles, organs, and tissues, that your body has in comparison to the amount of your body mass that is fat. People who are physically fit generally will have much more lean body mass than fat body mass.

Being active and exercising will give your body and muscles shape. People who exercise generally have less body fat than people who are inactive and are not in shape; additionally, adolescent boys and men tend to have less body fat than adolescent girls and women. If you want to know if your body composition is good ask a physical education or health teacher to measure your percent body fat or to calculate your Body Mass Index (BMI).

The President's Challenge Physical Fitness Test

American children have been earning a Presidential Physical Fitness Award (PPFA) for fitness since 1966. Those of you who reach or exceed the 85th percentile, meaning the top 15 percent of your age group, on all five items of the test are eligible to receive the PPFA for outstanding achievement. The PPFA is a round blue badge embroidered with an eagle.

Those who complete the President's Challenge physical fitness test items and exceed the 50th percentile on all of the test items, but do not achieve the 85th percentile on one or more, qualify for the National Physical Fitness Award (NPFA). The NPFA is a round red badge embroidered with an eagle.

Those who complete the President's Challenge physical fitness test but do not exceed the 50th percentile on all test items qualify to receive the Participant Physical Fitness Award (PA). The PA is a round white badge embroidered with an eagle.

Earning any of these awards is something of which to be proud. We encourage you to continue to try to improve from year to year.

Each of the five items in the President's Challenge physical fitness test measures a specific aspect of fitness.

- Curl-ups or Partial Curl-ups: abdominal strength/endurance

- Endurance Run/Walk: heart/lung endurance

- Pull-ups or Right Angle Push-ups: upper body strength/endurance

- Shuttle Run: leg strength/power/agility

- V-Sit Reach or Sit and Reach: lower back/hamstring flexibility

Remember!!

People who are trying to be fit and active are all winners.

Physical Fitness Award (Test Items)

The following exercises are ones that you will be asked to complete when you take the President's Challenge. Additionally, there are some suggested exercises that can help you meet the President's Challenge. When doing these exercises, make sure you follow the directions. If you are unsure about what to do or would like more or different exercises to perform, ask your instructor.

Curl-ups

Lie on a cushioned, clean surface with your knees flexed and feet about 12 inches from your buttocks. Place your hands on the opposite shoulders with your arms crossed. Have a partner hold your feet and count your curl-ups. Holding your elbows close to your chest raise your trunk up to touch your elbows to your thighs. A complete curl-up is counted for each time you lie back and touch your shoulders to the floor. Do as many curl-ups as you can in one minute. This should be used only for testing purposes—not regular exercise.

Partial Curl-up

Lie on a cushioned clean surface with your knees flexed and your feet 12 inches from your buttocks. Your arms will be extended forward with your fingers resting on your legs and pointed toward your knees. Have a partner cup his or her hands underneath your head. To do a partial curl-up you will slide your hands up your legs until your fingers touch your knees. A partial curl-up is complete when you place your head back in your partner's hands. Do one partial curl-up every 3 seconds until you cannot complete one at this pace. These should be used for regular exercise.

Endurance Walk/Run

At the signal "Ready, Go" begin the endurance run on a safe and marked course. You may walk during the test but you should try to complete the distance in the shortest time possible. Children who are 6 or 7 years old may run one-quarter of a mile and children who are 8 or 9 may run one-half of a mile.

Pull-ups

You should grasp a bar, with either an overhand or an underhand grip, and hang from the bar with your feet hanging freely (not touching the floor). You should raise your body until your chin clears the bar and lower yourself back to the beginning position. Try to complete as many pull-ups as you can.

Right Angle Push-ups

You should lie face down on a mat in the push-up position with your hands under your shoulders, fingers straight, and legs straight, parallel and slightly apart with your toes supporting your feet. Straighten your arms, keeping your back and knees straight while you lower your body until there is a 90-degree angle at your elbows and your upper arms are parallel to the floor, then push back up. Do one push-up every 3 seconds until you cannot complete one at this pace.

Shuttle Run

Start with two lines 30 feet apart. Place two blocks of wood or similar objects behind one line. Go to the opposite line and at the signal "Ready, Go" run to the other line, pick up one block, run back to the line you started at and place it on the floor behind the line. Run back to the other line, pick up the second block and run back and cross the starting line. Do this as fast as you can, without throwing the blocks.

V-Sit Reach

With your shoes off place your feet 8 to 12 inches apart on a line marked on the floor. This is the baseline, which will be crossed by a measuring line that will be used to measure your flexibility. Clasp your thumbs so your hands are together with palms facing down, then place them on the measuring line. Have a partner hold your legs straight and keep your toes facing upward. As you reach forward exhale, and reach as far as you can while staying in good position. Try this three times for practice and the fourth trial will be recorded.

Sit And Reach

Using a specially constructed box sit on the floor with your legs straight and your feet flat against the end of the box. A measuring line is marked on top of the box and is even with your feet. This line is marked 23 centimeters. Place your hands evenly along the measuring line and reach forward as far as you can. Do this three times for practice and your fourth trial will be recorded.

Getting In Shape To Meet The President's Challenge

Here are some suggested exercises that can help you meet the President's Challenge physical fitness award standards. When doing these exercises, make sure you follow the directions. If you are unsure about what to do or would like additional or different exercises to perform, ask your physical education or health teacher.

Warm-Up

Before you exercise you should always warm up your body. When you warm up your body you get your muscles and joints ready to exercise. Most people are warmed up when they begin to sweat and breathe more heavily. Warming up makes your muscles more limber and decreases your chance of being injured during exercise.

Flexibility

When training flexibility you should have already warmed up; you should never perform flexibility exercises when your muscles are cold. Once you have warmed up and are beginning to stretch, the proper form is to stretch until there is some tension on the muscle; do not bounce or try to reach repeatedly while holding a single stretch. When stretching you should reach and hold the stretch while maintaining the proper position for each specific stretching activity. Following are listed a few examples of flexibility exercises.

Figure 19.1. Neck Stretch. While sitting or standing with your head in its normal upright position, slowly tilt it to the right until tension is felt on the left side of your neck. Hold that tension for 10 to 30 seconds and then return your head to the upright position. Repeat to the left side, and then toward the front. Always return to the upright position before moving on.

Figure 19.2. Reach to the Sky. Stand with feet shoulder-width apart. Raise both arms overhead so that your hands are intertwined with palms together. Hold for 10 to 30 seconds and relax.

Figure 19.3. Reach Back. Stand with feet shoulder-width apart and hold your arms out to the sides with thumbs pointing down. Slowly move both arms back until you feel tension. Hold for 10 to 30 seconds and relax.

Figure 19.4. Arm Circles. Stand with feet shoulder-width apart and hold arms straight out to the side with your palms facing up. Start moving your arms slowly in small circles and gradually make larger and larger circles. Come back to the starting position and reverse the direction of your arm swing.

Figure 19.5. Side Bend. Stand with feet shoulder-width apart and place your hands on your
waist. Slowly bend to one side until you feel
tension. Hold for 10 to 30 seconds and relax.
Repeat on the other side.

Figure 19.6. Sit and Twist. Sit on a mat with your right leg straight in front of
you. Bend your left leg and cross it over your right leg so that your left foot is
alongside your right knee. Bring your right elbow across your body and place it on
the outside of your left thigh near the knee. Slowly twist your body as you look over
your left shoulder. Your right elbow should be exerting pressure against your left
thigh. Hold the stretch for 10 to 30 seconds, relax, and repeat for the other side.

Figure 19.7. Knee to Chest. Lie on
your back on a mat with your legs
straight. Bend your left knee and
bring it up toward your chest. Grasp
the underside of your thigh and
slowly pull your thigh to your chest.
Hold for 10 to 30 seconds. Release,
and repeat with the right leg.

Figure 19.8. Groin Stretch. Sit on a mat with your knees bent. Put the soles of your feet (or shoes) together and hold onto your ankles. Place your elbows on the inner sides of your knees and slowly apply downward pressure until you feel tension. Hold for 10 to 30 seconds and repeat.

Figure 19.9. Hurdler's Stretch. While seated, place one foot on the inside of the other leg just above your knee. Keep the other leg extended and straight. With your back straight, press forward toward the thigh of your extended leg. Use your hands for support. When you feel some tension in the back of your leg hold the stretch for 15 to 20 seconds. Do not bounce while holding this stretch. Repeat twice with legs in each position.

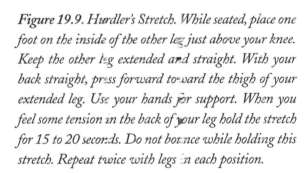

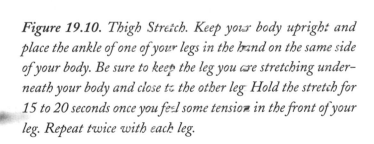

Figure 19.10. Thigh Stretch. Keep your body upright and place the ankle of one of your legs in the hand on the same side of your body. Be sure to keep the leg you are stretching underneath your body and close to the other leg. Hold the stretch for 15 to 20 seconds once you feel some tension in the front of your leg. Repeat twice with each leg.

Figure 19.11. Calf Stretch. Place your hands against a wall while standing upright. Bend one knee to be slightly in front of your body while you extend the opposite leg backward until the foot is placed flat on the floor. With your back straight you should feel some tension in the back of your leg. Hold the stretch for 15 to 20 seconds and repeat twice with each leg.

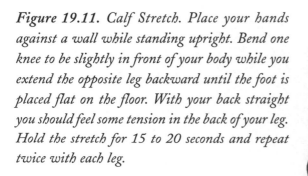

Figure 19.12. Back Flexibility. Kneel on all fours and raise first one arm and then the other arm. Next, raise one leg and then the other leg. Finally, raise the arm and leg from opposite sides and then repeat with the other arm and leg. Do all movements slowly and hold for a few seconds.

Figure 19.13. Cat and Camel. On your hands and knees with your head parallel to the floor, arch your back and then let it slowly sag toward the floor. Try to keep your arms straight.

Aerobic Exercises

Aerobic exercises are going to help you increase your cardiorespiratory fitness. See below for a few examples of activities that you can do that will help you improve your cardiorespiratory fitness.

- Bicycling
- Swimming
- Skating (Rollerblading)
- Running/Jogging/Walking/Hiking
- Cross-country Skiing
- Hurdler's Jumps
- Lateral Jumps
- Running Zig-Zags
- Soccer
- Full-court Basketball
- Singles Racquetball/Tennis/Badminton

Muscular Strength And Endurance Exercises

After you have warmed up you can begin to perform exercises that will strengthen your muscles and improve your muscular endurance. When doing these exercises always make sure you are using the correct form. Doing excessive repetitions or lifting more weight does not make you stronger sooner. By trying to do too much when performing strengthening exercises you can increase your risk of injury. Always pay attention to your body and its safety. Performing the exercises listed below are some ways you can improve your strength and muscular endurance.

Figure 19.14. Crunch. Lie down on the floor with your legs bent and your feet placed flat on the floor. Cross your arms on your chest. Lift your chest toward your knees until your shoulders come off of the floor. Lie back down once your shoulders come off the floor. Repeat for a predetermined number of repetitions.

Figure 19.15. Diagonal Curl. To strengthen different parts of the abdominal muscles than those developed with the curl-up, alternate the diagonal curl to the left and to the right.

Figure 19.16. Push Away. Start developing your upper body with the push-away until you can comfortably do three sets of 10 in one workout.

Figure 19.17. Bent Knee Push-up. Once you meet your goal for push-aways, try the bent-knee push-up, starting with two sets of 5 and increasing until you can do two sets of 10 in a single workout.

Figure 19.18. Right Angle Push-up. You should lie face down with your hands under your shoulders, fingers straight, legs straight, parallel and slightly apart with your toes supporting the feet. Straighten your arms while keeping your back and knees straight, lower your body until you have a 90-degree angle at the elbows. Repeat for a predetermined number of repetitions.

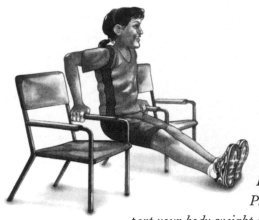

Figure 19.19. Modified Pull-up.
Place a pole or pipe that will sup-
port your body weight on the seat of two chairs that are
about four feet apart. Lie on your back underneath the bar and grasp it
with both hands about shoulder width apart. Pull your chest up to the bar keeping
your body straight from head to toe. Lower your body back to the floor, repeat for a
predetermined number of repetitions. Dip/Chair Dip. If you have a dip bar, place
your hands on the bars with your arms straight and your feet hanging free. Lower
your body by bending your elbows until your arms are bent at a 90-degree angle.
Repeat for a predetermined number of repetitions. Also, you can do these with
chairs as support if you do not have the proper dip bar. Place two chairs approximately shoulder width apart and use the arms of the chairs as your support. Place
both feet together in front of you with your heels resting on the floor and legs straight.
Perform the dip the same as it was performed on a dip bar.

Cooling Down

Once you have completed exercising you are ready to cool down. It is just
as important to cool down after exercise as it is to warm up before exercise.
When you cool down you should let your breathing return to normal. It is
best to walk around for a few minutes to make sure your breathing is normal
and let your heartbeat slow down. After you have walked around for a few
minutes following vigorous exercise you are ready to begin your cool-down
stretches. The stretching exercises you do after exercise can be the same exercises you did for your warm-up or you can add other stretches. Most importantly you should stretch all major muscle groups, especially those that
you used during exercise.

Chapter 20

Stretching

Flexible Benefits

We take part in aerobic activity to improve our cardiovascular endurance and burn fat. We weight-train to maintain lean muscle tissue and build strength. Those are the two most important elements of a fitness program, right?

Actually, there are three important elements. Often neglected is flexibility training. That neglect is regrettable, because flexibility training:

- Allows greater freedom of movement and improved posture
- Increases physical and mental relaxation
- Releases muscle tension and soreness
- Reduces risk of injury

Some people are naturally more flexible. Flexibility is primarily due to one's genetics, gender, age and level of physical activity. As we grow older, we tend to lose flexibility, usually as a result of inactivity rather than the aging process itself. The less active we are, the less flexible we are likely to be. As with cardiovascular endurance and muscle strength, flexibility will improve with regular training.

Stretch For Success

Before stretching, take a few minutes to warm up as stretching cold muscles can cause injury. Begin with a simple, low-intensity warm-up, such as easy walking while swinging the arms in a wide circle. Spend at least five to 10 minutes warming up prior to stretching.

When performing any stretch:

♣ It's A Fact!!

Since flexibility is one of the five components of fitness, stretching should be an integral part of every workout program. As we age our bodies naturally become less flexible and more prone to injury. With flexibility training, however, we can keep our bodies more limber and youthful. ACE (American Council on Exercise), America's authority on fitness, shares the following top ten reasons why every one should take time to stretch.

1. Decreases muscle stiffness and increases range of motion. Stretching helps improve your range of motion which may also slow the degeneration of the joints.

2. May reduce your risk of injury. A flexible muscle is less likely to become injured from a slightly extensive movement. By increasing the range of motion in a particular joint through stretching, you may decrease the resistance on your muscles during various activities.

3. Helps relieve post-exercise aches and pains. After a hard workout, stretching the muscles will keep them loose and lessen a shortening and tightening effect that can lead to post-workout aches and pains.

4. Improves posture. Stretching the muscles of the lower back, shoulders and chest will help keep your back in better alignment and improve your posture.

5. Helps reduce or manage stress. Well-stretched muscles hold less tension and, therefore, leave you feeling less stressed.

- Start each stretch slowly, exhaling as you gently stretch the muscle.

- Try to hold each stretch for at least 10 to 30 seconds.

Avoid these stretching mistakes:

- Don't bounce a stretch. Holding a stretch is more effective and there is less risk of injury.

- Don't stretch a muscle that is not warmed up.

- Don't strain or push a muscle too far. If a stretch hurts, ease up.

- Don't hold your breath.

---

6. Reduces muscular tension and enhances muscular relaxation. Stretching allows the muscles to relax. Habitually tense muscles tend to cut off their own circulation resulting in a lack of oxygen and essential nutrients.

7. Improves mechanical efficiency and overall functional performance. Since a flexible joint requires less energy to move through a wider range of motion, a flexible body improves overall performance by creating more energy-efficient movements.

8. Prepares the body for the stress of exercise. Stretching prior to exercise allows the muscles to loosen up and become resistant to the impact they are about to undergo.

9. Promotes circulation. Stretching increases blood supply to the muscles and joints which allow for greater nutrient transportation and improves the circulation of blood through the entire body.

10. Decreases the risk of low-back pain. Flexibility in the hamstrings, hip flexors, and muscles attached to the pelvis relieves stress on the lumbar spine which in turn reduces the risk of low-back pain.

Source: "ACE Lists Top Ten Reasons to Stretch," is reprinted with permission from the American Council on Exercise, www.acefitness.org.

Fitting Stretching Into A Compressed Schedule

Time constraints keep many people from stretching. Some complain they just don't have time to stretch; others hurry out of their fitness classes before the cool-down exercises are completed. Ideally, at least 30 minutes, three times per week, should be spent on flexibility training. But even a mere five minutes of stretching at the end of an exercise session is better than nothing. And all aerobic activity should be followed by at least a few minutes of stretching.

Here are some tips for fitting stretching into an overstuffed schedule:

1. If you don't have time to sufficiently warm up before stretching, try doing a few stretches immediately after a shower or while soaking in a hot tub. The hot water elevates muscle temperature enough to make them more pliable and receptive to stretching.

2. Try a few simple stretches before getting out of bed in the morning. Wake yourself up with a few full-body stretches by pointing the toes and reaching the arms above your head. This can clear your mind and help jump-start your morning.

3. Take a stretching class such as yoga or tai chi. Scheduling a class will help you to stick with a regular stretching program.

Flexibility Exercises

Preparing the body for exercise is important for persons at any age and fitness level. The key to preventing injuries before exercising is to warm up. One of the best ways to warm up is to do flexibility or stretching exercises.

The key to proper stretching lies in the way you perform the exercise. When you are stretching certain parts of your body, you should not feel pain. Staying relaxed is very important to stretching properly. Make sure your body is not tight. Your shoulders, hands and feet should be kept relaxed as you stretch. Breathe slowly.

Here are some exercises developed by the American Academy of Orthopaedic Surgeons. The exercises will help warm up various parts of your body.

Lower Back

While laying on your back, tighten your hip muscles and at the same time, tighten your abdominal muscles to flatten your lower back. Hold for 5 to 8 seconds, then relax. Repeat two or three times.

Pull your right leg toward your chest. If possible, keep the back of your head on the floor. Try to keep your lower back flat. Hold for 30 seconds. Repeat with your left leg.

Hip And Groin

While seated on the floor with bent legs in front of you and the bottoms of your feet touching each other, with arms supplying slight resistance on inside of legs, slowly push down your knees. Hold for 5 to 8 seconds.

While in a lunge position, place one leg forward, while your knee of the other leg is resting on the floor. Without changing the position of the knee on the floor or the forward leg, lower the front of your hip downward. Hold for 30 seconds.

Knee And Calf

While standing against a wall, hold the top of your left foot with right hand and gently pull heel toward buttocks. Hold for 30 seconds. Repeat with other leg.

Stand close to a solid support (such as a wall), and lean on it with your forearms, head resting on hands. Bend one leg and place your foot on the ground in front of you, with the other leg straight behind. Slowly move your hips forward, keeping your lower back flat. Hold for 15 to 30 seconds. Do not bounce.

Shoulder

In a standing or sitting position, interlace your fingers. With your palms facing upward, push your arms slightly back and up. Hold for 15 seconds.

With your arms overhead, hold the elbow of one arm with the hand of your other arm. Gently pull the elbow behind your arm. Do slowly. Hold for 15 seconds. Stretch both arms.

Gently pull your elbow across your chest toward your opposite shoulder. Hold for 10 seconds. Repeat with other elbow.

Hamstring

Sit down and straighten your left leg. The sole of your right foot should rest next to the inside of your straightened leg. Lean slightly forward and touch your foot with your fingers. Keep your left foot upright with the ankle and toes relaxed. Hold for 30 seconds. Repeat with right leg.

✔ **Quick Tip**

For more information on "Prevent Injuries America!®," call the American Academy of Orthopaedic Surgeons' public service telephone number 1-800-824-BONES (2663).

Chapter 21

Strength Training

As you leave your aerobics class, you may notice some guys and girls working out with dumbbells or crazy-looking machines. "Not for me," you think as you pass by. Then you notice that most of the kids in the weight room aren't muscle-bound football players. Most of them look like you— only a little more toned.

So why lift weights? Is aerobic exercise enough? The best way to a buff bod is to combine aerobic exercise with strength training. Read on to find out how.

What Is Strength Training?

Strength training is much more than quickly lifting a few weights. When you train with weights, you're using your muscles to push against the extra pounds; this strengthens and increases the amount of muscle mass in your body by making your muscles work harder than they're used to. Aerobic exercise, such as running or using a stationary bike, makes your muscles use more oxygen, strengthening your heart and lungs.

About This Chapter: This information was provided by TeensHealth, one of the largest resources online for medically reviewed health information written for parents, kids, and teens. For more articles like this one, visit www.TeensHealth.org, or www.KidsHealth.org. © 2001 The Nemours Center for Children's Health Media, a division of The Nemours Foundation.

Most people who work out with weights typically use two different kinds: free weights, which include barbells and dumbbells, and weight machines that are made by companies like Nautilus. Free weights help you to isolate and work on a specific muscle; weight machines tend to work a group of muscles at the same time.

For instance, when you do a bicep curl, raising a dumbbell up to touch your shoulder with your arm starting at a 90-degree angle, you isolate the muscle group known as the biceps. With a weight machine known as a leg press, you sit in a reclining position with your knees bent up against your chest to start. To perform the exercise, you push a heavy weight—typically a barbell or several weight plates—away from your body by straightening your legs. You can feel that this machine is working lots of different muscles in your upper legs, including the quadriceps (the front of the thigh), the hamstring (the back of the thigh), and even your behind.

Most gyms or weight rooms set up their machines in a circuit, or group, of exercises that you perform in a certain order to strengthen different groups of muscles.

Why Do Teens Strength Train?

With a regular weight-training program, you'll be able to increase your endurance and strength for other sports and fitness activities. In fact, many teens first discover weight training when a coach or gym teacher suggests lifting weights in order to improve their performance in a particular sport. And because it's important to have a spotter, someone to encourage you and help you safely handle the weights during a session, a bonus is that you'll be able to spend more time with your friends who also lift weights.

Believe it or not, another bonus to strength training is that it can also help improve your grades because any type of regular exercise can help develop your ability to focus and concentrate. Here's another surprise: strength training not only reduces your body fat while increasing your muscle mass, but in time you'll burn more calories even when you're sleeping because muscle burns more calories than fat. That means whether you're awake or asleep, your fat-burning furnace will be working overtime.

Finally, strength training can help reduce the risk of problems such as osteoporosis (weakening of the bones) when you get older.

Is It Safe For Teens To Strength Train?

If you're like most teens, you'll be able to start pumping iron the minute you decide to make it happen. Most trainers who work at gyms and in weight rooms are very knowledgeable about strength training but it's best to get your advice from someone who is a certified fitness trainer; you can also consult with a coach or physical education instructor.

Many schools offer weight or circuit training as units in their gym classes—check to see if you can sign up. Don't be afraid to ask for pointers and tips about how much weight you should start with, how to develop a routine, and what are the best foods to eat to increase energy levels and build muscle.

As is the case any time you start a new sport or activity, you should start out slowly so that your body gets used to the increase in activity. Even if you think you're not exerting yourself very much, if you've never pumped iron before, your muscles will be sore when you wake up the next day. Your coach or trainer can give you advice on how many times a week you should lift and what kinds of stretches you should do before and after lifting to avoid soreness or injury.

It's very important to make sure that when you are lifting weights—either free weights or on a machine—that there's always someone nearby to supervise, or spot you. A spotter also can act as your coach, telling you if you're not doing a particular exercise correctly.

Having a spotter nearby is particularly important when you are using free weights. Even if you're in great shape, sometimes you just can't make that last repetition. It's no big deal if you're doing bicep curls; all you'll have to do is drop the weight onto the floor. But if you're in the middle of a bench press—a chest exercise where you're lying on a bench and pushing a loaded barbell away from your chest—it's easy to become trapped under a heavy weight. A spotter can keep you from dropping the barbell on your chest.

✔ Quick Tip

Secrets Of Successful Strength Training

Are you getting bored with your strength training program, or not getting the same results you did when you started? It's easy to fall into a weight training rut, doing the same old routine of favorite exercises day in, day out. Unfortunately, too much "same old, same old" can be the enemy of effective physical conditioning. The key to successful training lies in varying the training stimuli, says William J. Kraemer, PhD, professor of applied physiology at the Pennsylvania State University's Laboratory for Sports Medicine.

The most effective way to add variety to your workouts is through periodization, which means making systematic changes to your training at regular intervals. Periodizing your strength workouts can help you avoid plateaus; prevent injury; and make greater gains in strength, power, muscular size and endurance, and athletic performance.

The Right Kinds Of Changes

A qualified personal trainer can design a periodized strength training program specifically for your needs, so, if at all possible, enlist the services of a professional when developing your program. Kraemer offers the following additional tips to help you succeed:

1. *List Your Goals and Plan to Achieve Them Over Time.* A typical way to plan your program is to set goals for one year and goals to achieve approximately every three months. Fitness assessment tests can help you determine these goals. If you have a variety of goals, you and your trainer will need to decide which to prioritize.

2. *Don't Try Too Much Too Soon.* Before you begin a periodized program, complete four to 12 weeks of basic training. Use this training to develop general conditioning and practice proper form and technique.

3. *Change Your Exercises.* Many fitness experts believe you should change your program at least every four to six weeks for maximum effectiveness. The muscle groups to be trained (based on your goals) should determine the type of exercises you perform.

4. *Change the Exercise Order.* Plan the order in which you do your exercises as seriously as you plan the exercises themselves. Try alternating between muscle

groups—for example, doing elbow curls (arms) followed by knee extensions (legs)—or "stacking" all the exercises for one muscle group (performing them consecutively). A third possibility is to start with the exercises of greatest priority to you and follow them with exercises of lesser importance.

5. *Change the Number of Sets.* Not all exercises require the same number of sets. Prioritizing your goals will help you determine which muscle groups or exercises need the most attention, and which need simply to be maintained.

6. *Vary the Recovery Time.* Your greatest physical gains are made during recovery, when your body makes the adaptations needed to support further physical development. The length of your rest periods should be based on your training goals, not on how long it takes to talk to a friend or get a drink of water, says Kraemer. Short rest periods (less than a minute) are normally used when the goal is to build local muscular endurance; long rest periods (more than three minutes) are used when the primary goal is to increase strength and power.

7. *Change the Resistance Load.* There is no consensus on what combination of reps and weights will yield the best training results. However, popular combinations include pyramid training (decreasing the number of reps per set as the weight increases, and then increasing the number of reps per set as the weight decreases); half-ascending pyramid training (just the first half of pyramid training); and half-descending pyramid training (just the second half of pyramid training). Note that your genetic makeup plays a large part in determining your ability to lift heavy weights.

8. *Evaluate Your Progress Every Four to Eight Weeks.* Keep a detailed record of your workouts, noting exercises performed, number of reps and sets, amount of resistance, and length of rest periods. Monitor your results.

9. *Be Flexible With Your Training.* Remember, be prepared to change your workouts to accommodate personal circumstances such as illness, mood, soreness, etc.

10. *Give Purpose to Every Workout.* The more carefully you plan your weight training program, the more meaningful, exciting and effective each session will be.

Source: Reproduced with permission of IDEA Health & Fitness Association, (800) 999-IDEA, www.IDEAift.com.

What Are Some Dangers Of Strength Training?

You may love the challenge of lifting, especially if you and your friends do it together. You'll definitely see results in both your muscles and in your ability to progressively lift more weight. But there are a few things to look out for.

Because your bones, joints, and tendons are still growing and developing, it's easy to overdo it and strain or even permanently damage them. When you're in the middle of a strength-training session and something doesn't feel right to you, or if you hear or feel a "pop" when you're in the middle of a workout, stop what you're doing and have a doctor check it out immediately. It's possible you may need to modify your training or even stop lifting weights for a while to allow the injury to heal.

Another danger surrounding strength training is the use of anabolic steroids or other performance-enhancing drugs and preparations that supposedly help muscles develop. You may have even heard rumors about some of the athletes at your school who use them. Steroid use is widespread in many sports—including bodybuilding, swimming, and track and field—but because many of their long-term effects on the body are still unknown, and because they are linked to health problems like cancer, heart disease, and sterility, you should resist the urge to try them.

What Is A Healthy Routine?

If you take a few minutes to watch the guys and girls pump iron at your school, you'll see there are lots of different ways to train with weights. However, there are a few good basic routines that you can modify as you start to train harder later on.

If you're just starting out in the weight room, most fitness experts recommend you begin by training three sessions a week, ranging from 20 minutes to an hour, allowing at least one day off between sessions. It's best to work only two or three muscle groups during each session, for example, legs and arms one session and chest and back the next. Before you head for the weight bench, you should warm up by spending 10 minutes pedaling on a stationary bicycle or by taking a brisk walk around the gym.

There are many different exercises you can use for each body part, but the basics—like bench presses, bicep curls, and squats—are great to start with. Perform three sets of 8 to 10 repetitions (or "reps") of each exercise starting out with a light weight to warm up and increasing the weight slightly with the second and third sets. Perform two to three different exercises for each body part to make sure you work each muscle in the group effectively.

Don't rely on strength training as your only form of exercise; you still need to get your heart and lungs pumping by doing some kind of additional aerobic exercise at least 3 days a week for at least 20 to 30 minutes per session. If you're pressed for time, you can schedule a short jog or bicycle ride either before or after a strength-training session.

☞ Remember!!

Strength training is a great way for teens to improve their strength, endurance, and muscle tone. Just a few short sessions a couple of days a week will really pay off—besides a buff bod, you may find that you have more energy and focus.

Part 3

Activities To Try

Chapter 22

Aerobic Dancing

From humble beginnings in the late 1960s, aerobic dance has become a major symbol of the fitness craze that exploded into American culture in the 1980s. It's still one of the most popular ways to get fit—and stay fit—around the world.

More than 24 million people participate in aerobics. Once confined primarily to young women, aerobic dance has blossomed into a sport for both sexes and all age groups to have fun while losing weight and keeping in shape.

Essentially an hour's workout set to music, a typical aerobics program begins with 5–10 minutes of warm-ups and stretching, peaks with 20–30 minutes of target heart range dance, can include 20 minutes of a muscle stretching floor program known as body sculpting, and ends with 5–10 minutes of cool-down and more stretching. Programs typically run three to four times a week.

The benefits of aerobics include increased cardiopulmonary efficiency, strengthened heart and lungs, improved circulation, lowered cholesterol levels, and stress and anxiety reduction. But it is a strenuous form of exercise,

About This Chapter: Reprinted with permission from, "Your Podiatric Physician Talks About Aerobics and Your Feet," a brochure produced by the American Podiatric Medical Association, www.apma.org. © 2003 APMA. Reprinted by permission.

and thorough preparation, wise choice of routines, proper equipment, and consideration of floor surfaces are essential to avoid injury.

Don't Forget The Feet

Because aerobic dancing involves quick lateral movements, jumping, and leaping for extended periods of time, proper care of the foot plays a crucial part in keeping the entire body fit to endure the "pain" that precedes the "gain" of a more fit physique and efficient heart and respiratory system.

If your feet suffer from excess pronation or supination (your ankles tend to turn inward or outward too much), it's especially important to see a podiatric physician, who may recommend controlling the sometimes harmful motions with an orthotic shoe insert.

Proper shoes are crucial to successful, injury-free aerobics. Shoes should provide sufficient cushioning and shock absorption to compensate for pressure on the foot many times greater than found in walking. They must also have good medial-lateral stability. Impact forces from aerobics can reach up to six times the force of gravity, which is transmitted to each of the 26 bones in the foot.

Because of the many side-to-side motions, shoes need an arch design that will compensate for these forces, and sufficiently thick upper leather or strap support to provide forefoot stability and prevent slippage of the foot and lateral shoe "breakup." Make sure shoes have a toe box that is high enough to prevent irritation of toes and nails.

According to the American Aerobics Association International (AAAI), the old sneakers in your closet are probably not proper shoes for aerobics. Major shoe companies today have designed special shoes for aerobics, which provide the necessary arch and side support; they also have soles that allow for the twisting and turning of an aerobics regimen.

> ✔ **Quick Tip**
> It's a good idea to see a doctor of podiatric medicine specializing in sports medicine before beginning an aerobics regimen. The podiatrist will perform a biomechanical or gait analysis to assess your risk of injury.

Running shoes, perhaps the most popular athletic shoes, lack the necessary lateral stability and lift the heel too high to be considered proper for aerobics. They also often have an acute outside flare that may put the athlete at greater risk of injury in sports, like aerobics, that require side-by-side motion. Running shoes are not recommended by podiatric physicians for aerobics.

✔ Quick Tip

Purchase shoes in the afternoon, when the feet swell slightly. Wear the same socks (podiatrists recommend athletic socks made of an acrylic blend) that you will wear in training.

Once you've found the proper shoes, tie them securely, but not too tight, in the toe box to allow toes to spread, and tightly around the arch. Double-tie the laces to prevent accidental slippage in mid-routine.

Prevention Of Injuries

In a physically challenging sport such as aerobics, injuries are common, and often involve the foot, ankle, and lower leg. (Other susceptible parts of the body are the knee and back.)

Physicians say most injuries from aerobics result from improper shoes, surfaces, or routines, and overuse of muscles through too vigorous a regimen.

New, properly tied, well-fitted aerobic-specific shoes will address the first problem, and common sense will help the with the others. The key to injury prevention is proper conditioning, which will provide muscles the flexibility and strength needed to avoid injury.

If you are attending an aerobics class, make sure it is led by a certified instructor. Hardwood floors, especially with padded mats, are the best surfaces possible. If you can, start with a multi-impact class, where you can start at a low-impact level and work your way up as your conditioning improves.

If your routine is at home with a video, be very careful. Read the label to determine whether the video is produced by certified aerobics instructors and whether you can handle the degree of impact. While it's safe to do low-to-moderate impact aerobics on the living room carpet, that's not a proper surface for high-impact routines.

In addition, make sure the video includes a proper warm-up period. Make sure there are no rapid, violent movements. Do not bounce or use ballistic stretching, or stretches known as the Yoga plow or hurdler's stretch. Knees should always be loose during warm-up. A static stretch held for 10 seconds can help avoid overstretching injury.

As you work out, monitor your heart rate to stay near the target heart range (start with 220, subtract your age, then multiply by 0.8 to find target heart range). You should be within five of the target range. Monitor pulse at peak and after final cool-off and compare. The difference is known as your cardiac reserve.

Drink lots of water to avoid dehydration during workouts; it can cause nausea, dizziness, muscle fatigue, and cramping.

Don't underestimate the importance of the cool-off period. It burns off lactic acid (which makes muscles feel tired) and adrenalin, while keeping blood from pooling in the extremities.

> ## ✔ Quick Tip
> ### Tips From The American Podiatric Medical Association
>
> - Start easy and build up your time slowly.
>
> - Start at a low-impact level and work your way up as your conditioning improves.
>
> - Don't forget to stretch regularly.
>
> - Use aerobics shoes not running shoes.
>
> - Fit your shoes with the socks that you plan to wear during aerobics activity.

While fitness professionals exercise vigorously six times a week, it's best to start slower. Although it varies by the individual, it's safe to start exercising twice a week for several weeks, then gradually increase to a maximum of five times a week. Remember to pace yourself, and listen to your body. If you feel pain, stop. Don't attempt to exercise through pain, or you may aggravate an acute injury into a chronic or even permanent one. If you continue to be bothered by pain more than 24 hours after exercising, see a physician.

Common Aerobics Injuries

Plantar fasciitis (arch pain): Arch pain is often caused by frequent stress on the plantar aspect, or bottom of the foot, in an aerobics routine. When the plantar fascia, a supportive, fibrous band of tissue running from the heel to the ball of the foot, becomes inflamed, pain on the bottom of the foot results. Forefoot and rearfoot instability, with excessive pronation, may result in plantar fasciitis. Shoes with proper support in the arch often prevent plantar fasciitis; if not, see your podiatrist for a custom orthotic device or a recommendation for another shoe.

Heel spurs: Heel spur syndrome, related to plantar fasciitis, occurs after calcium deposits build up on the underside of the heel bone. Heel spurs form gradually over many months. Both plantar fasciitis and heel spurs can be avoided by a proper warm-up that includes stretching the band of tissue on the bottom of the foot.

Sesamoiditis: Sometimes referred to as the ball bearings of the foot, the sesamoids are a set of accessory bones found beneath the large first metatarsal bone. Incredible forces are exerted on the sesamoid bones during aerobics, and inflammation and fractures can occur. Proper shoe selection and custom orthotic devices can help avoid sesamoiditis.

Shin splints: Aside from ankle sprains, shin splints are perhaps the most common injury to the lower body, as the muscles attached to the shin bone bring the foot up and down. The pain is usually an inflammation of the shin muscle and tendon due to stress factors. Treat shin pain with cold compresses immediately after the workout to reduce inflammation. Proper stretching before the workout should prevent the onset of shin splints. Strengthening of muscles also helps reduce shin splints.

Achilles tendon and calf pain: The frequent rising on the toes of an aerobics routine often creates pain and tightness in the large muscles in the back of the legs, which can create pain and tightness in the calf and inflammation of the Achilles tendon. Again, stretching the calf muscles gently and gradually before and after the workout will ordinarily help alleviate the pain and stiffness.

Stress fractures: Probably the most common injuries to aerobics instructors, stress fractures are caused by poor shoe selection, hard surfaces, and overuse. Women are more likely to develop stress fractures, usually in the lesser metatarsal bones, than men. When swelling and pain surface, see a podiatrist. X-ray evaluation and early treatment can prevent a disabling injury.

If you experience any of these injuries, see a physician (a podiatrist can treat most of them), who will prescribe treatments to alleviate the pain, and make recommendations to prevent recurrence of any discomfort. As foot specialists trained in all aspects of foot care, podiatrists are also qualified to perform foot surgery if the condition requires it.

The Bottom Line

The bottom line when undertaking an aerobic dance program is to be careful and responsible. Aerobics may even provide a more vigorous workout than jogging, and injuries will inevitably occur if you don't listen to your body and exercise your common sense as well as your muscles.

☞ Remember!!

Remember there are good aerobics programs and bad ones. Use discretion in choosing both a class to attend or home video to purchase that is right for you. Always pace yourself, and stop if you feel pain. Remember, foot pain is not normal, so don't ignore it. Chances are, a successful aerobics regimen will bring out the body you've always dreamed of, and a better feeling about yourself both physically and mentally.

Chapter 23

Biking

Thirty million Americans regularly ride bikes either for recreation or for fitness training. Cycling for fitness can be an activity for just about everybody. Riding a bike is a non-impact exercise that can produce as high a level of cardiovascular training as desired. In the category of exercise activities requiring equipment, it is one of the highest rated participation sports. The fact that it is non-impact, makes cycling more therapeutic than injurious. For the elderly or those recovering from accident or injury, cycling can be the primary form of fitness.

Before choosing a bike, you must know the type of riding you want to do. There are several types of bikes. The road/racing bike is what people think of as a "10 speed". This is the bike used for riding long distances on paved roads. People who want to go distances of 25 miles or more per ride should have one of these bikes. The beginning cyclist should use low gears and fast pedaling to increase the stamina needed for long rides. Touring, or long-distance riding, places big demands on the muscles of the back, arms, legs, and neck. By cycling several times a week and doing a weight training program 2–3 times a week, an exerciser can improve cycling skills quickly. The miles covered with each ride should be gradually increased over a period of weeks.

About This Chapter: Text in this chapter is from "Biking Basics," by Pam Germain, reprinted with permission from The National Association for Fitness Certification (NAFC), Pam Germain, Director. © 2003 NAFC. All rights reserved. For additional information, visit www.body-basics.com.

♣ **It's A Fact!!**

Equipment You'll Need

A Bike. Think of the type of riding you want to do before you buy one. Mountain bikes are strong and stable and built for gravel roads and tricky trails. Racing bikes are built to go super fast on pavement, and sport bikes, a combination of both, are good for many different purposes.

A Helmet. Your helmet should sit right above your eyebrows and be tightly buckled so it doesn't slip while you are riding. It should be flat—make sure it is level and is not tilted back or forward. The front of the helmet should sit low—about two finger widths above your eyebrows to protect your forehead. The straps on each side of your head should for a "Y" over your ears, with one part of the strop in front of your ear, and one behind—just below your earlobes. If the helmet leans forward, adjust the rear straps. If it tilts backward, tighten the front straps. Buckle the chinstrap securely at your throat so that the helmet feels snug on your head and does not move up and down or from side to side.

Source: "Bicycling Activity Card," BAM! (Body And Mind), Centers for Disease Control and Prevention, April 2002.

Mountain bikes or all-terrain bikes have fat tires and place the rider in a more upright position than road bikes. Mountain biking is a fast paced, off-road sport that uses every muscle in the body and every brain cell in the head. For safe mountain biking the rider and the bike must operate as a unit as they brave the hills, constantly in motion and out of balance. The rider learns how to steer with the entire body and react to gravity and centrifugal force. Mountain biking requires muscular and cardiovascular strength, balance, and good reflexes. A resistance training program can certainly be an asset to the serious mountain cyclist.

There is a third type of bike called a hybrid or fitness bike. It is similar in looks to the mountain bike, but with tires similar to a road bike. These are designed for comfort and have a wide range of gears. An exerciser can ride on pavement or dirt roads easily with these bikes, making them a good choice for the average individual who likes to exercise outdoors.

Recumbent bicycles look totally different from the upright bikes. On a recumbent bike you sit upright, leaning back on the seatback. The pedals are in front of your torso instead of under you. Your body weight is supported by the seat, removing the pressure from your shoulders and arms. Many people are surprised to learn that riding a bike can actually be comfortable on a recumbent. For individuals with back problems or shoulder/wrist injuries, a recumbent may be an exercise alternative. There is another advantage of being able to easily look around and admire the view. For the serious cross-training exerciser, these bikes use the leg muscles differently than upright bikes, with more effort placed on the hamstring muscle. Recumbent bicycles can be a fun outdoor exercise choice.

Whatever kind of cycling activity appeals to you, it's important to choose a bicycle that fits properly. Everyone is built differently and bikes from a good bike shop can supply a custom fit, even if the least expensive style is purchased. A good fitting bike is essential to enjoyable cycling.

Also essential to pleasant and safe cycling is a helmet. Head injury is the most disastrous thing that can happen if you fall off your bike. If your head hits the ground without a helmet on, there is a 100% chance you will be

Be Safe

Use your head and wear a helmet. You should always wear a helmet when you ride—plus, it's the law in many states. It's also important that your helmet is approved by one of the groups who test helmets to see which ones are the best: the Consumer Product Safety Commission (CPSC) or Snell B-95 standards are best for bicycling helmets. Try not to ride at night or in bad weather, and wear brightly colored, or reflective clothes whenever you ride so you can be seen. You can even put reflectors or funky reflective stickers on your bike—who knew being safe could look so cool? Also, watch out for loose pant legs and shoe laces that could get caught in your bike chain.

Be street smart. Ride on the right side of the road, moving with traffic, and obey all traffic signs and signals. Discuss the best riding routes with your parents—they'll help you determine safe places to ride near your home.

When you reach an intersection, be sure to stop and look left, right, and then left again to check for cars—then go. Use hand signals to show when you're going to turn, and be sure to keep an eye out for rough pavement ahead so you can avoid it. And although you may think you can't go out without your favorite tunes, never wear headphones when you're on your bike.

The faster you are going, the longer it will take you to completely stop your bike once you hit the brakes. Science says that if you are going 20 MPH and you hit the brakes, it will take 15 feet to stop if you are on dry pavement, and 23½ feet if you are on wet pavement, so make sure you brake early.

Source: "Bicycling Activity Card," BAM! (Body And Mind), Centers for Disease Control and Prevention, April 2002.

injured. With a helmet, the chance of head injury is only 2%, even if it does bounce on the pavement.

Cycling is an activity for the multitudes. It's great cardiovascular exercise and fun.. There are so many variations of cycling routines that almost anyone can find an enjoyable way to include this sport in a fitness plan.

Cycling Comfort

Individuals who participate in indoor cycling, whether in a class or solo training can improve the safety and effectiveness of the training by making sure the bike is adjusted properly to fit the body.

1. **Seat Height:** The maximum total tension a muscle can exert is greater in an elongated position than in shortened position. Proper seat height results in increased efficiency and muscular conditioning. Higher seat positions are recommended up to a point.

   Seats that are too high cause the exerciser to rock the hips side to side in an effort to keep the feet on the pedals. This can result in posterior knee pain.

   Seats that are too low can cause anterior knee pain.

   For most riders, a seat height allowing 25 degrees of knee flexion when the pedal is at the lowest position is recommended.

2. **Fore And Aft Seat Position:** The position of the seat forward and backward can affect the leverage by changing the leg position Proper seat placement toward or away from the front of the bike can improve the body's weight distribution and pedaling efficiency and increase the comfort.

   A recommended neutral position to help determine good seat position is with the knee directly above the pedal when it is forward and horizontal.

3. **Foot Position:** Where the foot is placed on the pedal can affect the leverage also. Toe clips help keep the foot properly positioned.

4. **Torso Position:** The upper body position during indoor cycling does not have to compromise comfort as it does in outdoor cycling or racing. If an upright position with higher handlebars is the most comfortable for the exerciser's back, then it is recommended. However, most people feel more comfortable in a forward flexed position with lower handlebars during high-intensity cycling. For comfort and safety, avoid riding with locked elbows and change hand position frequently.

☞ Remember!!

If you like recreational activities that involve wheels, concrete, or asphalt, then protect your brain by wearing a helmet. Today's helmets are lightweight, well ventilated, and have lots of padding. Try on your helmet to make sure it fits properly and comfortably on your head before you buy it.

Really good riders still need to wear helmets. Bike crashes or collisions can happen at any time. Even professional bike racers get in serious wrecks. In three out of four bike crashes, bikers usually get some sort of injury to their head.

Source: "Survival for the Fittest," BAM! (Body And Mind), Centers for Disease Control and Prevention, April 2002.

Chapter 24

Courtside: Tennis And Volleyball

Tennis

Gear Up

What's all the racket about racquets? Well, you can't play tennis without one. If you're buying a junior racquet, choose the longest one that you can comfortably use. Want more information on selecting a junior racquet? If you weigh more than 85 pounds you should look for an adult racquet.

When you have a racquet, you'll need to find a court. Look around at school or at parks in your neighborhood. Then, put on socks (if they're not cotton, they'll help you avoid blisters) and sneakers with good ankle support. Don't forget the tennis balls.

- Advanced players can serve a ball at more than 100 miles per hour, making it travel 80 feet across the court in less than one second.

- The world's first tennis tournament took place in Wimbledon, England in 1877.

- You might have heard tennis players saying the word "love" a lot around the courts. Unless it's Valentine's Day, they're probably talking about

About This Chapter: This chapter includes text from "Tennis Activity Card," and "Volleyball Activity Card," BAM! (Body and Mind), Centers for Disease Control and Prevention (CDC), reviewed November 5, 2002.

the score. In tennis, "love" means that your opponent has not scored any points yet and has a score of zero. Also, in tennis one point = 15, two points = 30, three points = 40, and usually, 4 points = a win.

Play It Safe

Tennis is an activity that forces you to turn your body quickly in many different directions, so make sure you warm up and stretch before playing. Wear tennis shoes with good support to protect your ankles and thick (not cotton) socks that fit well to prevent blisters on your feet. To prevent hand blisters, keep your racquet handle dry by using sawdust or hand chalk. Always bend your arm when you swing, or else it might start to hurt—a problem known as "tennis elbow." Clip your toenails and make sure there is extra room in your shoes, because "tennis toe" can be nasty too.

To protect other players, never throw your racquet or tennis balls, and try to keep loose balls off the courts. Be courteous and keep yourself and others safe by staying off courts where other people are playing.

When you're outside waiting to play, sit in the shade and drink lots of water—that way you'll stay cool and won't get sunburned. While you are playing, take a break between games or sets to cool off. And you may want to keep a wet towel around your neck while you wait. Also, you can look and feel cool by wearing a cold, wet bandana on your head while you play. And always wear sunscreen.

> ♣ **It's A Fact!!**
> Wondering why tennis balls are so fuzzy? The fuzz increases the wind resistance, which slows down the ball and helps the players to volley (hit the ball back and forth without stopping) longer. Without it, the ball would fly off the court after every serve. The fuzz also helps players control the ball, by keeping it stuck to their racquet strings for just a little longer when they hit it.

How To Play

Tennis is a fun activity that two people (a "singles" match) or four people on two separate teams ("doubles") can play. You can play with friends at your local tennis courts, or join an organized team. When you start playing tennis, some of the key strokes you should learn are: serve, forehand, backhand, two-handed backhand, volley, and smash. But first, check out these basic skills to get you started.

Holding the Racquet. The racquet handle has eight sides—four are flat and four are angled. Take the racquet handle between your thumb and index finger of your dominant hand (the one you write with) as if you were shaking hands. The knuckle on your index finger should be on the top right angle. Then, grip and make sure it feels comfortable. Separate your third and fourth fingers slightly.

Serving. Hold the ball with the thumb, index finger, and middle finger of your free hand (hand not holding the racquet). Extend the arm with the ball just in front of you and then raise it above your head. Toss the ball gently, so it goes a few inches higher than the full height of the racquet extended above your head. Keep your eye on the ball. Bring the racquet around above your shoulder and hit the ball while it's in the air. Try to use the same toss every time.

Receiving and Returning the Ball. Stand in the middle of the court and hold the racquet gently with both hands so you can run in either direction when the ball comes over the net. When the ball is hit to your forehand side (e.g., right if you're right-handed), step toward the ball with your opposite leg and swing. If the ball comes to your backhand side (left if you're right-handed), go for the ball with your dominant arm in front of your chest and your other hand holding the racquet as well. Swing without moving your wrists.

Parts Of The Body Worked

- Upper and lower legs
- Heart and lungs
- Arms
- Abs

Volleyball

Gear Up

- **A ball.** Volleyballs are about 26 inches around and weigh a bit more than half a pound.

- **A net.** The net is stretched across the middle of the court and adjusts to different heights—7 1/2 feet for girls and 8 feet for guys.

- **Elbow and knee pads.** When you're playing volleyball, you're probably going to hit the ground a few times. Protect yourself with pads.

- **Volleyball shoes.** The bottoms of volleyball shoes are made of special rubber to keep you from slipping as you move around the court. Your shoes should also give you good ankle support and have lots of cushioning to protect your feet while you're jumping.

Play It Safe

Be sure to wear knee and elbow pads when you're playing on a hard court to protect you when you dive for the ball. When you go up for the ball, try landing on the balls of your feet with your knees bent and your hips lowered a little. Also, warm up and stretch before you play, and take off any jewelry.

Communicate with your teammates while you're playing to keep from running into each other. Make sure everyone on the team knows to "call" the ball by saying "got it" or "mine" if they plan to go for it.

If you're playing outside, find a soft court made of sand or grass, and clean up any sharp objects that you see. Be sure that there aren't any trees or basketball hoops in your way. And, wear sunscreen and always drink plenty of water. If you're playing inside, the court should be made of wood.

If your volleyball net is held up by wires, make sure they are covered with soft materials. That way you won't get hurt if you accidentally jump or run into the net.

♣ It's A Fact!!

- Volleyball was invented by William G. Morgan in 1895. He blended ideas from basketball, baseball, tennis, and handball to create the game, which he originally called "mintonette."

- Volleyball became an Olympic sport at the Tokyo games in 1964.

- Beach volleyball was added to the Olympics in 1993.

✤ It's A Fact!!

Volleyball is all about physics. The force of the volleyball hitting your arms is the action, and the force of you hitting the ball is the reaction. If these forces were equal, you wouldn't be able to move the ball off your arms. But since the force of you pushing the ball is stronger than the force of the ball pushing into you, you're able to change the ball's direction and pass it to your teammate. If the ball's force ever became stronger than your own, it would knock you to the ground.

How To Play

Volleyball is fun to play because everybody gets involved. The game is unique because the same player isn't allowed to hit the ball twice in a row, so everyone takes turns serving, passing, and setting the ball A team can hit the ball up to three times before they get it over then net. Before you play, check out these moves.

Serving the ball. Stand at the back of the court and face the net. Hold the ball in the palm of your non-dominant hand (for example, left if you're right-handed) and stretch out your arm at waist level. Lean forward and swing your dominant hand (the one you write with) up toward the bottom of the ball. Now, drop the ball and hit it with your fist or the bottom of your hitting hand. Follow through, pointing your hitting arm toward your target. Finally, get ready to score. Only the team that's serving can score points. After you have practiced this underhand for a while, you can try a powerful overhead serve.

Passing the ball. Move to the place where you think the ball will land and stand with your feet shoulder-width apart. Bend your knees and put your arms straight out in front of you. Lock your hands together with your thumbs pointed forward. Watch the ball make contact with your arms and then push it forward with your forearms. Aim with your shoulders and straighten your legs, using the force from your legs to move the ball where you want it to go.

Setting the ball. Stand with your feet shoulder-width apart, facing your target. Bend your knees and raise your hands above your head with your elbows bent. Put your hands together about six inches above and in front of your forehead, and make a diamond shape with your thumbs and pointer fingers. When the ball comes to you, use only your thumbs and the tops of your fingers to push the ball up in the direction you want it to go. Your palms should not touch the ball.

Parts Of The Body Worked

- Upper and lower legs
- Arms
- Shoulders and neck
- Knees and ankles
- Hips
- Butt

Chapter 25

Golf

Meet The Expert

Meet Brandon Edge—a 12-year old golfer from Lakeworth, Florida. Brandon was born with cerebral palsy (a disorder that causes the loss of movement parts of the body), which made it almost impossible for him to get involved in his favorite sport... golf. But, he didn't let that stop him.

Brandon first became interested in golf when he and his family played "goonie" golf (also known as putt-putt or miniature golf) at a local course, and at the end, the course manager awarded Brandon the ball. That was the beginning of his love for the game.

Gear Up

Don't worry about buying an entire set of golf clubs right away. If you're just starting out, all you really need are the 5, 6, or 7 irons, a driver, and a putter. You'll use a driver off of the tee for long distance shots, followed up by your irons, which give more control for shorter shots. And don't forget your putter—the putter is used on the green.

About This Chapter: From "Golf Activity Card," BAM! (Body and Mind), Centers for Disease Control and Prevention, 2003.

Next on your list should be golf balls and tees. Tees look like a round peg with a flat top, and are used to raise the ball off of the ground so you can get your club under it better. Put the tee into the ground and sit your golf ball on top of it. Make sure you have plenty of tees on hand—they sometimes break when you hit the ball. Don't get over-whelmed by the number of golf balls there are to choose from. You don't have to use an expensive ball because a lot of them will prob-ably end up in the woods or water anyway.

> ✔ **Quick Tip**
> Don't forget a hat and sunscreen. On those hot, sunny days, it's important to protect yourself from the sun.

Also, don't forget that some courses have a dress code. This means that they can ask you to wear certain types of clothing like shirts with collars and shorts or pants without holes in them. As a rule of thumb, keep your clothing simple. Dress in com-fortable, loose fitting shirts, pants, or shorts. Sneakers are fine for beginners.

Once you've got all of your gear, hit the links and have some fun.

Play It Safe

It's important to warm-up and stretch before you step onto your local golf course. Before swinging, make sure that no one is standing too close—it's a good rule of thumb to stand at least four club lengths away from the person swinging the club. Don't play until the group in front of you is out of the way. Stand still and stay quiet while others are in play. If your ball lands in the rough of the course (in high grass, brush, or trees), watch out for creepy, crawly animals and poisonous plants.

Check the weather forecast before going out onto the course. The gen-eral rule for avoiding storms is: If you can see lightning, flee it, if you can hear thunder, clear it. Get away from small metal vehicles like golf carts, and put your clubs away. Stay away from trees because they attract lightning, and avoid small on-course shelters—they are made to protect you from rain show-ers and provide shade.

Whether you're walking the course or riding in a cart, don't forget your water bottle. It's important to drink plenty of water before, during, and after your round. Need a rest? Sit down in a shady area, or under a tree—put a cold towel around your neck to keep you cool.

How To Play

Golf is played on a course with either nine or 18 different holes—a complete game of golf is called a round. It's important to know the basics of the game and how to use (and choose) your clubs. You may want to take a few lessons from the pro at your local golf course, or rent an instructional video to learn more about the proper swing, grip, and stance.

Check out these tips to get you swinging in the right direction.

The Clubs: If your clubs are too long or too short, you're likely to have problems. To find the right size clubs for you, try swinging with a few different lengths. A good rule of thumb is to choose clubs that are about as long as the distance from your belly button to the floor. You don't need to decide right away—lots of courses and driving ranges have sample clubs that you can practice with until you find the perfect fit.

The Swing: The key to the swing is to keep your eyes on the ball. Focus on the ball and keep your head down (and still) when you swing. Your eyes should stay on the ball through your entire swing.

Jack Nicklaus, one of the best players in golf, learned one basic thing from his father—hit the ball hard, and not worry about where it goes—you can always fix that later. By trying to hit the ball far, you'll naturally try to make the biggest swing with your arms that you can. Swing them back as far

---

♣ **It's A Fact!!**
- When walking on the moon, astronaut Alan Sheppard hit a golf ball that went 2,400 feet, nearly one-half a mile.
- In 1997, at the age of 21, Tiger Woods became the youngest player ever to win the Masters (by the largest margin in a major championship in the 20th century).

as you can—getting your hands behind your head, and follow through as far as you can. You'll feel your body turn and you'll notice that while swinging back, your weight will shift to your right foot, and then to your left as you swing through the ball.

Tee It Up: If you're a beginner, hit the ball off of a tee every time—it's much easier to get under the ball. Put the tee into the ground at different heights to see where you like it best. If you're a more experienced player, only use a tee when using your drivers. Experiment with your irons once you're in the fairway to get the ball onto the green. Just remember that the iron you choose depends on how far (and high) you need to hit the ball. Use a 3 iron for long shots to the hole—a 9 iron can be used for those shorter shots.

♣ It's A Fact!!

There are 336 dimples on a regulation golf ball. The dimples make it travel farther. It has to do with air flow. As air flows around a ball without dimples, it breaks away from the surface of the ball forming a pocket of swirling currents behind it—like the wake behind a speedboat. This creates a "drag" on the ball, slowing it down. Dimpled golf balls can easily sail two hundred yards from the tee, while a smooth one (with no dimples) would only go about fifty yards. Golfers discovered this about a hundred years ago, when they noticed their old golf balls, covered with scratches and nicks, sailed farther down the fairway than shiny new ones.

Chapter 26

Gymnastics And Cheerleading

Gymnastics

Gear Up

Unlike some other sports, gymnastics doesn't require a lot of equipment, but there are certain things you'll need for specific events, and some standard gear that all gymnasts should have.

Female gymnasts usually wear leotards (one or two piece outfits that fit snugly to the body). Boys can wear running shorts or sweatpants with fitted tops, or with your shirt tucked in. Just make sure you don't wear clothing that is too loose—it could get caught on the equipment when you are performing your tricks and cause you serious problems. For those of you with long locks, you'll need to pull it back with a hair band or in a braid—this will prevent it from getting in your face during your routine which could cause you to lose concentration and sight.

Gymnasts also wear hand guards and use chalk to prevent their hands from slipping when working on the floor mats, rings, or bars. The hand guards help prevent blisters and make it easier to swing around on the bars.

About This Chapter: This chapter includes text from "Gymnastics Activity Card," and "Cheerleading Activity Card," United States Department of Health and Human Services, Centers for Disease Control and Prevention (CDC), reviewed April 30, 2002.

Play It Safe

The most important gymnastics rule to remember is to know what you're doing. Never attempt a trick you are not familiar with. Make sure you always have a trained spotter (someone who stands near you in case you need help while doing your tricks) just in case you lose your balance on the beam, or attempt a wobbly handstand.

Before you attempt any trick or stunt, always make sure the equipment is sturdy and has been set up properly (always ask a coach or another grown-up for help). Floors should be padded with mats that are secured under every piece of equipment. Also, make sure there is enough distance between each piece of equipment before you start swinging. Collisions can cause you, or others around you, to get hurt if you don't watch out. Use your head. Pay attention and be serious about your practice—horseplay and goofing around can get you into trouble. Always know what your teammates are doing and where they are.

And last but not least, never eat or chew gum while doing gymnastics— the moment you become unaware of what is in your mouth, it can easily become lodged in your throat and you could choke.

How To Play

Gymnastics is known as the sport of all sports. It's a great way to improve strength, flexibility, balance, and coordination for other types of physical activities, and it's a great way to meet new people and have fun.

It doesn't matter if you're a guy or a girl—gymnastics has a few different categories to choose from so you can find your favorite. Artistic gymnasts use lots of skills to perform on many different kinds of apparatuses (pieces of equipment). Boys participate in six events (floor, vault, parallel bars, high bar, still rings, and pommel horse) and girls in four (floor, vault, uneven parallel bars, balance beam). Gymnasts who participate in rhythmic gymnastics jump, tumble, flip, and dance to music while using rope, hoops, bars, or ribbons as part of their routines. In gymnastics, there's something for everyone.

But, before you get started, you need to know (and master) the basics.

Hit The Mat

The handstand is one of the basic skills of gymnastics. If you're a beginner, it's a good idea to practice your handstands against a wall until you get your balance and build up your strength and confidence. And remember, it is always good to have a spotter—just in case you need some help along the way.

Follow these tips to a perfect handstand:

- Face the wall.

- Get in a squatted position so that your knees are bent and your body is close to the ground.

- Put your hands on the floor with the tips of your fingers facing the wall (your hands should not be any wider than shoulder width apart).

- Bend your head down to the floor—keeping it between your arms.

- Kick your legs up putting all your weight on your hands—keeping your upper body straight and tight.

- Once your feet hit the wall, straighten out your legs.

Parts Of The Body Worked

- Hips and butt
- Upper and lower legs
- Abs
- Shoulders and neck

♣ It's A Fact!!

A standard balance beam is only four inches wide (that's about the width of a loaf of bread), and almost four feet off of the ground.

Cheerleading

Gear Up

You'll need a good comfortable pair of sneakers that provide a lot of support and cushion for your feet. Also, many cheerleaders use spirit-raising tools such as pom-pons and megaphones.

Play It Safe

Today's cheerleading is super fun, but it's risky too—especially if you perform stunts. On this team sport, each squad member's position is key to completing the stunts safely and dazzling the crowd.

Make sure you're well conditioned for all those kicks, jumps, and splits—warm up before each practice and game, and do lots of stretching. Focus on stretching your legs and back. If you do stunts and build pyramids, make sure you stretch your arms and shoulders too.

✔ **Quick Tip**

Stunt Safety

Practice safe stunts. If your squad does lifts, tosses, or builds pyramids, make sure you follow these important safety rules.

- Always practice stunts on mats or pads.

- Never attempt a stunt unless a coach is there.

- Always use spotters for each and every stunt.

- If you are new to stunting, start with easier stunts and gradually move up to harder ones.

- Remember that if someone in the stunt yells "Down," the stunt should come down immediately.

How To Play

When you hear the word "cheerleading," what do you think of? How about a fast-paced competitive sport for both guys and girls that involves a high level of endurance, strength and precision? For many cheerleaders, that is exactly what cheering is. Cheerleading is coming into its own as a competitive sport. Cheer squads compete up to the national level, developing cheer and dance routines that include complex pyramids, lifts, and tosses.

If you're just starting out, here are some basic cheerleading motions:

Arm Motions

- *Goal Post.* Arms should be above your head, straight up in the air, and touching the side of your head. Your fists should be closed with your thumbs facing each other.

- *High V.* From the goal post position, move your arms out slightly wider to form a high V. Fists should be closed and thumbs facing away from your body. Your arms should be slightly in front of you so that you can see your fists out of the corner of your eyes.

- *Low V.* For this motion, the opposite of a high V, move your arms down into a v-like position by your sides. Keep your fists closed with your thumbs facing away from your body.

- *Basic T.* Your arms should be straight out on each side, in line with your shoulders. Keep your fists closed with your thumbs facing down, and your arms straight and level. Your body should look like a T.

Jump Tips

There are four main parts to a jump:

- *The Prep.* Begin with your feet together with your weight on your toes. Move your arms to a high V position and keep your shoulders back.

- *The Whip.* Next, lift your body up through your shoulders, quickly swinging your arms forward in a circle. Bend at the knees, keeping on the balls of your feet, building up to the lift.

- *The Lift.* When your arms complete their circle to the high V position, jump off the ground, pushing through your toes. Once you are in the air, pull your legs up toward your arms. Keep your toes pointed, your arms stiff, and your head up.

- *The Landing.* Bring your legs together quickly so that your feet are together when they hit the ground. Bend your knees slightly to absorb the weight and take the pressure of your legs.

Parts Of The Body Worked

- Upper and lower legs

- Upper body

- Arms

- Knees and ankles

- Hips and butt

- Lower back

- Heart and lungs

♣ **It's A Fact!!**

- About 98% of all female college cheerleaders are former gymnasts.

- Madonna, Halle Berry, Kim Basinger, Cameron Diaz and Kirsten Dunst were all cheerleaders.

- Male celebrities who were cheerleaders include Samuel L. Jackson, Steve Martin, Aaron Spelling, and even President George W. Bush.

Chapter 27

Horseback Riding

Meet The Expert

Who's the barrel racing queen? She's Tanya Steinhoff, a 12-year-old from Vinita, Oklahoma. What makes her horseback riding royalty? Last year, she won tons of competitions, including the National Barrel Horse Association's youth and open (kids and adults) championships.

Whoa... Do you know what barrel racing is? It's when you race a horse around three big barrels in a special pattern. The horse and its owner have to work together to turn quickly and go super fast.

Gear Up

You'll need a horse, riding gear, and a helmet. Most riding schools will let you borrow these. Pick the horse that's right for you. If you're a beginner, go for a horse that is five-years-old or older—they are calmer and give a smoother ride. Your helmet has gotta be ASTM-F 1163 standard [American Society for Testing and Materials] and SEI certified [Safety Equipment Institute], and on right. If your hair is long, tie it up. Wear clothes that aren't baggy or loose, make sure to button them up, and leave your jewelry at home.

About This Chapter: From "Horseback Riding Activity Card," BAM! (Body and Mind), Centers for Disease Control and Prevention, 2003. Available online at www.bam.gov.

You don't want to get caught on stuff. Your pants should let you throw your leg over the horse when you're getting on. If it's cold out, wear a long-sleeved shirt with a jacket or sweatshirt on top. Waterproof jackets aren't good because the noise they make could spook (scare) your horse. Riding gloves will stop the reins from slipping out of your hands. Wear hard-toed leather boots or shoes that completely cover your ankles and have heels (not sneakers).

How To Participate

Riding tall in the saddle is an awesome feeling. You'll have a blast. Start out by riding with a guide at a riding facility—it's best to take some lessons to learn the basics. To find a place to ride, look in the yellow pages or do an internet search. There are many different ways to ride horses, and lots of equestrian (horse riding) activities But before you start, you'll need to know how to:

Mount 'Em: Stand next to the horse's left shoulder and face its tail. (Make sure it's saddled first.) Take the reins in your left hand and grab hold of the bottom of the horse's mane with your left hand as well. Put your left foot in the left stirrup. Grab the back of the saddle with your right hand. Bounce a little on your right foot and push off, pulling on the saddle and the horse's mane at the same time to help yourself up. (It doesn't hurt him.) Swing your right foot over the horse as you let go of the saddle, and put your right foot in the right stirrup.

Ride 'Em: Squeeze both legs against the horse's sides and push your hips forward. When the horse starts going, stop squeezing and move your hands forward a bit to loosen the reins. Hold the reins so that you can guide the horse's head in the direction you want to go—kinda like a steering wheel. But don't pull back too hard—he'll start backing up or just stop. Relax and follow the horse's body.

Play It Safe

Approach your horse carefully and from the side—not from behind. You might get kicked. Also, watch your feet, because it hurts when a horse steps on you. Keep a good grip on the reins at all times so you can control the horse. Lead the horse from its left side with your right hand. Your left hand should hold most of the rope, folded accordion-style. Don't wrap the rope around your wrist, hand, or body, because if the horse takes off, you don't want to go with him.

Wear the right gear. Wear a helmet and sturdy boots in the stable and anywhere there are horses—not just when you are riding. Check all your stuff...the saddle (leather seat), bridle (part that goes on horse's head and reins), and cinch (strap around the horse's belly that holds the saddle on) should be fastened and sturdy.

Until you have some experience in saddle, don't ride alone. If you are riding in a group, keep at least a horse length away from the others. Know the area where you're riding. Ride slowly and carefully until you and your horse are familiar with a new route, and where objects or animals could scare the horse. Try to stay away from soft muddy ground, holes, and ditches— horses can trip too.

♣ It's A Fact!!

- When they take down the famous Rockefeller Center Christmas tree in New York City, they give it to the U.S. Equestrian Team headquarters in New Jersey to make into jumps for their Olympics training course.

- Horses sleep standing up...without falling over. How do they do it? The muscles and ligaments in their legs "lock up" at bedtime.

Chapter 28

Kickboxing And Martial Arts

Kickboxing

Are you looking for a total body workout that totally kicks butt? How about a way to increase your stamina, flexibility, and strength while listening to your favorite dance mixes?

If this sounds good to you, keep reading to find what you need to know before you take the kickboxing challenge.

What Is Kickboxing?

Competitive kickboxing actually started in the 1970s, when American karate experts arranged competitions that allowed full contact kicks and punches that had been banned in karate. Because of health and safety concerns, padding and protective clothing and safety rules were introduced into the sport over the years, which led to the various forms of competitive kickboxing practiced in the United States today. The forms differ in the

About This Chapter: This chapter begins with "Kickboxing," provided by TeensHealth, one of the largest resources online for medically reviewed health information written for parents, kids, and teens. For more articles like this one, visit www.TeensHealth.org, or www.KidsHealth.org. © 2001 The Nemours Center for Children's Health Media, a division of The Nemours Foundation. "Martial Arts' is from "Martial Arts Activity Card," BAM! (Body And Mind), Centers for Disease Control and Prevention (CDC), reviewed June 2, 2003.

techniques used and the amount of physical contact that is allowed between the competitors.

Currently, one popular form of kickboxing is known as aerobic or cardio-vascular ("cardio") kickboxing, which combines elements of boxing, martial arts, and aerobics to provide overall physical conditioning and toning. Unlike other types of kickboxing, cardio kickboxing does not involve physical contact between competitors—it's a cardiovascular workout that's done because of its many benefits to the body.

Cardio kickboxing classes are usually comprised of 10 to 15 minutes of warm-ups, which may include stretching and traditional exercises such as jumping jacks and push-ups; then about a 30-minute kickboxing session that includes movements such as knee strikes, kicks, and punches. Some instructors may use equipment like punching bags or jump ropes.

After this, at least 5 minutes should be devoted to cooling down, followed by about 10 minutes of stretching and muscle conditioning. Stretching is really important because beginners are prone to strained ("pulled") muscles, and slow, proper stretching helps relax muscles after vigorous activity and prevent injury.

The Basics

Before you decide to jump in and sign up for a class, you should keep a few basic guidelines in mind:

- **Know your current fitness level.** Kickboxing is a high-intensity, high-impact form of exercise, so it's probably not a good idea to plunge in after a long stint as a couch potato. You might try preparing yourself by first taking a low-impact aerobics course or less physical form of exercise and working up to a higher level of endurance. When you do begin kickboxing, allow yourself to be a beginner by working at your own pace and not overexerting yourself to the point of exhaustion.

- **Check it out before you sign up.** If possible, observe or try a class beforehand to see whether it's right for you and to make sure the instructor is willing to modify the routine a bit to accommodate people's different proficiency levels. Try to avoid classes that seem to move too fast, are too complicated, or don't provide the chance for any individual instruction during or after the class.

- **It's a class act.** Look for an instructor that has both a high-level belt in martial arts and is certified as a fitness instructor by an organization such as the American Council on Exercise (ACE). Also, try to start at a level that suits you and slowly progress to a more intense, fast-paced kickboxing class. Many classes call for intermediate levels of fitness and meet two to three times a week.

- **Comfort is key.** Wear loose, comfortable clothing that allows your arms and legs to move easily in all directions. The best shoes are cross-trainers—not tennis shoes—because cross-trainers allow for side-to-side movements. Gloves or hand wraps are sometimes used during classes—you may be able to purchase these at the facility where your class is held. Give your instructor a call beforehand so you can be fully prepared.

- **Start slowly and don't overdo it.** The key to a good kickboxing workout is controlled movement. Overextending yourself by kicking too high or locking your arms and legs during movements can cause pulled muscles and tendons and sprained knee or ankle joints. Start with low kicks as you slowly learn proper kickboxing technique. This is very important for beginners, who are more prone to developing injuries while attempting quick, complicated kickboxing moves.

- **Drink up.** Drink plenty of water before, during, and after your class to quench your thirst and keep yourself hydrated. Recommended amounts are:

  - 1 to 2 hours before exercising: 10 to 12 ounces of cold water (about 1 1/2 cups or 1/3 liter)

  - 10 to 15 minutes before exercising: 10 ounces of cold water (about 1 1/4 cups or 1/3 liter)

  - While exercising: 3 to 4 ounces of cold water every 15 minutes (about a 1/2 cup)

- After exercising: 2 cups of cold water for every pound of weight loss through sweat (this means about a cup or 2 for most teens; if it's a hot day, you may feel thirsty enough to drink even more)

- **Talk to your doctor.** It's always a good idea to see your doctor and have a complete physical exam before you begin any type of exercise program—especially one with a lot of aerobic activity like kickboxing. This is extremely important if you have any chronic medical conditions such as asthma or diabetes or are very overweight.

Moves You Can Use

Here are a few moves that you can try at home:

- **Roundhouse kick:** Stand with the right side of your body facing an imaginary target with your knees bent and your feet shoulders' width apart. Lift your right knee, pointing it just to the right of the target and pivoting your body toward the same direction. Kick with your right leg, as though you are hitting the target. Repeat with your other leg.

- **Front kick:** Stand with feet shoulders' width apart and arms at a 90-degree angle in front of your shoulders. Bend your knees slightly, and pull your right knee up to your chest. Point your knee in the direction of an imaginary target. Then, kick out with the ball of your foot. Repeat with your other leg.

- **Side kick:** Start with the right side of your body facing a target. Pull your right knee up to your left shoulder, and bend your knees slightly as you kick in the direction of your target. The outside of your foot or heel should be the part that would hit the target. Repeat with your other leg.

Why Kickboxing?

Besides keeping your body fit, kickboxing has tons of other benefits. According to a study by the ACE, you can burn anywhere from 350 to 450 calories an hour with kickboxing.

Kickboxing also reduces and relieves stress. Its rigorous workout—controlled punching and kicking movements carried out with the discipline and skills required for martial arts—can do wonders for feelings of frustration and anger. Practicing kickboxing moves can also help to improve balance, flexibility, coordination, and endurance.

Kickboxing is also a great way to get a total body workout while learning simple self-defense moves. Kickboxing fans say the sport helps them to feel more empowered and confident.

So get out there and jab, punch, and kick your way to fitness.

Martial Arts

Meet The Expert

Who's that guy in the cool black belt? It's Kenny Hashimoto, star of the second most popular sport in the world—judo. Kenny is a 16-year-old from Thornton, Colorado. He loves judo…and is totally good at it too. Judo is a martial art that was founded in Japan. It's full of wrestling moves and also teaches you how to be mentally strong.

Kenny first tried judo when he was five because "it was a family thing." (His dad and his uncle were into it.) He always had fun, but like most judokas (judo players), he started to get into competition too. He qualified for a national competition in Hawaii when he was just seven.

Gear Up

Most martial arts students wear white pants, a white jacket, and a cloth belt. For some martial arts, the belt color shows the student's skill level and personal development—from white (beginner) to black (expert). The colors reflect nature. For example, the white belt that students start out with stands for a seed. The yellow belt that they get next stands for the sunshine that opens the seed. To advance from one grade level to another, you have to pass loads of tests—five for the green belt, nine for the brown belt, and 10 for the black belt. You can get a first-degree black belt in two to four years, but after that, there's still more to learn… There are 10 black belt levels.

For sparring (practice fighting), go for full gear, including a mouthpiece and padding on your head, hands, feet, and shins.

Play It Safe

Look for an instructor who's into respect and discipline, but still has plenty of patience. The class area should have lots of space and a smooth, flat floor with padding. The fewer students the better—more attention for you.

Wear all the right gear. Warm up and stretch so you're loose and ready to go. You need good instruction before launching into any moves. And when you do learn the moves, remember your limits. For example, white belt students shouldn't spar (practice fight).

♣ It's A Fact!!
If you open your hands wide and shove something, your force spreads out across your palm and fingers. But if you hold all of your fingers together and hit with only the side of your hand or your finger-tips, that same amount of force goes to a much smaller area and the hit is harder. If you try this on yourself, you'll see the difference. Just don't beat yourself up too much.

When you are ready for matches, you've gotta have an instructor around to regulate. Some martial artists use special weapons (like swords), but it's almost a sure thing that you'll get hurt with them unless you're totally advanced… so, no weapons. During your match, make sure that your partner knows when you're ready to stop. If you let your guard down, your partner may think it's a good chance to take you down.

How To Play

Martial arts—a special type of defense skills—started in the Orient (East Asia). Today, they're taught all over the world for self-defense and avoiding conflict, too. Body and mind control, discipline, and confidence are key. There are a lot of martial arts styles, but since certain types rough up the joints (like knees) more than others, these are some of the best for kids your age:

- Judo comes from Japan and means "gentle way." It's like Jujitsu, one of the oldest martial arts, but not as hard core. Judo has lots of wrestling moves. It also teaches participants how to make good decisions and be mentally strong. Judokas (judo players) focus on competition.

- Karate comes from Japan, and means "empty hand." It's Japan's most popular martial art. Feet, legs, elbows, head, and fists get used for kicking, punching, defensive blocks, and more. Karate stresses defense and uses weapons.

- Tae Kwon Do comes from Korea and means "the way of the foot and fist." It's famous for high kicks. Tae Kwon Do became Korea's national sport in 1955 and is now the world's most popular martial art.

Other martial arts include Aikido, Hwarang Do, Kung Fu, Jujitsu, Kendo, Ninjutsu, Northern and Southern Shaolin Boxing, Tai Chi, and T'an Su Do.

Interested? The first thing you need to do is to decide on the style you want to study. Do you want to enter tournaments, or simply know how to defend yourself? After that, just get into a good class.

Games

You know the balloon game, right? The one where you bat around a balloon and don't let it touch the ground? We'll, here's something new… When you play the martial arts way, you only get to hit the balloon with martial arts

---

♣ It's A Fact!!

- In karate competitions, opponents are not allowed to actually hit each other. Their moves have to stop short of the other person.

- The original five Chinese fighting styles that we call Kung Fu mimic the moves of tigers, cranes, leopards, snakes, and dragons.

- Judo was the first martial art accepted at the Olympic Games. 197 countries participate.

moves. You can punch, block, use feet, elbows, knees, head—anything they teach you in class.

Parts Of The Body Worked

- Upper and lower legs

- Knees and ankles

- Arms

- Abs

- Hips and butt

Chapter 29

Pilates

What's the hot new way to exercise that has celebrities like Julia Roberts, Uma Thurman, and Leonardo DiCaprio hooked? The answer: Pilates (pronounced: puh-lah-teez).

Pilates improves your mental and physical well-being, increases flexibility, and strengthens muscles without the strain and impact of sports like running or tennis. That's because Pilates focuses on your breathing and uses slow, controlled movements. So sit yourself down, get comfortable, and get ready to learn about Pilates!

What Is Pilates?

Pilates is a body conditioning routine that seeks to build flexibility, strength, endurance, and coordination without adding muscle bulk. In addition, Pilates increases circulation and helps to sculpt the body and strengthen the body's "core" or "powerhouse" (torso). As a result, you should be less prone to injury, have better posture, and experience better overall health.

About This Chapter: "Pilates," reviewed by Kim Rutherford, MD, This information was provided by TeensHealth, one of the largest resources online for medically reviewed health information written for parents, kids, and teens. For more articles like this one, visit www.TeensHealth.org, or www.KidsHealth.org. © 2001 The Nemours Center for Children's Health Media, a division of The Nemours Foundation.

♣ **It's A Fact!!**

The founder of Pilates was Joseph H. Pilates, a man who was born in Germany and as a child found it hard to participate in sports because of his frail body. Later, though, he trained himself to become an accomplished athlete. While interning as a nurse for the British during World War II, he designed exercise apparatuses for immobilized patients as well as the men in his regiment. These apparatuses later became the inspiration for the machine comprised of pulleys, cables, and springs that Joseph Pilates designed for his exercise program.

Pilates also developed 500 specific exercises that focus on the torso. He later became a trainer for dancers who wished to tone their muscles and achieve coordination, strength, and flexibility.

The eight principles of Pilates are: relaxation, coordination, concentration, breathing, flowing movements, alignment, stamina, and centering.

There are two types of Pilates. The kind that is linked closest with Joseph Pilates requires several components: the use of his machine, a certified teacher who has the appropriate qualifications, and either a one-on-one training session or a small class made up of four to five people. Today, the machine most people use is called the Reformer.

The other form of Pilates, called body-control Pilates, requires only a floor mat. With this type of Pilates, you don't need a machine, weights, or other equipment. The exercises are designed so that your body uses its own weight as resistance.

Before You Begin

Before you begin any type of exercise program, it's a good idea to talk to your doctor, especially if you have a health problem.

Keep these tips in mind so that you can get the most out of your Pilates workout.

- Staying calm is key. Breathe deeply and keep your breathing even. Pilates is designed to combine your breathing rhythm with your body movements. Also, remember to concentrate on your muscles and what you are doing. The goal of Pilates is to unite your mind and body, which relieves stress and anxiety.

- Be cool and comfortable. The best thing about Pilates is that you rarely break a sweat, so if you find that you are, you might want to take a couple minutes to rest up before you continue. Also, you should wear comfortable clothes (as you would for yoga—shorts or tights and a T-shirt or tank top are good choices), and keep in mind that Pilates is usually done without shoes. If you start feeling uncomfortable, strained, or experience pain, you should stop.

- Let it flow. When you perform your exercises, avoid quick, jerky movements. Every movement should be slow, but still strong and flexible. Remember that Joseph Pilates worked with dancers, and your movements should flow like a dance.

- Don't leave out the heart. Pilates offers numerous benefits, but it doesn't take the place of a cardiovascular workout. It's a good idea to pair Pilates with another form of exercise like swimming or brisk walking.

Getting Started

The great thing about Pilates is that just about everyone—from couch potatoes to fitness buffs—can do it.

Because Pilates has gained lots of attention and was recently recognized as a generic form of exercise like kickboxing, you have lots of options if you'd like to take a class. You'll probably find that many fitness centers and YMCAs offer Pilates classes, and some Pilates instructors also offer private classes that can be purchased class by class or in blocks of classes. Instructors should be certified by a group such as Pilates, Inc.

Keep in mind that these classes will most likely consist only of mat work—not the type of Pilates that requires a machine.

Here are a few basic exercises you can try out at home:

- **The Hundred:** Lie with your back flat on the floor, and your knees bent over your chest and at a 90° angle. Place your arms at your sides, with your palms down. Let your belly relax as you breathe. With your head and neck lifted off the mat, start pumping your arms straight up and down. Breathe each time you pump. Start at 20 to 30 repetitions and slowly work up to 100.

- **Rolling Ball:** Sit on the floor with your knees bent. Roll slightly backward until you're balancing on your tailbone, with your arms locked underneath your knees. Tuck your chin into your chest, exhale, and roll all the way backward until you reach your shoulder blades, stopping at the neck. Inhale and slowly use the muscles in your torso to bring you back to the starting position. Try doing six repetitions.

- **Straight Leg Stretch:** Lie with your back flat on the floor and your arms at your sides, with your palms down. Bring your right leg straight up (pretend you're going to touch the ceiling), while keeping your back flat on the mat. Slowly make giant clockwise circles with your right heel, still keeping your back flat. Pretend that the center of the circle you're making is your left kneecap. Make three to five circles with each leg.

☞ **Remember!!**

The important thing to remember when doing Pilates is to go slowly and concentrate. If you keep it up and learn to perfect your movements, you should be stronger, more toned, and more flexible—and less stressed.

Chapter 30

Play Ball: Baseball, Softball, Football, Basketball, And Soccer

Baseball

Gear Up

All ball players will need a ball, a bat, and a glove. All baseballs are pretty much the same, but bats can be either wooden or aluminum. These days, only the pros use wooden bats full time. Aluminum bats are lighter and easier to handle and don't break as often. There are a couple of different types of gloves, depending on your field position.

All batters should wear a helmet while at the plate and on base to protect the head. For better base running, try wearing baseball cleats instead of sneakers.

Catchers have a special set of protective gear that includes a helmet, a mask, shin guards, and a chest protector. All of these pieces are very important to protect you if you play behind the plate.

About This Chapter: This chapter includes text from "Baseball Activity Card," "Softball Activity Card," "Basketball Activity Card," "Football Activity Card," "Soccer Activity Card," BAM! (Body And Mind), Centers for Disease Control and Prevention (CDC), reviewed April 30, 2002.

Play It Safe

Wear your protective gear during all practices and games, especially if you're a catcher—those fast balls can pack a punch. Don't forget to warm up and stretch before each practice or game.

In the infield? Stay behind the base on any throw. You'll avoid hurting yourself—and the base runner. In the outfield? Avoid bloopers with your teammates by calling every fly ball loudly, even if you think nobody else is close by. And in the batters' box, wear a batting helmet and use a batting glove to protect your knuckles from those inside pitches. If you think a pitch is going to hit you, turn away from the ball and take it in the back.

Throwing those fastballs can really take a toll, so if you're a pitcher, make sure to get plenty of rest between games, and don't pitch more than 4–10 innings per week.

How To Play

Baseball is known as America's favorite pastime. This sport uses many different skills from pitching, catching, and batting (which require lots of hand-eye coordination), to base running which means going from a standing start to a full sprint. To get started, you just need a bat and a ball.

How to hit the ball. First, get hold of that bat by stacking your hands on the handle (right hand on top if you're a righty, left hand on top if you're a lefty), making sure the curve of the bat is in the middle of your fingers and that your knuckles are in a straight line. Balance on the balls of your feet, with your weight on your back foot, and bend your knees slightly. Your hands should be shoulder height, elbows in, and keep your head in line with your

> **♣ It's A Fact!!**
>
> - There are exactly 108 stitches on a baseball.
>
> - In 1974, girls started playing on Little League teams.
>
> - A major league pitcher can throw a baseball up to 95 miles an hour—which takes less than 1/2 second for the ball to cross the plate.

torso, turned toward your front shoulder. As the pitcher throws, step toward the pitch, and swivel toward the ball with your hips, keeping your arms steady as you move toward the ball. Keep your eye on the ball, and complete your swing by pivoting forward and shifting your weight to your front foot, following through with the bat after you hit the ball.

♣ It's A Fact!!

How does a professional baseball player hit the ball so far? It's science. When the bat hits the ball, the bat exchanges momentum with the ball and the ball takes off. The faster the bat is swung, the harder it hits the ball and the harder the bat hits the ball, the faster and further the ball goes. So if you want to hit like a pro, pump up those arm muscles and take some practice swings.

How to throw the ball. Did you know that throwing the ball accurately requires a little footwork? First, step toward the target with the glove side foot, making sure the toe of your shoe is pointing directly to where you want the ball to go. Aim the leading shoulder at the target. Aim the bill of your hat (the "duckbill") at the target and throw.

How to catch the ball. Keep your eye on the pitch and stay low with your feet apart and knees bent so you can move quickly in any direction. Have your glove ready at or below knee level, pocket side out. When scooping up a ground ball, bend down and use both hands to scoop it to the middle of your body so you have it securely.

Softball

Gear Up

You'll need a glove that fits your hand and skill level, and is geared to the position you play. There's a lot of truth to the old saying, "Fits like a glove"—if your glove is too big, or small, you may have problems catching and fielding the ball. For beginners, gloves that are about 9½ to 11 inches long are a good start.

You can't play without a bat and ball. Try aluminum or other non-wooden bats—they are lighter and easier to handle. As for the ball, you can find softballs at most stores that sell sports equipment.

Also, for organized team play, you'll need a pair of shoes with rubber cleats—they dig into the ground and can give you more traction while running the bases or fielding a ball. If you're playing a pick-up game with your friends, a pair of sneakers will do. If you're a catcher, you'll need special protective gear like a helmet with a face mask, shin guards, and a chest protector.

And remember, always wear a helmet to protect your head while at the plate or on base.

Play It Safe

Before you hit the field, warm up. Get all of your muscles ready to play by stretching before every game.

Whether you're in the field or up to bat, don't forget to wear your safety gear in games and in practices. A helmet is important when batting, waiting to bat, or running the bases. If you're a catcher, make sure you wear your protective gear during all practices and games, and wear it properly—have your coach or a parent check it out for you. Don't wear jewelry like rings, watches, or necklaces—they could cut you (or someone else), or get caught when you're running the bases.

Did you know that an umpire could call you out for throwing your bat? Well, they can. And, it's not just the out you have to worry about—it's your teammates' safety. Always drop your bat next to your side in the batters box before you head for first base.

Be a team player—always know where your teammates are before throwing the ball or swinging your bat. Make sure they are ready and have their glove up as a target before you throw the ball to them. Call loudly for every fly ball or pop up in the field, even if you don't think any of your teammates are close by. Teams that play together win together.

How To Play

Softball is a game of speed, skill, and smarts. Whether you're looking to play in your backyard or at the state championships, softball is a great team sport that everyone can play.

Many of the skills in softball are similar to those in baseball, but there are some unique differences that make softball a game of its own.

✔ **Quick Tip**

If you're interested in playing at a more competitive level, fast-pitch softball is what you'll see— you can steal bases and bunt, and you only need nine players to get a game going. If you're playing a pickup game with your friends, you'll probably play slow pitch softball. You only need ten players to field a team, but invite as many people as you want—it's more fun that way.

Did you know that a softball isn't really soft at all, and that it's almost two times bigger than a baseball? Because a softball is bigger than a baseball, it doesn't go as far when you hit it. But, keep your eye on the ball—a softball can sometimes cross the plate at a very fast speed. Even with their underhanded pitching style (unlike baseball's overhand style), softball pitchers can put a lot of heat on the ball. Most beginners play in slow pitch leagues where the hitting game is having a sharp eye and timing your swing. Keep your eyes peeled for pitches that are shoulder high and that drop right over the plate—they are perfect for driving into the field.

♣ **It's A Fact!!**

Did you know that it's easier to hit a home run in outer space? That's because the density (thickness) of the air on earth plays a role in how far a ball travels when it's been hit. The particles that make up air on earth are close together—this makes it difficult for things (like a softball) to travel through it. If you took away the air altogether, the ball would keep going. In places like Colorado where the altitude (height of the land above water level) is higher, the air is thinner, and a ball can fly much farther. Under these conditions, a hit that might be a routine fly ball can sail over the fence with no problem.

Basketball

Gear Up

A Basketball. Basketballs come in different sizes depending on your age and whether you're a girl or boy. There are also different basketballs for inside and outside use. If you're buying a new basketball, make sure you ask the salesperson for help to figure out what size and type ball you need.

A Hoop. Basketball hoops are available in most gyms and in many parks. You can even buy a hoop and attach it to the side of your house or garage, if you have one. To create your own regulation court at your house, make sure you set your foul line 15 feet from the backboard.

Play It Safe

Basketball can really make you work, so make sure you stretch and warm up before playing. Because of all of the quick moves and jumping, it can put a lot of wear and tear on your ankles, so protect them by wearing the right pair of shoes—medium or high tops do the best job of supporting your ankles. Protect those knees by learning how to cut, stop, and land a jump safely.

Be careful not to misuse basketball equipment. It's great if you've got the skills to put up a mean slam dunk, but hanging on the rim is dangerous and could cause you to get hurt. Also, make sure the court and sidelines are clear of any obstacles such as other basketballs or water bottles. If you're playing outside, make sure the baskets and sidelines are not too close to walls, fences, or bleachers and there are no holes on your court.

If you're a serious player, you may want to invest in a mouth guard to keep your teeth safe from flying elbows; knee and elbow pads so you don't get scraped up (especially if you're playing on an outdoor court); and sports glasses to protect your eyes.

How To Play

Basketball is fun to play in pick up games in the yard with your pals, or you can join an organized league. Different positions rely on different skills— point guards should focus on their dribbling and passing, while centers and forwards should be powerful rebounders and shooters. Outside guards need to be quick and strong to make those 3-point shots. Want some basics?

♣ It's A Fact!!

- Former pro, Wilt Chamberlain, once scored 100 points in a single NBA game.

- Michael Jordan was cut from the varsity basketball team when he was in the 10th grade— and went on to be the NBA's Most Valuable Player for 5 seasons.

How to Dribble. Bounce the ball on the floor with your strongest arm. When it bounces back, use your fingertips to stop the upward motion and push it back to the floor, keeping it about waist high when it bounces. Once you've mastered dribbling in place with one hand, switch to the other and begin to move around as you dribble. Practicing dribbling by moving the ball in a figure eight between your legs is one good way to build your skills.

How to Pass the Ball. Face the person you're passing to, with your head up and knees slightly bent. Spread your fingers wide and hold the ball at chest level, elbows out. Extend your arms, take a step toward the person you're passing to, and snap your wrists forward and up as you release the ball.

How to Shoot a Lay-up. Start about 10 feet in front of and to the right of the basket. Dribble toward the basket, timing it so that your last step is with your left foot. Holding the ball with both hands (left in front, right in back), jump off your left foot, let go with your left hand, and extend your right arm fully to release the ball at the top of your jump. Keeping your eyes on where you want the ball to go really helps land this shot.

♣ **It's A Fact!!**

Did you ever wonder how Michael Jordan seems to hang in the air longer than everyone else when he goes up for a slam dunk? Well, actually, he doesn't—it just seems that way because MJ holds on to the ball longer than most players before shooting or dunking. Hang time depends entirely on the force generated by a player's legs when he or she leaves the ground (how hard they push off the ground) and the jump's height (the higher the jump, the longer the hang time). The average NBA player can make a 3-foot high jump when going up for a shot or dunk, with a hang time of less than 1 second (.87 seconds to be exact).

How to Cut, Stop, and Land a Jump. Ease up on your cuts or pivots by making them less sharp to avoid rotating your knees. When stopping, rather than coming to a sudden stop or bringing your weight down on one foot with a single step, use the "stutter step" to slow yourself down by taking two extra steps. When landing your jumps, do it softly by bending your knees over your feet (which should be pointed straight ahead) when you hit the ground. Instead of landing flat-footed, land on either the balls or toes of your feet and rock back toward your heels.

Football

Gear Up

Obviously, you need a football to play, and you should choose the size based on your age. Always wear a helmet with a face mask and jaw pads, and a mouthpiece to protect against those hard hits. Because football is a contact sport, there are many different pieces of gear you should wear to protect different areas of your body. For upper body protection, you should wear a neck roll to prevent whiplash, shoulder pads, rib pads, arm pads, and elbow pads. For leg protection, you should wear hip pads, tailbone pads, thigh pads, and knee pads. Most leagues require all this, but it's a good idea to protect yourself even in backyard games.

Play It Safe

Be sure to stretch and warm up before every practice and game and always wear your protective gear. To avoid getting hurt, learn from your coaches how to block and tackle correctly. Don't tackle with the top of your head or helmet—not only is it illegal, but it can cause injury to both players. If you play in an organized league, there are lots of rules—and they are there for a reason—to keep you safe. If you break these rules, you risk not only getting hurt, or hurting someone else, but your team will be penalized. If you're playing in the backyard with your friends, stay safe by sticking to touch or flag football, and only play with kids who are around your age and size.

How To Play

There are lots of skills needed to play football from throwing and catching the ball to blocking and tackling the other players. There's even a national Punt, Pass, and Kick contest devoted just to the main skills you need.

♣ It's A Fact!!

- Champs. Notre Dame has won a record 9 NCAA National Championships, and the Dallas Cowboys and San Francisco 49ers have each won 5 Super Bowls.

- The numbers worn on players' uniforms represent the positions they play. For example, wide receivers and tight ends have numbers between 80–89.

- A football field is 120 yards long (including the 2 end zones), and 53 1/3 yards wide.

League teams are a great way to learn all the rules and strategies of football. Pop Warner is the most popular youth football league, but there are many others nationwide. Want the basics?

Throwing the ball. Grip the ball by placing each of your fingers between each lace of the ball. Bring your throwing arm back with your elbow bent. Extend your free arm (the one without the ball) in front of you and point to your target. Snap your throwing arm forward, releasing the ball, and follow through with your shoulders and hips. When you are finished, your throwing arm should be pointing toward your target with your palm facing the ground.

> **♣ It's A Fact!!**
>
> You'd think more football players would study physics, since how far you can throw a football is definitely a science. How far a football goes is a combination of the "velocity" (or speed) of the football after you throw it, the angle (or arc) the football is thrown at, and how the ball rotates in the air (that's why it's best to throw a spiral).

Catching the ball. Hold your arms out with your elbows slightly bent in front of your chest. Bring your hands together, touching the thumbs and index fingers to make a triangle with your fingers. Catch the nose of the ball in the triangle, and use your chest to help trap the ball. Bring your arms in around the ball and hold it tight against you.

Punting the ball. Place your feet shoulder-width apart with your kicking foot slightly in front. Slightly bend your knees and bend your body forward a little. Hold the ball out in front of you with the laces facing upward. Take two steps forward, beginning with your kicking foot and drop the ball toward your kicking foot. Kick the ball hard with the top of your foot and follow through with your leg as high as you can.

Soccer

Gear Up

A ball. Soccer balls come in different sizes depending on how old you are. Kids 8–12 should use a size 4 ball, and kids 13 and over should use a size 5 ball. Synthetic leather balls are best for beginners, because they don't absorb water and get heavy.

If you play in a league, a goal will usually be provided for you, and you can buy a smaller goal if you want to play in your backyard—just make sure it is anchored to the ground. No goal? No problem. Just set up any two objects (cones or water bottles are good) to shoot between.

Two pieces of equipment you need to wear at all times when playing soccer are shin guards and cleats. Shin guards are designed to protect your legs from the ball, and from being kicked by other players. They are required in most leagues. The right cleats to wear for soccer are ones that are plastic or rubber—they'll help you with your quick starts, stops and turns.

Play It Safe

Be sure to wear shin guards and appropriate soccer cleats during games as well as practices. Warming up, especially your leg muscles, is very important. To avoid headaches and dizziness, use your head and learn the proper technique for heading a ball in a game. Many leagues have strict rules about wearing jewelry, watches, and barrettes during games. Since any of these items can cause you to get hurt if you're hit with a ball, it's a good idea to not wear them when you play. Also, to protect your mouth from collisions (especially if you have braces), wear a mouthguard.

♣ It's A Fact!!

- Nikolai Kutsenko of the Ukraine juggled a soccer ball for 24½ hours nonstop with his feet, legs and head—the ball never touched the ground.

- Soccer players can run as many as 6 or 7 miles during the course of a game.

How To Play

In addition to a good strong kick, you'll want to master basic skills like passing (moving the ball to a teammate with a controlled kick), dribbling (tapping the ball with your feet to move it down the field), trapping (stopping the ball with your feet, legs, or chest), and heading (using your head to stop or pass the ball). Once you get these skills down, you'll be unstoppable.

Here are some great passing and trapping tips.

Passing. Pick your target out before you start the pass. Keep your head down to make sure you kick the ball correctly. Plant your non-kicking foot next to the ball and kick the ball right in the center using the inside of your foot and follow through with your leg.

Chest trap. As the ball comes toward you, get in front of it and let it hit your chest. Bring your shoulders around and slightly inward, creating a cavity for ball. Make sure you keep your arms down, so the ball doesn't accidentally hit your hands and cause a foul. When the ball hits your chest, arch your back, so your chest pops the ball upward and then lands at your feet.

♣ **It's A Fact!!**

If you played soccer on top of a mountain, you'd be able to kick the ball much further. Why? The air pressure on top of a mountain is lower than at the bottom. When a soccer ball is kicked into the air, the air pressure pushes against the ball and slows it down. Since the air pressure on top of a mountain is much lower, there is less pressure to push against the ball and slow it down. As a result, the ball will go further.

Chapter 31

Skating And Skateboards

Inline Skating

Meet The Expert

Anthony Lobello sprints at 40 miles per hour in carbon fiber boots, with boot bottoms made from airplane aluminum, and bearings (hardware that helps the wheels spin fast) made like those in Formula 1 racecars. "They're just a little smaller," he explains.

Gear Up

There are several different types of inline skates, depending on the type of skating you do. Recreational skates have a plastic boot and 4 wheels. These skates are best for beginners. Hockey skates have laces and are made of leather with small wheels for quick movement. Racing skates have 5 wheels and, usually, no brake. Freestyle skates have three wheels and a pick stop for tricks. Fitness skates have larger wheels and are used for cross-training. Aggressive skates, the kind worn by X Games competitors, are made of thick plastic with small wheels for quick movement, and grind plates to protect the skate when doing tricks. No matter what kind of skates you wear, always wear a helmet, as well as wrist guards, elbow pads, and knee pads.

About This Chapter: This chapter includes "Inline Skating Activity Card," "Figure Skating Activity Card," "Skateboarding Activity Card." BAM! (Body And Mind), Centers for Disease Control and Prevention (CDC), April 30, 2002.

Play It Safe

Avoid getting hurt by making sure your helmet and pads are on correctly. Your helmet should be tightly buckled, with the front coming down to right over your eyebrow, and your pads should be on tight, so they don't slip while you are skating. It's also important that your helmet is approved by one of the groups who test helmets to see which ones are the best: the Consumer Product Safety Commission (CPSC), or Snell B-95 standards are best for inline skating helmets. Make sure you are always in control of your speed, turns and stops, and be careful of cracks in the pavement where you are skating—they can be dangerous if your wheels get caught in them. It's best to go skating out of the way of traffic and other people (skating rinks are great places to skate).

> **♣ It's A Fact!!**
>
> • Inline skates were invented by a Minnesota hockey player so that he could skate during the off-season.
>
> • California has the most inline skaters—3.6 million residents of the Golden State regularly go inline skating.
>
> • Many professional skiers use inline skating to train during the off-season, because some of the skills of each activity are the same.

How To Play

If you're just beginning inline skating, here are some tips to get you rolling.

Practice balancing on your skates by walking in them on a flat, grassy area. As you move to the pavement, balance yourself without trying to move. Gradually begin to skate by moving forward, but not too fast. Keep your knees bent and flexible when you skate—it will keep you more stable. And if you fall—fall forward. Then you will fall on your kneepads—they're there to protect you.

It's also a good idea to take lessons from a certified instructor—you can find one through the International Inline Skating Association. As you get more skilled on your skates, there are several types of competitive inline skating activities—like speed skating and aggressive skating, which includes events like those at the X Games. There are also sports leagues just for those who play on wheels, such as roller hockey, roller soccer, and roller basketball.

Games

- Skate on one foot. Practice balancing on one foot at a time while you're skating. See how long you can glide on each foot. This is a great way to work on your balance.

- Skate with friends. Go inline skating at the local park or skating rink, or join a skate club in your town.

- Combine activities. Tired of just skating around in circles? Grab some friends for a game of inline hockey, inline basketball, or even inline soccer.

Parts Of The Body Worked

- Heart and lungs
- Upper and lower legs
- Hips and butt
- Lower back

Figure Skating

Meet The Expert

Jimmy is a 13-year-old figure skater who skates in events organized by the Skating Association for the Blind and Handicapped (SABAH). At the age of three, Jimmy was introduced to figure skating by a skating instructor who visited his school (a school specifically for visually-impaired kids) to tell them about ice skating, and how to get involved. Jimmy says, "I went home that day and told my mom all about it. She thought it was cool, and that's when I got started."

Gear Up

Figure skates are very thick and heavy and have a toe pick attached for tricks. Figure skates are made up of two parts, the boot and the blade. If you are just starting out, you can buy skates with both a boot and a blade, but more advanced skaters can buy each separately. The boot should be snug in the heel and supportive of the ankle. The blade is attached to the boot with screws, and is wider than the blade on an ice hockey skate, so that the edge grips the ice. You should not use figure skates to play ice hockey, because the blades extend past the boot and can cause other players to get injured.

If you are a beginning skater, along with your skates, you may want to wear a helmet to protect your head against any falls.

Be sure to wear layers so that you can put on or take off clothes depending on whether you are cold or warm. It's important to be able to move, so sweatpants or warm-up pants are perfect. You should only wear one pair of lightweight socks inside your skates, though, and remember to wear mittens and a hat to keep warm.

Play It Safe

Be a courteous skater—always be aware of other skaters and follow the traffic flow of the rink. Be careful not to get too close to other skaters with your exposed blades. And keep your skate laces tied tightly so that you don't trip yourself or anyone else up.

If you feel yourself beginning to fall, bring your hands, arms, and head into your body to absorb the shock of hitting the ice. And make sure you hop up quickly so that you are not in the way of other skaters.

How To Play

Did you ever watch the figure skaters in the Olympics wondering how the heck they did all those jumps and spins? Well, according to the experts, the key to becoming a successful skater is one simple thing—balance. Good posture is an important part of

♣ It's A Fact!!

• The "Axel," a figure skating jump, is named for Axel Paulsen, who performed the first jump ever during a competition in 1882.

• In order to compete in the Olympics, figure skaters must be at least 15 years old.

• The blade on a figure skate is only 3–4 millimeters thick—that's the same width as two pennies.

balance, because it helps even out your weight over the skates. This keeps you from falling and helps you glide smoothly and work up some speed. Keep your head and chin up and imagine that they are connected with an imaginary line that runs down the center of your chest and connects with the toes of both of your feet.

It's also important to know how to stop. The basic stop is called a snow-plow. Keeping both knees bent, shift your weight to one foot, then turn the other foot inward at an angle. Gradually shift your weight to the angled foot, which will slow you down and eventually bring you to a stop. A hockey stop is a more advanced move. To do it, quickly turn your feet sideways until they are perpendicular to the direction you were moving, putting more weight on your back foot.

Parts Of The Body Worked

- Heart and lungs
- Upper and lower legs
- Upper body
- Knees and ankles

> ✔ **Quick Tip**
>
> Skating can be hard work, and puts a lot of stress on your leg and back muscles, so be sure to warm up before you skate and stretch those muscles well.

Skateboarding

Meet The Expert

Kanten Russell began skateboarding when he was 14, turned pro at 19, and he's still pushing the limits today. Kanten's a street skater from San Diego, California. His awesome showing in *The Storm*, a video voted #1 by *Transworld Skateboarding* magazine, at the ESPN X Games, and on the cover of *Big Brother* skating magazine, puts him on top of the street skating scene. You can buy the video and check him out, but remember, he's a pro...you definitely shouldn't try this stuff at home.

Gear Up

Skateboards can be bought pre-assembled, or you can buy all of the pieces and put it together yourself. Pre-assembled boards are best for beginners, until you decide if skateboarding is really for you. If you are putting your own board together, you'll need a deck (the board itself), grip tape for the top of the deck so your feet don't slip, 2 trucks (the metal parts that are the axles of the wheels), 4 wheels, and 2 bearings per wheel (these keep the wheels spinning on the truck's axle). Before each time you ride, make sure your trucks are tightened and your wheels are spinning properly. Don't forget to wear a helmet, knee and elbow pads, and wrist guards. It's important that your helmet is approved by one of the groups who test helmets to see which ones are the best: the Snell B-95 standard is best for skateboarding helmets. Non-slippery shoes are a good idea too, so you can have better control of your board.

♣ **It's A Fact!!**

- If you ride with your right foot forward, you have what's called a goofy stance. If you ride with your left foot forward, you have a regular stance.

- Professional skateboarder Tony Hawk is in the *Guinness Book of World Records* for being the only skateboarder to successfully do a "900." That's 2½ rotations in the air from a ramp.

- The first X Games competition was held in June 1995 in Rhode Island.

Play It Safe

Before you ride, make sure you give your board a safety check to make sure everything is put together right. Always wear all of your protective gear including a helmet, knee and elbow pads, and wrist guards. If you do tricks with your board, you may also want to wear gloves to protect your hands from the pavement. If you're just starting out, skate on a smooth, flat surface so you can practice keeping control of your board. And no matter how experienced you are—never hold on to the back of a moving vehicle. It's best to skate out of the way of traffic and other people (skate parks are great places to skate). But if you are skating in streets near your house, be aware of cars and people around you, and stay out of their way. Also, once the sun sets, it's a good idea to put up your board for the night, since skating in the dark can be dangerous.

How To Play

If you're just starting out, follow these steps to develop your skateboarding skills. Put one foot on the board, toward the front, with the other on the ground. Push off the ground with your foot and put it on the rear of the board while you glide. Push again when you slow down. If you start going too fast, step off the board with your back foot. To turn, shift your weight to your back foot so that the front truck lifts off the ground and then move your body in the direction you want to go—the board will go with you.

If you want to find half pipes, vert ramps, and skate courses near you to practice your moves, look for a nearby skate park, designed to give skateboarders a great ride.

There are several different styles of skateboarding:

- Street skating is skateboarding on streets, curbs, benches, and handrails—anything involving common street objects. Street skating is best left to the pros though—it's very dangerous.

- Downhill skating is racing down big hills, usually on a longer skateboard called a longboard.

- Freestyle skating is more artistic, involving a series of tricks and stunts.

- Vert skating is skateboarding on mini-ramps and half pipes, which are U-shaped ramps.

Parts Of The Body Worked

- Upper and lower leg

- Knees and ankles

Chapter 32

Walking, Running, Jumping, Hiking, And Climbing

The Walking Workout

Research results could hardly be clearer: Taking a walk is one of the best ways to take charge of your health. A study in the *Journal of the American Medical Association* (February 11, 1998) showed that walking briskly for half an hour just six times a month cut the risk of premature death in men and women by 44 percent. A study in the *New England Journal of Medicine* (January 8, 1997) reported that men 61 to 81 years old sharply reduced their risk of death from all causes, including cancer and heart disease, by walking two miles a day. Other research has shown similar results for women.

Besides the well-documented health benefits, the beauty of walking is you can go at your own pace. If you are new to exercise or recovering from injury or childbirth, you can aim to walk for 20 to 45 minutes four or five days a week at the good fitness walking speed of three miles an hour. When (and if) you want to power up, you can take longer walks and work up to walking each mile in 15 minutes or less.

Once you're ready to hit the road (or the trail, track, treadmill or mall), how do you make the most of your walking workout? Minneapolis, Minnesota, walking instructor Kate Larsen, who has developed the LifeWalk™ Easy Audio Coach tape (888-LIF-WALK), offers these 10 practical tips for getting maximum aerobic, strength, postural and conditioning benefits from your walking program:

1. **Warm Up First, Then Stretch.** Start by walking for just seven to 10 minutes (wear a watch) and then do a few gentle stretches. Your muscles will stretch better if you've warmed them up first. Ask a fitness professional which stretches are best for you.

2. **Take Short, Quick Steps.** By taking short, quick steps, rather than long strides, you will work your glute muscles (in your buttocks) as you log miles.

3. **Practice the Heel-Toe Roll.** Push off from your heel, roll through the outside of the foot, then push through the big toe. Think of the big toe as the "go" button and push off with propulsion. Keep the other toes relaxed. (This takes practice.)

4. **Squeeze Your Glutes.** Imagine squeezing and lifting your glutes up and back, as if you were holding a $50 bill between them. This will strengthen your low-back muscles. Developing the ability to maintain this deep contraction throughout your walk will take a while.

5. **Zip Up Your Abs.** During your walk, imagine you're zipping up a tight pair of jeans. Stand tall and pull your abdominal muscles up and in. You can practice this even when you're not walking.

6. **Pump Your Arms.** Imagine you are holding the rubber grips of ski poles in your hands. Stand straight, drop your shoulders, squeeze your shoulder blades behind you and push back your elbows with each step. Keep your arm movements smooth and strong.

7. **Keep Your Chest Up, Shoulders Back.** Use your walk as an opportunity to practice perfect posture. Imagine someone dumped ice down your

back. That's the feeling you want to have as you hold your chest up and shoulders back.

8. **Keep Your Head Up.** Look about 10 feet ahead of you. Imagine you're wearing a baseball cap and have to look up just enough to see the road. This keeps your neck aligned properly.

9. **Smile and Have Fun.** Learning these techniques takes time and concentration. Be patient and enjoy your workout. Dress comfortably, find a partner or wear a headset and listen to music you love and, if you're walking outdoors, vary your route.

10. **Practice Mental Fitness.** Don't replay the problems of the day while you walk. Try to maintain a state of relaxed awareness by paying attention to your breathing and noticing how your body feels. Visualize yourself getting healthier, stronger and leaner.

A Habit You Can Live With

Consistency is probably the most important part of your walking workout. The more committed you are to walking all or most days of the week, the healthier you'll be. Remember that short walks are better than none at all. As Larsen says, health, like life, is a journey. All you have to do is take the first step.

Walk Safely

Shoes are the most important part of your walking gear. Good walking shoes are generally flat, but flexible, so your foot rolls with each step. They should fit well, but leave enough room for your feet to spread out while walking. Wear socks that are comfortable. Try socks made of cotton or other sweat-wicking materials—they will keep your feet drier and help

✔ **Quick Tip**

Don't forget your sunscreen and a hat. The sunscreen protects your skin from the sun. In the summer, a hat keeps the sun out of your face, and in the winter it helps to keep you warm by trapping the heat that is lost from the top of your head. A bright colored hat will also make it easy for drivers to see and avoid you.

prevent blisters. Running shoes are okay to use for walking. Don't forget to trade in the old shoes when the treads start wearing out—which is about 500 miles.

Wear comfortable clothing when walking. Try to dress in layers, so you can always take off something as you warm up. Layering with a t-shirt, sweatshirt, or windproof jacket is a good idea if it's windy or chilly outside.

Before you walk out the door, talk about the best walking routes with your parents so you know your safety zones and how to avoid traffic. And, only walk in those areas so your parents will know where you are.

It's always best to walk where you can avoid traffic—like parks or even the mall. Or try to find an area where there are sidewalks. If you have to walk on a street without sidewalks, walk close to the curb facing traffic. Remember to cross the street only at marked crosswalks or at corners, keep your ears and eyes open, and watch out for traffic in front and back of you. Wear bright-colored clothing or reflectors so drivers can see you. If you are walking alone, don't wear headphones—if they are too loud, they can keep you from hearing any oncoming traffic.

Water, water, water. It's a good idea to drink some water before you head out to walk, while you are walking, and when you get back—even if it's cold outside or you don't feel thirsty. In the summer, late afternoons (not nights) and mornings are the best times to walk to avoid the midday heat and humidity.

♣ It's A Fact!!

- If you walk 6,000 steps each day, you will walk a mile.

- Racewalking has been an Olympic sport since 1908. It is the longest foot race (31 miles) in the Olympics.

- The distance to the sun is 93.5 million miles. If you walk about 4 miles every hour (which is fairly fast) it would take you 23.4 million hours, which is 974,000 days or 2,670 years to reach the sun.

It is best to warm up your muscles before stretching them. So warm up for 5 minutes at an easy walking pace before stretching. Then stretch by starting at the top of your body and working your way down. Make sure to cool down and stretch after your walk too.

☞ **Remember!!**
Start out slowly and gradually increase the speed and distance you walk—don't try walking a marathon your first time out. And no matter where you are walking, be aware of what is going on around you.

Running For Pleasure

Besides walking, running is one of the least expensive forms of exercise. All you need is a good pair of shoes. (If you really want to give running a try, make sure you invest in the best fitting running shoes you can find.) Next, plan a safe route and follow this beginning schedule.

If you are totally new to exercise, ease into movement. After a five minute walking warm-up, start with a short run every other day (even as little as 5 minutes) and follow it with 10 or more minutes of walking, or as far as you can or feel like going. Gradually increase the duration of each run in a 2x forward/1x backward duration plan.

Example—5 minutes, 8 minutes, 5 minutes/8 minutes, 11 minutes, 8 minutes/11 minutes, 14 minutes, 11 minutes, and so on.

You can also begin your program with a Walk/Run routine, alternating 5 minutes of walking with short runs up to five minutes. You can use the 2x forward/1x backward method with your running segments. Gradually build up your running time to 30 minutes. Always complete your workout with a 5 minute slow paced cool-down and stretching of the calves, hamstrings, hip flexors, and back.

While you are building up your running stamina, practice good running form:

1. Run tall with good posture. Your trunk will lean forward from the hips slightly, but try to lengthen your body, lift your chest, and hold your abdominals in.

2. Let your arms swing at a 90 degree angle between the chest and hipbone, not crossing them over your body. Your arm swing should compliment your stride. Relax your wrists and hands. Do not clench your fists.

3. Power your stride from your thighs, hips, and buttocks muscles. Plant your heel on the ground first and roll onto the toes.

4. Stay relaxed and peaceful.

Take regular days off to prevent injury. Remember, physical training has 2 parts:

1. Tissue breakdown—caused by the running.

2. Tissue regeneration—caused by the rest period.

Proper training and resting will strengthen your body optimally. Running every other day, and not two days in a row, is good injury prevention. When you are conditioned enough to train for a race, you may add an extra running day to your week.

When you can run continuously for 30 minutes, you can begin to adjust your running workout toward specific training goals. Some new training techniques may include:

1. Train to cover extra ground. Once a week push yourself until you can run 2–3 times farther than normal distance. Longer runs will boost aerobic capacity.

2. Train for increased speed. To boost your anaerobic capacity and power, 1–2 times a week add several sprints into the middle of your running workout. To sprint, run faster than normal until you reach breathlessness, then back off to your normal pace and recover. This can be done 2–4 times in a run.

Tips for increasing your enjoyment of running include:

1. Set running goals—for speed, distance, races, etc.

2. Run with a partner

3. Change the route when you get bored

4. Record your progress in a log

Distance/Marathon Running

Your casual running workout may be so enjoyable that you want to push yourself and enter races. Sometimes the thought of training to run a long distance may seem daunting to the casual runner, but have no fear. Runners do not train for a marathon by running the distance of the race. It is not necessary to run the length of the race before race day. The buildup of steady training with shorter runs plus the flow of adrenalin on the race day will allow you to run the race.

About three months in advance of a 10K race, you will begin to gradually increase your mileage until you have a running schedule that will train you specifically for the run you want to enter.

10K Marathon Prerequisite (suggested): Running regularly for several months, 8–10 miles per week, at least 3 miles duration.

Start adding distance gradually to your runs so that the weekly total increases from 13 miles per week to 21 miles per week over a 12 week timetable. Alternate short run days (2–3 miles) with longer run days (4–8miles), including some sprints in the long run days. Maintain 2–3 rest days each week.

Longer Marathons Prerequisite (suggested): Able to run the 10 K marathon. Gradually build your running schedule to a total of 50 miles a week. A weekly schedule may resemble this:

- Sunday: Long day—12 miles built up to 18 miles
- Monday: Short day—4 miles built up to 9 miles
- Tuesday: Rest from running—do weight training
- Wednesday: Medium day—8 miles built up to 12 miles

- Thursday: Rest from running—weight training

- Friday: Medium day—8 miles built up to 12 miles

- Saturday: Bicycle

The week before the race the workouts are tapered off so that you will be well rested for the race. During that week the first two workouts can be fairly hard, followed by two days of light workouts, and 2 days of complete rest before race day.

Remember to eat lots of nutritious energy providing food while training and drink plenty of water. Food is your friend, not the enemy.

Cross Training For Running

Many runners use cycling and water jogging to increase aerobic endurance by reducing the stress on leg muscles. These cross training activities are usually done one workout a week, substituting for the running.

There are also specific exercises to train running muscles. Do the following 1–2 times a week. They can be done after a thorough warm-up and before the actual run.

1. **Hopping:** increases ankle strength and hip flexors. Start with feet shoulder width apart. Hop up and down on one foot for 30 seconds then switch. Hop on each leg for two 30-second sets. You can hop forward or stay in place.

2. **Skipping:** strengthen ankles and calves. Skip like you did when you were a child only exaggerated. Push off your toes and lift your knees high, propelling yourself up and forward. Coordinate arm movements with legs. Skip for 2–3 minutes.

3. **Butt Kicks:** Leaning slightly forward, alternately kick each heel toward your butt as you move forward. Do 2 sets for 30–60 seconds.

Weight Training Program

Most runners today recognize the need to get complete conditioning by adding weight/resistance training to their programs. The goal of weight training program is to prevent injuries and balance the muscle groups. A split routine takes less time and adds more variety to the program. It may be done 2–3 times weekly, alternating the routines. Here is a sample workout performing 1–3 sets of 8–15 repetitions:

Routine #1	*Routine #2*
• Incline chest press	• Leg Extensions
• Seated Row	• Leg Curls
• Squats	• Upright Row
• Overhead Tricep Extension	• Over head Press
• Incline Bicep Curls (alternating)	• Low Back Extensions
• Curl-ups (abdominals)	• Oblique Twist (abdominals)

As you get more involved in your running program, you will encounter joys and challenges. Two highly recommended websites dedicated to running are:

• http://www.kicksports.com

• http://www.runnersworld.com

Jumprope

Meet The Expert

If you think that jumping rope is just for girls, you haven't checked out Ben Raznick's power moves.

Who is Ben Raznick? Ben is 15 and a member of the Skip-It jump rope team in his hometown of Boulder, Colorado. He has been jumping competitively for over half his life.

Gear Up

You'll need a rope. But not all ropes are actually made of rope. Ropes come in cloth (regular rope), speed (skinny cord), beaded (plastic beads that CLACK when they hit the ground), and even electric.

Play It Safe

Avoid spills—set the right length for your rope. To find out what that is, stand on the center of the cord and pull the handles up so they fit right under your arms. When you jump over the rope, the rope should just brush the floor under your feet. If it doesn't touch the floor, it's too short. If it hits the floor in front of your feet, it's too long.

How To Play

Jump rope is just a fun game that girls play in their backyards or on the playground, right? NO WAY! Betcha didn't know that aside from being a great aerobic workout, jumpers of all ages can compete nationally in categories such as speed, freestyle, and double dutch, which is where two ropes are turned like an egg-beater by two turners, while one or two people jump within the moving ropes.

Parts Of The Body Worked

- Upper and lower legs

- Heart and lungs

- Upper arms

> ## ♣ It's A Fact!!
>
> - Every year, schools across the country participate in Jump Rope for Heart (JRFH), an activity to raise money to stop heart disease and stroke. JRFH has donated more than $327 million to the American Heart Association.
>
> - Speed, freestyle, single rope, and double dutch are all different ways to jump rope.
>
> - The 2001, 11–under year old national champ jumped 304 times in one minute.

Hiking

Meet The Expert

Ben Mourer's only 17, but he's already teaching lots of adults about hiking. As an official hike guide for the North Country Trail Association and the American Hiking Society, Ben leads adults and kids of all ages on trails near his hometown of Chicora, Pennsylvania. He sets up the hike, points out cool trees and animals along the trail, and helps keep hikers safe by bringing along first aid kits and extra water.

Gear Up

First, you'll need a good pair of shoes and thick socks designed for this type of activity. You can start with some sturdy sneakers with thick bottoms. When you begin to take on more difficult trails, try a pair of hiking boots, and make sure they fit. Make sure they fit. Also, get a backpack or fanny pack to carry all of your hiking supplies. Dress in layers and bring along a waterproof jacket with a hood in case you get caught in the rain. And don't forget a hat, sunscreen, and sunglasses because the higher you hike, the more dangerous the sun's rays become.

To keep hiking fun, you always need to be prepared to beat problems that could happen while you're out, like finding the trail if you get lost or stuck in bad weather. Make sure you bring a map of the area you'll be hiking in and a sturdy compass. You'll also need to bring plenty of water and extra food, like sports bars or trail mix, in case you have to stay out late and get hungry. The adults on your hike should bring a box of waterproof matches and an Army-style knife. A flashlight and extra batteries will help you find your way if you end up out after dark. Finally, you'll need to bring a first aid kit, in case someone gets hurt during your hike.

Play It Safe

Prep. Get in shape before you head out on your hike. Try walking around your neighborhood with your pack loaded with five pounds more gear than you'll actually carry on your hike. If that goes well, plan a short hike to test your abilities on the trail.

Buddies. Take a friend and an adult along on your hike. That way you can look out for each other and you'll have people to talk to. Also, be sure to let someone who's not going know where you'll be hiking and what time you'll be back.

H2O. Carry lots of water even if you are only planning a short hike. For warm-weather hikes, bring six to eight quarts of water per day. In the cold weather or higher elevations, you can be safe with half that amount. Whenever you are near water, make sure you wet yourself down. Dampen a bandana and wipe your face, neck, and arms or wrap it around your head while you hike.

Blisters and more. To prevent blisters, try spraying your feet with an antiperspirant before heading out. Bring extra pairs of socks that you can change into if your feet get wet or sweaty—if they aren't made of cotton, they'll keep your feet drier. Once you're on the trail, stop as soon as you feel a "hot spot" on your feet and apply special type of bandage called "moleskin" to the sore area. Also, try using a hiking stick to keep some pressure off of your legs and knees.

Buzz. Don't get bugged by bugs. Protect yourself from bites and stings by using a bug repellant that includes DEET. Repellents that contain DEET are the most effective, but make sure you rub them on according to the directions. A good rule of thumb from the experts is that kids should use repellents with less than 10% DEET. Get your parents to help you put it on your face so you don't get it in your mouth or eyes. And wash your hands after you apply it. Remember that stuff that smells good to you smells good to bugs too, so don't use scented shampoos or lotions before hiking.

Weather watcher. When it's hot, pick trails that are shaded and run near streams. If you need to hike uphill in the sun, first soak yourself down to stay cool. You can also try wearing a wet bandana around your head or neck. Also, try to stay out of cotton clothes. Keep yourself out of bad weather by checking forecasts before you hike and watching the skies once you're out on the trail. During lightening storms, head downhill and away from the direction of the storm, and then squat down and keep your head low.

♣ It's A Fact!!

- In the year 2000, 67 million people went hiking.

- America's National Parks have more that 12,000 miles of trails.

- The Appalachian Trail starts in northern Georgia and continues through South Carolina, North Carolina, Tennessee, Virginia, Maryland, Pennsylvania, New Jersey, New York, Connecticut, Massachusetts, Vermont, and ends in Maine at Mt. Katahdin, Baxter Peak, Baxter State Park.

Keep it yummy. To stay healthy on your hike, you'll need to know how to keep your food and water safe. Remember the four C's: contain, clean, cook, and chill.

How To Play

Take a hike. No, really, take the time to go hiking. Hiking with your friends or family is a great chance to get outdoors, breathe some fresh air, and get active. It's easy to get started. Just look for a trail in a national park near you.

For your first day hike (hiking for a day or less without camping overnight), choose a safe, well-marked trail that doesn't have too many steep climbs. Otherwise, you'll get tired too early and won't make it as far as you want to go. Each time you go hiking, try going a little farther and take a slightly steeper trail. Before you know it you'll be hiking the Appalachian Trail—a 2,167-mile trail that goes all the way from Maine to Georgia.

Parts Of The Body Worked

- Upper and lower legs

- Back

- Heart and lungs

- Hips and butt

- Abs

Try Rock Climbing

Climbing stretches and strengthens the mind and body and can be enjoyed at any level, and any age. Not all climbing is straight up and treacherous, there are climbs to suit any ability.

- Rock climbing will make you sweat. The cardiovascular benefits will improve the stamina of your body.

- Rock climbing will stretch you. Flexibility is essential in climbing, especially in the hips. It will stretch your muscles, therefore there is less soreness after exercise.

- Rock climbing will strengthen your muscles and add to your muscular endurance.

In the upper body you will gain strength in your fingers, forearms, shoulders, chest, and back. Your calves and toes will also benefit in the lower body. Climbing improves agility, muscular endurance, flexibility, and strength. It strengthens and stretches the mind and body so it is easier to work out longer, and each movement is new, challenging, and without impact.

Chapter 33

Water Sports

Aquatic Fitness

Aquatic fitness is defined as activities performed in the water that promote and enhance physical and mental fitness. Aquatic fitness is typically performed in a vertical position in shallow and/or deep water. There are numerous applications to appeal to a wide variety of participants.

The water's unique properties allow the pool to provide an environment for people of all abilities. Buoyancy creates a reduced impact exercise alternative that is easy on the joints, while the water's resistance challenges the muscles. Water lends itself to a well-balanced workout that improves all major components of physical fitness—aerobic training, muscular strength and endurance, flexibility, and body composition.

Shallow water programming is performed in waist to chest depth. The feet remain in contact with the pool bottom during most of the workout providing a low impact training option. Deep water programs, on the other hand, are performed in water depths that allow the participant to remain vertical (upright) and yet not touch the bottom. Flotation equipment is utilized to maintain correct alignment and provide a truly non-impact workout.

About This Chapter: "Aquatic Fitness" is reprinted with permission from the Aquatic Exercise Association, www.aeawave.com. © 2002 Aquatic Exercise Association. All rights reserved. Additional information is taken from BAM! (Body And Mind) Activity Cards (www.bam.gov), Centers for Disease Control and Prevention, April 2002.

How Is Water Exercise Different?

Buoyancy: In the water your body is buoyant and the impact to the joints during exercise is significantly less than on land.

- A body immersed to the neck bears approximately 10% of its body weight.

- A body immersed to the chest bears approximately 25–35% of its body weight.

- A body immersed to the waist bears approximately 50% of its body weight.

A properly designed program in the water provides a highly effective workout in a safe and gentle environment due to the principle of buoyancy. Shallow water programs are generally best performed in water that is about mid-chest depth for maximum comfort, control of movement, and optimum toning benefits for the upper body.

Resistance: Muscles must work against resistance to become developed and toned. Water provides substantially more resistance than air—at least 12 times the resistance—making each movement in the pool more challenging to the muscles. Also, muscles typically work in pairs; i.e. biceps and triceps or quadriceps and hamstrings. When you move your body, or your limbs, through the water you are always encountering resistance. This helps to provide a more balanced workout as opposing muscles are involved, unlike on land where you typically need to reposition the body, or select a separate exercise, to provide adequate stimulation to both muscles of the pair.

Cooling Effect: Water cools more efficiently than air, so when exercising in the water the body is able to eliminate excess heat more effectively. This is not to say that you will not sweat during a workout in the pool, but water helps prevent overheating and washes away the perspiration as you exercise. Because the water cools the body quickly, it is imperative that you begin every workout with a "thermal warmup" designed to elevate the body's core temperature, warm the muscles and prepare the joints for the increased workload to come. Even at the recommended temperature of 80–85 degrees Fahrenheit (special populations and specialty training may require deviations from this recommended range), a proper warm up is necessary to prevent injury and provide comfort.

Heart Rates: Heart rate responses differ when exercising in the water than when exercising on land. Typically, aquatic exercisers experience a reduced heart rates response (that is, a lowered pulse rate), but the water should not be considered less effective. Studies have shown that oxygen consumption (the true measure of the cardiovascular benefits) is comparable to a similar program on land, although the heart rate response is lower. Several factors, some of which have been previously mentioned, influence the exercising heart rate when submerged in the water to mid-chest:

- The effect of buoyancy allows a more efficient return of blood to the heart from the extremities.

- The cooling affect of water reduces the workload on the heart. (One function of the heart is to keep the body cool during sustained exercise.)

- Hydrostatic pressure, the pressure that the water exerts on the body while submerged, assists in blood flow and improves the exchange of oxygen into the blood.

How Does Water Exercise Compare To Land Exercise In Regards To Calorie Burning?

As on land, there are several variables that affect caloric consumption during vertical water exercise. Variables include:

- Water depth in which the person is exercising.

- Speed of movement through the water.

- Amount of force applied (how "hard" you work) to movements.

- Length of the persons limbs.

- Environmental factors such as water temperature, air temperature, humidity, etc.

On land, weight bearing is a primary factor for increasing calorie consumption, but in the water it appears that using the water's resistance is more of a factor. Based upon the finding of a study that compared energy expenditure (calories burned) for upper and lower body exercises performed in the water and out of the water (Cassedy 1992), one can estimate that combining upper and lower body movements in the pool would expend somewhere between 400 and 500 calories in a one hour class. This is comparable to running at 10–11 minutes per mile.

Is It Safe To Exercise Alone In The Pool?

The Aquatic Exercise Association (AEA) advises against exercising alone in the pool because of the risk of drowning should something unexpected occur. Most people find it more enjoyable to exercise with a friend, so even if you plan to workout in your home pool, invite someone to join you. It is also easier to maintain a regular exercise program since your are accountable to someone besides yourself. At the least, have someone remain on deck to provide assistance. Stay safe, never exercise alone in the water.

What Is The Purpose Of Wearing Shoes While Exercising In The Water?

Although impact is greatly reduced in the pool, you will still experience some impact stress to the weight bearing joints of the body (unless you remain in a suspended position, such as deep water exercise). Therefore AEA recommends that you wear shoes for added cushion, shock absorption and comfort during bouncing movements. Shoes also provide ankle support which is important in programs that include twisting or turning activities. Footwear can also protect your feet from rough surfaces—whether the pool bottom, pool deck, or locker rooms; this is critical for individuals with diabetes. The best news—water shoes can make your workout more effective.

Do I Need To Bring A Water Bottle To My Aquatic Fitness Classes?

Yes. Even though the water cools the body more effectively, you will lose fluids from perspiration during a vigorous aquatic program. To prevent overheating and related problems (muscle cramps, heat exhaustion, and heat stroke) it is suggested to drink water before, during, and after exercise. Keep your water bottle handy at the side of the pool and your workout can continue uninterrupted.

My Aquatic Classes Are Outdoors, How Do I Protect My Skin?

Unfortunately, most all tanning has some damaging influence on your skin. Cloudy days and water submersion are not effective for preventing sun damage; up to 80% of ultraviolet radiation penetrates cloud cover and up to 50% reaches swimmers in the water. Typical cotton t-shirts can allow 30–50% of harmful ultraviolet rays through to your skin when dry; even more when wet. Special sun-protective clothing is available. Wear a waterproof sunscreen with at least an SPF of 15 and apply 30–40 minutes before exposure, consider sun-protective clothing and hats, and always wear your sunglasses.

What If I Cannot Keep Up With The Rest Of The Class During The Exercise Program?

First of all, this is YOUR exercise class and you need to feel comfortable listening to your own body's needs and abilities. Pace yourself and do not be afraid to do things a little differently. Also, make sure to select a class that is appropriate for your abilities. Most facilities offer a variety of programs—from special needs to advanced fitness. Observe different classes and find the one that is right for you. Also, make sure that your instructor in properly trained and certified. The instructor should be able to assist you with making necessary modifications without feeling "singled out" from the group. And finally, as you continue to exercise you will see your energy, enthusiasm and abilities continue to advance.

I Love Exercising In The Water, But My Skin Gets So Dry. What Can I Do?

The best way to prevent dry skin is to drink—yes, drink—plenty of water everyday. However, being submerged in the pool for an hour or more will tend to dry the skin. Do NOT put on lotions (except waterproof sunscreens) before your class; it will simply wash off, waste your money, and adversely affect the pool's water quality. Immediately after class, shower and apply a good quality moisturizing lotion to your damp skin (now is a good time to moisturize the hair too). Your swim suit will also last longer if you rinse thoroughly immediately after exercising in the pool, chlorine and other chemicals necessary to provide a safe environment will gradually deteriorate the

Survival For The Fittest: Top Ten Tips

1. DO learn to swim. If you like to have a good time doing water activities, being a strong swimmer is a must.

2. DO take a friend along. Even though you may be a good swimmer, you never know when you may need help. Having friends around is safer and just more fun.

3. DO know your limits. Watch out for the "too's"—too tired, too cold, too far from safety, too much sun, too much hard activity.

4. DO swim in supervised (watched) areas only, and follow all signs and warnings.

5. DO wear a life jacket when boating, jet skiing, water skiing, rafting, or fishing.

6. DO stay alert to currents. They can change quickly. If you get caught in a strong current, don't fight it. Swim parallel to the shore until you have passed through it. Near piers, jetties (lines of big rocks), small dams, and docks, the current gets unpredictable and could knock you around. If you find it hard to move around, head to shore. Learn to recognize and watch for dangerous waves and signs of rip currents—water that is a weird color, really choppy, foamy, or filled with pieces of stuff.

7. DO keep an eye on the weather. If you spot bad weather (dark clouds, lighting), pack up and take the fun inside.

8. DON'T mess around in the water. Pushing or dunking your friends can get easily out of hand.

9. DON'T dive into shallow water. If you don't know how deep the water is, don't dive.

10. DON'T float where you can't swim. Keep checking to see if the water is too deep, or if you are too far away from the shore or the poolside.

Source: BAM! (Body and Mind), Centers for Disease Control and Prevention, April 2002.

material of your suit. Products are available to help remove the chlorine residue from your skin/hair and suit, and some companies manufacturer chlorine resistant swim wear/exercise wear.

I Am Young And Athletic—Can Water Exercise Really Provide The Workout I Need?

Definitely! Water fitness programming has progressed and diversified over the past several years which is one of the reasons we are seeing such a big "wave" of participation. Although a significant part of the workout intensity is up to the individual (you can employ various training principles to alter the intensity), the type of program selected is also very important. Most facilities offer a variety of options for water exercise participants—just as they do for land-based group exercise. Check out aquatic programs featuring kick boxing, sports specific training, intervals, and circuits. Or, if you prefer the one-on-one approach, consider aquatic personal training to more specifically target your goals and needs. And don't forget, specialized aquatic fitness equipment can further enhance your training results.

The Deal On Boating And Jet Skiing

Skimming over the water is a great ride. You probably aren't driving a boat or jet ski yourself just yet, but they are lots of fun to ride with an adult. (Remember, they like to have fun too.) You and your parents can check the state rules for how old you have to be, and cruise through this boating site.

Stay alert! When you're riding, keep a lookout for other boats, jet skiers, water skiers, divers, and swimmers. Who has the right-of-way? Generally, drivers should keep to their right when they are passing other boats—just like you do when you are walking in the hall at school.

Always ride at a speed that will let you stay in control so you can stop or go another way if you need to. It's also not a good idea to jump wakes (tracks in the water left by other boats or jet skis) or speed through choppy water, because it's easy to loose control.

Do not ride with a driver who has been drinking alcohol.

Make sure you know and practice what to do if someone falls out of the boat.

Some people teak surf (hold on to the back of the boat and then let go to ride the wave that the boat makes), but you shouldn't copy them. Teak surfers get too close to the boat, don't wear life jackets, and breathe exhaust fumes (chemicals) that the boat makes. Sounds like a bad idea to us.

Swimming

Gear Up

Pick out a swimsuit that fits your style. If you plan to swim competitively, you'll need a suit that is lightweight and stretchy. It should also fit snugly so it won't slow you down when you're racing or slip off as you dive into the water.

A pair of goggles will allow you to see where you are going underwater without your eyes feeling itchy and irritated. They even make prescription goggles so you can see underwater if you wear glasses.

Finally, if you're outside, you'll wanna guard against the sun. So, rub on some sunscreen.

Play It Safe

Learn to swim and always swim with a friend. It's more fun and having a friend there if you need one is just plain smart.

Make sure to respect rules and lifeguards. Pool rules like "no running" or beach rules like "no swimming outside the flags" are there to protect you. (And lifeguards enforce them so that you can

> ### ✔ Quick Tip
>
> Look out for signs warning you that the water is not clean, because polluted water could make you sick. (And even if it is clean, try not to swallow it.)
>
> It's also smart to keep clear of objects in the water like water plants and animals. They can cause problems for you so, if you see them—go the other way. (You've heard about what jellyfish and snapping turtles can do, right?)
>
> Finally, if you're outside, you need to guard against the sun. Those burning rays reflect off the water and sand onto you…and they can really spoil the fun. So, rub on some sunscreen to get sun proof.

stay safe, not to ruin your fun.) Make sure a lifeguard or an adult can see you just in case you need help.

Don't try to keep up with stronger or more experienced swimmers, especially if they swim out further than you think you can swim back.

Swimming is real workout. So, take breaks. If you get tired while you're in the water, float on your back for a few minutes until you get your power back.

Make sure to keep an eye on mother nature. If you spot bad weather (dark clouds, lightening), it's time to take the fun inside.

And when you get out of the water, tilt and shake your head to let all of the water drain out of your ears—"swimmers ear" can be a real pain.

Diving makes a splash, but make sure you know how deep the water is before you leap.

How To Play

Swimming is more than a great way to cool off when it's hot, it's also a fun activity that helps you work out your whole body. If you don't know how to swim, or you want to brush up your skills, you'll want to take some lessons at your local pool. There, you'll master the basics to help keep your head above water.

Floating. Our bodies have a natural tendency to float—so go with it. Relax and let the water support your body. Lie back with your arms stretched out to the side. Turn your palms up and keep the backs of your hands in the water. Arch your back, stretch out your legs (some gentle kicking will help you float easier), and take short breaths to stay relaxed. Floating is a great way to rest, or rest while you call for help if you don't have enough energy to swim to shore or the side of a pool.

Treading water. Another way to keep afloat is to tread water. Get into the water and pretend you are gently riding a bicycle, with your back straight and your arms straight out in front of you. Sweep your arms together with your palms facing down and in. Then, sweep them back out with your palms facing down and away from each other.

Swimming underwater. Breathe in as much air as you can and then let it all out, take one more breath and hold it, and slide under the water. (Even though it seems like taking lots of quick breaths before going underwater could help you, doing that is called "hyperventilating" and it can actually make you pass out underwater. Not good.) Stretch out your body with your legs together and your arms straight out a little bit above your head. Pull your legs up then kick them apart to start gliding. Next, bring your legs together and kick in a scissor motion to move around. While you kick, put your arms out to your sides and push them back towards your legs. Glide as far as you can, and then come back up when you need a breath. Try to stay relaxed and don't push yourself too far. The more you practice, the stronger your lungs will become.

Parts Of The Body Worked

- Upper and lower legs
- Arms
- Shoulder and neck
- Heart and lungs
- Back

Water Skiing

Gear Up

First you'll need water skis. There are four types: combination pairs, slalom, tick, and jump skis. New skiers should start with combination pairs, since they are wider and easiest to learn on. Make sure your skis have been checked and that they fit properly. You will also need a flexible towrope that has a floating handle.

All water skiers wear life vests (also known as personal floatation devices or PFDs). You should wear a special water skiing life vest that is approved by the Coast Guard. You and your parents should check this out to get the official word on which life vest is right for you. Finally, since you're outside, you need to guard against the sun.

> ♣ **It's A Fact!!**
>
> Elephants can swim up to 20 miles a day. They stick their trunks above the water like snorkels.
>
> At the 2000 Summer Olympics in Sydney, Australia, the USA won 33 swimming medals, including 14 gold medals.
>
> It takes about 800,000 gallons of water to fill up an Olympic-size pool.

> **✤ It's A Fact!!**
>
> Wondering why water skiers don't sink? Skiers weigh the same whether they're stopped or skiing, so the pressure on top of the skis stays the same. As a skier gets pulled faster, the water pushes against the bottom of the skis, balancing out the pressure from the top. The bigger the skis and the faster the boat goes, the easier it is for the skier to stay up on top of the water.

Play It Safe

Water skiers need to be good swimmers and always wear a life jacket that fits properly.

Safe water skiing requires three people: the skier, an experienced boat driver, and the spotter to look out for the skier's signals. Since the noise from the boat is so loud, it's important that everyone agrees on and understands the hand signals to use so you can talk without saying a word. Remember, you need to master hand signals before you begin cutting across the water on your skis.

When you're out on the water, be sure you're in a safe area to ski. Don't ski near docks, boats, rocks, or in shallow water. The only place to start is in the water—dock or land starts should be left to the pros.

If you start to lose your balance while skiing, just bend your knees and crouch down so you don't fall. If you do fall—and everyone does—remember to let go of the rope. Then, find your skis and hold one of them up to signal you're okay and to let other boaters know you're in the water.

How To Play

Want to walk on water? Try water skiing. Water skiers hold onto a rope and are pulled on their skis behind a boat going fast. They glide across the water with the wind in their faces. It's a great activity that you can do with your family or friends and it can be competitive. Check out these tips and you'll be skiing in no time.

Getting Started. Before you get in the water to ski, make sure you're wearing a life vest that is the right size and is on the right way. Get in the water with your skis. Wet your ski bindings before you put on your skis, and keep the bindings loose enough that the skis will come off if you fall. Bend your knees up towards your chest with your arms straight out in front of you. As the boat pulls the rope toward you, grab the rope handle with both hands and hold it between your knees. You should almost be sitting on the skis. Facing the boat, lift the tips of your skis a bit above the water, keep your skis shoulder width apart, and keep your arms straight. Nod your head to let the boat driver know you are ready to go, and begin straightening your legs as you are pulled out of the water. If you stand too soon you'll fall down, so take it slow and be patient.

Steering. To turn, just lean in the direction you want to go. Move your weight to the edge of the skis on the side you want to turn toward while you keep the skis pointed forward. If you want to turn faster, crouch down while you lean.

Parts Of The Body Worked

- Upper and lower legs

- Arms heart and lungs

- Knees and ankles

- Hips and butt

- Upper body

> **♣ It's A Fact!!**
>
> - In 1922, Ralph Samuelson became the first person to try water skiing. First he strapped boards from a barrel to the bottom of his feet, and later on he decided to try skis.
>
> - The best water skiers can go up to 60 mph.
>
> - The men's world record for jumping is 233 feet, which is about as far as kicking a 77-yard field goal in football.

Surfing

Gear Up

All you really need is a bathing suit or a wetsuit (for cold water or if it's cold out), and of course, a surfboard. Here are some tips: You may want to get a used or inexpensive board at first. It wouldn't be smart to mess up a cool, new board making beginner's mistakes. The fins should be in good

---

♣ It's A Fact!!

- The movie *Blue Crush* was filmed in Hawaii, on the north shore of the island of Oahu.

- Among board riders across the world, female surfers are known as "wahines."

- "Surf forecasters" use information from satellites in space to find big waves.

---

condition, and it should have a place to attach a leash (cord that hooks your ankle to the board so it doesn't get away). Long boards are easier to ride and control. Your board should be 12 to 14 inches taller than you. Also, put two coats of wax on your board if the deck (top) doesn't have a pad that keeps you from slipping.

Play It Safe

First things first…You've gotta be a strong swimmer. As a beginner, you are going to be in the water more than riding your board. And always surf with someone else.

While you're a beginner, stick to waves no bigger than three feet. If you are a real beginner, surf only broken (white) waves. Never paddle out farther than you can swim back with your board. Most of all, if it doesn't feel right or you are too scared, just don't go.

Always leash your board to control it. When you begin the wipeout (fall at the end of a ride), kick your board out and away from you.

Bad weather = No surfing.

Finally, make sure to wear sunscreen.

How To Play

What do surfing and walking a dog have in common? Well, surfboards don't bark, but they still need a "leash" to keep them from getting away.

Surfing takes lots of practice, but when you're riding that wave, it's incredible. Here's how to start:

Goofy Foot? Put your best foot forward—find out whether you are regular or goofy-footed. Try sliding across a smooth floor with socks on. If you lead with your left foot, you're "regular," and the left foot goes near the front of the board when you're surfing. If your right foot goes first, you're "goofy," and the right foot goes up front.

Paddling. To get around in the water, lay chest-down on your board, keeping your legs straight behind you. With each arm, make an overhand swimming stroke that starts at the front of the board and finishes under the board near your legs. (It's like swimming the crawl stroke, except you're on top of the board.) As you finish the stroke with one hand, the other hand is just starting. Try practicing in shallow water or a pool first.

Catching the Wave. When you see white water (breaking waves) coming, turn around to face the shore, aim your board the direction the wave is coming, and start to paddle in. When the wave reaches you, it will push you forward. Stop paddling, grab the side of the board, push up your body, and quickly get your feet under you. Both should land at the same time, toes pointing sideways. Move your lead (regular or goofy) foot in front. Hey, you're surfing.

> ✔ **Quick Tip**
> Did you know that surfers have rules for who "owns" a wave? Surfers riding waves have to get out of the way of those paddling out, and everyone has to stay clear of swimmers. A surfer who is standing and riding a wave gets to keep it—no one should "drop in" (try to catch the same wave).

Parts Of The Body Worked

- Hips and butt
- Upper and lower legs
- Lower back
- Shoulders and neck
- Knees and ankles

Diving

Gear Up

It's simple—all you need is a swimsuit and a pool with a diving board. Check out your neighborhood or a community center in your area for a pool you can use.

Play It Safe

Here's the deal: Know how to swim well before stepping on the

> ♣ **It's A Fact!!**
>
> - Platform diving became an Olympic event in 1904. Springboard diving made it in 1908.
>
> - In January 1991, Fu Mingxia from China became the world's youngest platform champion. She was only 12.
>
> - Divers hit the water at speeds of up to 34 miles per hour.

board. Always dive with someone else. And… Protect your noggin. You've gotta know the water depth before you dive, and never ever dive into shallow water. Check around for signs or ask a lifeguard. Diving areas are usually marked. In case you haven't figured this out yet, above-ground pools are not designed for diving. They're way too shallow. (Lots of in-ground pools aren't deep enough either, so check out the water before you dive.)

When you are on the board, enter the water straight on and make sure there's nothing in your way before you leap. If people come into the diving area from other parts of the pool, wait until they're gone, or just ask the lifeguard to clear the area for you. If you jump when there is someone else in the diving area, or even just mess around while diving, you could land on top of someone and get hurt.

Don't run up to a dive. Always stand at the edge of the board or pool and then dive. And dive straight ahead—not off to the side.

Most of all, only try dives that are in your comfort zone. Leave those fancy or stunt leaps to experienced divers. An adult can help you decide which dives are safe to try.

How To Play

Diving is about precision, flexibility, and strength—all in one. Experienced divers leap 5–10 meters (about 16–33 feet) into the air from a springboard or platform, do stunts like somersaults or twists, and then plunge into the water below.

A certified diving instructor can help you master the diving board, but for now, try this beginners' dive… Point your arms straight over your head, with your shoulders by your ears. Keep your head between your arms and tuck your chin to your chest. Bend at the waist, but don't bend the knees. Keep your legs straight. Fall towards the water, making sure not to lift your head or shoulders. Follow through with your fingers into the water. That's it—you've made the plunge.

Parts Of The Body Worked

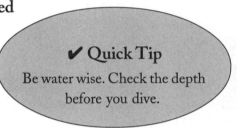

✔ Quick Tip
Be water wise. Check the depth before you dive.

- Heart and lungs

- Arms

- Abs

- Upper and lower legs

Canoeing And Kayaking

Gear Up

You'll need a kayak (boat that's almost completely closed on top with space for just one person) or a canoe (open boat that can fit you and a friend or two) plus the right kind of paddle. Kayak paddles have a blade on both sides, but canoe paddles have one blade. Be sure to pick the right size paddle— the stick part of a canoe paddle should be about six to eight inches longer than the length of your arm with your fingers out. Don't forget another essential: the life vest. Water shoes or sneakers—not sandals—that grip on the bottom will help your feet stay put when you are pulling the paddle through the water. Keep a whistle attached to your life vest so you are always ready to get attention if trouble strikes.

Play It Safe

You need to be a strong swimmer because you might have to swim underwater, or in moving water. Always go paddling with another person—not just for times of trouble, but because someone should help you carry, load, and launch your boat, right?

Make sure your life jacket fits. Since paddling is an activity that you can do all through the year, leave enough room to put clothes under it when it is cold out. Be prepared to get wet. Take along extra dry clothing, just in case. Remember to keep sun proof with sunscreen.

Save paddling for good weather days. Since you don't know what mother nature will throw at you, know where your float trip will take you, spots where you can get out or camp for the night, and different ways to go in case unexpected trouble strikes your route. Avoid whitewater rapids, dams, and falls—only experienced whitewater paddlers should take these on.

Sure, you want all your friends and their stuff to come along, but don't put too much weight in the boat—you should have more than six inches of side between the top of the fully loaded boat and the water. Spread out the weight (including people) so the boat will stay balanced.

Take lessons to help you learn ways to get yourself back in your boat if it tips over—before you take your first trip. And then practice them. The main thing to remember is… Don't panic. If you can't get back in, stay with your boat and flip it back over—it'll float—and try to swim the boat to shore. (Remember, you're wearing a life jacket.)

How To Play

Paddlers (people who canoe or kayak) really know how to have fun on the water— just a boat, a paddle, nature, and you.

♣ It's A Fact!!

- Native Americans used animal skins and a variety of tree barks to make canoes. The very best canoe covering was made from paper birch bark because it was lightweight and very strong.

- Thirty thousand years ago, canoes helped ancient people move to new places along the Pacific Ocean: first in Asia, then along the coasts of Canada, the U.S., and South America.

Canoeing. Hold the paddle with your inside hand on top and your water-side hand two to three feet down. Your knuckles should be facing out. Without stretching, insert the blade of the paddle all the way in the water as far forward as you can reach. Push your top hand forward and pull your bottom hand back, turning your shoulders to move the paddle blade straight through the water to your hip. Keep the top of the paddle handle lower than your eyes and don't follow the curve of the canoe. Have a friend paddle on the other side of the canoe, or switch sides as you paddle, to keep the boat gliding along straight.

Kayaking. Kayak paddles have a blade on each side. Lift your paddle with both hands and hold it across your chest. Place your hands the same distance from each blade, just outside your shoulders. Hold the paddle out in front of you, just a few inches above the kayak. Keeping your left elbow straight, bring your right hand straight back, letting your right elbow bend back toward your body. Your body will twist to the right a bit. Paddle. Now, use the other arm. You're kayaking.

✔ Quick Tip

- Only get to the water through marked paths—not through someone else's property. Take your paddling breaks in public places too.

- Keep your lunch spots and campsites clean—don't leave garbage in the water or lying around. If there's nowhere to put your trash, take it with you and dump it when you get home.

- Give people fishing plenty of room and try not to disturb the water too much where they are—it'll scare the fish off.

- Keep away from the wildlife—even if they are as cute as pets.

Chapter 34

Winter Sports

Gear Up

Are your skis the right size? If the tip of your upright ski reaches your face between your nose and chin, they are. If you're a beginner, shorter skis will be easier to control. The bindings (the part that holds your boot to the ski) are the most important parts of the ski—to make sure they don't break, get them tested regularly by a pro.

Make sure your boots fit and are comfortable. In general, ski boots are ½ size smaller than your normal shoe size.

Be a trendsetter by picking up the helmet habit. Choose an ASTM [American Society for Testing and Materials] approved model that fits right, is ventilated, and doesn't affect your hearing or field of vision.

Ski poles are used to give you balance and help you get up if you fall, or need to side-step up a hill.

Goggles are important to protect your eyes from flying dirt or snow, as well as stopping the sun's glare while whooshing down the slopes. Some goggles come with fun tinted lenses. If you don't have goggles, you can use sunglasses instead.

About This Chapter: The main text of this chapter is excerpted from "Snow Skiing Activity Card," Body and Mind (BAM!), Centers for Disease Control and Prevention, April 2002.

If you are renting equipment, the staff at the ski shop can help you find all the right stuff.

Stay Warm On The Slopes

1. Long underwear to keep you warm and absorb sweat.

2. Insulated tops and pants such as sweaters and leggings—this layer should be warm, but not baggy.

✔ **Quick Tip**
Skiing And Snowboarding: Get Ready For Winter

Alpine skiing is a skill sport that demands top physical conditioning from virtually every aspect of fitness: upper and lower body strength, endurance and flexibility, and explosive power. The leg muscles are the primary focus for strength training. During a downhill run sustained muscular contractions of the legs maintain proper form and control. Quick turning requires bursts of power from the legs, hips, and upper extremities. Balance and good form are enhanced by training the abdominals and low back for strength.

Snowboarding is more like surfing or skateboarding than skiing, so the training for it is a bit different. A snowboarder's lower body needs explosive power and the ankles need special attention with stabilization exercises. The inconsistent properties of snow cause a need for balance, reaction time, and agility for both sports. Snowboarders should include calf raises and ankle rotation while skiers should focus some attention on the tibialis anterior (shin), which pulls the top of the foot toward the knee, while leaning forward.

You should already have good general fitness before beginning sport-specific training. During the off-season, participating in a variety of activities will maintain or improve fitness. For the skier or snowboarder, a solid foundation of cardiovascular and muscular endurance will enhance posture and skill development and help insure a stronger, safer ski season. A good aerobic base prepares the athlete for strenuous training later that will focus on coordination, agility, and power. Recreational skiers and snowboarders can train at a heart rate of 130–180 beats per minute, depending on their abilities and goals.

---

3. Ski pants and jackets to protect you from snow and wetness.

4. A hat, because 60 percent of heat loss is through the head.

Play It Safe

If you can, sign up for lessons from a ski school, even if you've taken lessons before—your instructor can teach you all the right moves, for beginners as well as for more advanced students.

A core strength base through strength training lays the foundation for snow sport-specific muscular endurance. Resistance training for both skiing and snowboarding should be moderate weight and a lot of repetitions. Flexibility through regular stretching will help prevent injuries.

Sport specific training ideally begins 8–10 weeks before the first planned trip. Higher intensity exercise improves stamina and speed, and sport specific drills work on the skills needed. It's important to start pre-ski or snowboard training at least one month before hitting the slopes.

Circuit training and intervals can be adapted to emphasize the muscles used most during the sports and prepare the cardiovascular system. Working out on stair climbers emphasizes the major skiing support muscles. There are many ways to manipulate a stepping workout that will prepare your balance and posture for skiing and snowboarding, as well as work the cardiovascular system.

Cross training sports that help prepare for skiing and snowboarding include ice skating, inline skating, skateboarding, bicycling, running, tennis, racquetball, and volleyball.

Source: From "Skiing and Snowboarding," reprinted with permission from The National Association for Fitness Certification (NAFC), Pam Germain, Director. © 2003 NAFC. All rights reserved. For additional information, visit www.body-basics.com.

The key to skiing is control of your equipment and your speed. If you feel yourself start to lose control, fall onto your backside or your side and don't attempt to get up until you stop sliding.

The easiest way to get hurt while skiing is to try a run or a move that is too hard. Always ski on trails that match your skill level and never attempt a jumping move, or other trick, unless taught by an instructor.

Did you know that it is just as important to drink water when you are active in the cold as in the heat? Why? Higher altitudes and colder air can

---

✔ Quick Tip

Here is some additional advice if you will be a beginner in snow sports:

- Take a group lesson to get going.

- Concentrate on your form and practice those basics.

- If an instructor confuses you, let him/her know that you aren't "getting it" and you need a different tip to work on.

- Go to the library and flip through the ski or snowboarding magazines. Really read the articles on tips and techniques.

- Ski or snowboard as often as you can. Borrow gear and clothes if you have to so that you can afford extra lift tickets.

- Mental practice before you hit the slopes can really help with form. Think about your form while you're on the ski lift. Visualization in the chair can make a difference in the snow.

- To improve once you've got the basics, take time away from the more challenging runs (maybe at the end of the day) to practice the skill you've learned on the easier slopes. The goal is mastery.

- Make friends with other who are more advanced than you are. Try to imitate their technique.

Source: From "Skiing and Snowboarding," reprinted with permission from The National Association for Fitness Certification (NAFC), Pam Germain, Director. © 2003 NAFC. All rights reserved. For additional information, visit www.body-basics.com.

cause your body to lose water. If you experience dizziness or have dry mouth, headache, or muscle cramps, take a water break. A good rule would be to drink water or sports drinks before, during, and after your ski runs.

Always check the snow conditions of the slope before you go up—you'll need to ski differently in icy conditions than you would if you were on wet snow or in deep powder.

Altitude can zap your energy. Don't push it. Ski the easier runs later in the day when you are tired. Most importantly—know when to quit.

While on the slopes, set a meeting time and place to check in with your parents or friends. And always ski with a buddy. And wear plenty of sunblock, because those rays are strong on the mountain due to high altitude and reflection off the snow.

Be sure to keep the Responsibility Code for Skiers in mind:

- Always stay in control and be able to stop or avoid other people or objects.

- People ahead of you have the right of way. It is your responsibility to avoid them.

- Do not stop where you obstruct a trail or are not visible from above.

- Whenever starting downhill or merging into a trail, look uphill and yield to others.

- Always use devices to help prevent runaway equipment.

- Observe all posted signs and warnings. Keep off closed trails and out of closed areas.

- Before using any lift, you must have the knowledge and ability to load, ride, and unload safely.

How To Play

Skiing can be done as a fun activity with your family or friends, and as your skills increase, you might even want to ski competitively There are several main skiing categories including alpine skiing, which is the fast-n-furious downhill skiing; freestyle skiing, in which skiers perform jumps and tricks over moguls (large bumps on the ski slope) while skiing downhill; and cross country skiing, where skiers race long distances over flatter land.

Here are some key tips to get you started:

- *To get on a lift*, put both your poles in your inside hand. Turn to the outside and watch for the next chair. As it gets to you, grab the outside pole and sit normally on the chair. Keep your skis apart, with the tips up, as you're lifted off the ground.

> ### ♣ It's A Fact!!
>
> - Competitive freestyle skiers can jump as high as a 3 or 4 story building, when performing tricks in the air.
>
> - Before it was a sport, skiing was used as a form of transportation in the mountains of Europe.
>
> - Men are allowed to compete in the Olympic ski jumping event, but women are not.

- *To get off the lift*, grab a pole in each hand, but don't put on your wrist straps. Point the pole tips toward the outside of the chair, and hold them up so they don't catch on the snow. Hold the bar on the outside of the chair for balance, relax your legs, and ease yourself forward, pushing off once your skis touch the snow. Don't stand up until the chair has passed over the top of the mound, and move away from the chairlift before you prepare to ski so that others can get off behind you.

- *Getting up after a fall.* Make sure your skis are below you on the hill. Grab the top of both poles in one hand, grab the bottom of both with the other, and plant your poles in the snow just above your hip. Push up with both arms to shift yourself forward and over your skis. Make sure your weight is forward and over your skis before you stand up.

Chapter 35

Yoga

Gear Up

Before you begin to relax your mind and body, make sure you suit up properly by wearing comfortable clothing that won't get in the way of your stretching. T-shirts, shorts, sweats, and tank tops are all great to wear for yoga because their fabric is movable and breaths easily. Jeans are definitely out.

Bare feet are ideal when you practice yoga, both for the traction they give you for standing poses, as well as the workout your feet will get.

One of the most important things you will need is a yoga or exercise mat to use during seated or floor postures. Don't worry if you don't have a special mat, use a firm pillow or folded up blanket—they work just as well.

Play It Safe

It's important to make sure your muscles are warmed up before you begin your yoga routine. Never force your body into a posture or try to go beyond your limits—you could strain your muscles. Using the correct form is also key to getting the most out of your yoga experience, so get into a class that's

About This Chapter: The information in this chapter is from "Yoga Activity Card," BAM! (Body and Mind), Centers for Disease Control and Prevention (CDC), reviewed April 30, 2002.

right for you (whether you're a beginner or an expert). And, don't be afraid to ask your teacher for help. Learning the correct way to do each pose is important for overall mind and body development.

Feeling stiff or sore? If you are, you've overdone it. If you're just getting into yoga, it's important to start off slowly. Since yoga is not a competitive sport, your progress may be slow, but with time your body will become more flexible and you'll be able to achieve more difficult poses.

Interested in giving yoga a try, but not sure where to find classes in your area? It's important to find a class that you feel comfortable in, and has an experienced teacher. Try asking friends and family members if they know of a good

> ✔ **Quick Tip**
>
> If you're feeling stressed out, meditation can help reduce those stressful feelings and increase your ability to remember things more clearly. Sometimes when the pressure is on, the memory centers (chakras) of your brain take a time out. This means you could forget things like what math problems you have to do for homework, or where you are supposed to meet your friends after school. So, before you panic—close your eyes, take a deep breath, and relax. It does your body (and mind) a lot of good.

place, or check out your local YMCA, county recreation centers, and fitness clubs—they sometimes have classes for all ages and skill levels. Also, don't forget about your local library—there you can find more information on yoga itself, as well as magazines or books that may have a listing of classes in your area.

How To Play

Did you know that yoga has been around for more than 5,000 years? Today, you see lots of super stars and athletes practicing yoga, but it's a great activity for anyone. No matter what other activities you participate in, yoga can strengthen your abilities by increasing flexibility, staying power (endurance), and your ability to focus.

Lots of physical activities build your muscles and strength, but many times other parts of your body are left out. Because yoga is a full body workout, it can help to check any imbalance in your muscles.

In addition, yoga strengthens, tones, and stretches your muscles, helping to increase your flexibility. If your body is flexible you will be less likely to get injured.

Most yoga practices focus on physical postures called "asanas," breathing exercises called "pranayama," and meditation to bring your body and mind together through slow, careful movements. But, there's more to it than that. Yoga leads to improved physical fitness, increased ability to concentrate, and decreased stress. Yoga is an activity that helps both your body and mind work a little better.

When To Practice

Yoga can fit easily into your schedule—taking 10–15 minutes each day to practice can make a difference (just make sure to wait at least two to three hours after you've eaten). Yoga is a perfect way to chill out and take some time just for yourself. So, set aside a special time each day and relax, release, and rejuvenate.

Where To Practice

Find a quiet spot where you won't be distracted. Look for a level area that is large enough for you to stretch upwards as well as to the sides for standing and floor positions or stretches.

♣ It's A Fact!!

- The word yoga comes from an ancient language and means yoke or unite—to bring together your body, mind, and spirit.

- A "yogin" is a male student while a "yogini" is a female student.

- Many yoga poses are based on animals and the different postures they do in nature.

- More than 6 million people practice yoga including Madonna, Kareem Abdul Jabar, and Michelle Pfeiffer.

How To Practice

Always warm up. Plan a well-rounded workout that includes lots of different positions from all of the major muscle groups (arms, legs, abs, back, chest). Most importantly, remember to breathe. It's a good idea to start with several arm stretches over your head and deep breaths. Inhale when you try upward and expanded movements, and exhale during downward or forward bending motions.

Concentrate on each position—move slowly making controlled movements until you feel your muscles tensing and resisting (you should feel your muscles stretching, not straining). Each pose in yoga is an experiment, so go slowly and listen to your body. Know when you are pushing yourself too hard or need to challenge yourself a little more.

Last but not least, remember to take 5–10 minutes to relax your body at the end of your workout. This will help to prevent sore muscles and is a way to unwind your body.

Parts Of The Body Worked

- Chest and back

- Abs

- Upper and lower legs

- Arms

- Heart and lungs

- Shoulders and neck

- Hips and butt

- Wrist and forearm

- Knees and ankles

Part 4

Maintaining Health And Fitness

Chapter 36

Nutrition Basics

Different foods contain different nutrients and other healthful substances. No single food can supply all the nutrients in the amounts you need. For example, oranges provide vitamin C and folate but no vitamin B_{12}; cheese provides calcium and vitamin B_{12}; but no vitamin C. To make sure you get all the nutrients and other substances you need for health, build a healthy base by using the Food Guide Pyramid as a starting point. Choose the recommended number of daily servings from each of the five major food groups. If you avoid all foods from any of the five food groups, seek guidance to help ensure that you get all the nutrients you need.

There are many ways to create a healthy eating pattern, but they all start with the three food groups at the base of the Pyramid: grains, fruits, and vegetables. Eating a variety of grains (especially whole grain foods), fruits, and vegetables is the basis of healthy eating. Enjoy meals that have rice, pasta, tortillas, or whole grain bread at the center of the plate, accompanied by plenty of fruits and vegetables and a moderate amount of low-fat foods from the milk group and the meat and beans group. Go easy on foods high in fat or sugars.

About This Chapter: Text in this chapter is excerpted from "Dietary Guidelines: Build a Healthy Base," *Nutrition and Your Health: Dietary Guidelines for Americans, Fifth Edition*, 2000, U.S. Department of Agriculture.

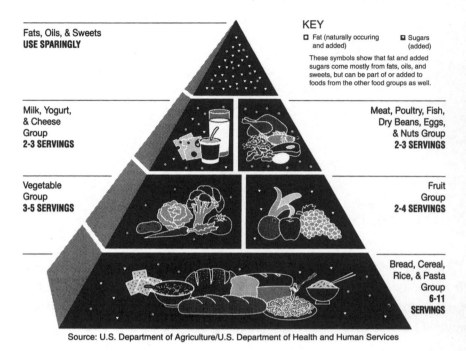

Figure 36.1. The Food Guide Pyramid

Also, notice that many of the meals and snacks you eat contain items from several food groups. For example, a sandwich may provide bread from the grains group, turkey from the meat and beans group, and cheese from the milk group.

Choose a variety of foods for good nutrition. Since foods within most food groups differ in their content of nutrients and other beneficial substances, choosing a variety helps you get all the nutrients and fiber you need. It can also help keep your meals interesting from day to day.

Use Of Dietary Supplements

Some people need a vitamin-mineral supplement to meet specific nutrient needs. For example, women who could become pregnant are advised to eat foods fortified with folic acid or to take a folic acid supplement in addition to consuming folate-rich foods to reduce the risk of some serious birth

Table 36.1. What Counts As A Serving?

Bread, Cereal, Rice, and Pasta Group (Grains Group)—whole grain and refined

- 1 slice of bread
- About 1 cup of ready-to-eat cereal
- 1/2 cup of cooked cereal, rice, or pasta

Vegetable Group

- 1 cup of raw leafy vegetables
- 1/2 cup of other vegetables cooked or raw
- 3/4 cup of vegetable juice

Fruit Group

- 1 medium apple, banana, orange, pear
- 1/2 cup of chopped, cooked, or canned fruit
- 3/4 cup of fruit juice

Milk, Yogurt, and Cheese Group (Milk Group)*

- 1 cup of milk** or yogurt**
- 1 1/2 ounces of natural cheese** (such as Cheddar)
- 2 ounces of processed cheese** (such as American)

Meat, Poultry, Fish, Dry Beans, Eggs, and Nuts Group (Meat and Beans Group)

- 2–3 ounces of cooked lean meat, poultry, or fish
- 1/2 cup of cooked dry beans# or 1/2 cup of tofu counts as 1 ounce of lean meat
- 2 1/2-ounce soyburger or 1 egg counts as 1 ounce of lean meat
- 2 tablespoons of peanut butter or 1/3 cup of nuts counts as 1 ounce of meat

NOTE: Many of the serving sizes given above are smaller than those on the Nutrition Facts Label. For example, 1 serving of cooked cereal, rice, or pasta is 1 cup for the label but only 1/2 cup for the Pyramid.

* This includes lactose-free and lactose-reduced milk products. One cup of soy-based beverage with added calcium is an option for those who prefer a non-dairy source of calcium.

** Choose fat-free or reduced-fat dairy products most often.

Dry beans, peas, and lentils can be counted as servings in either the meat and beans group or the vegetable group. As a vegetable, 1/2 cup of cooked, dry beans counts as 1 serving. As a meat substitute, 1 cup of cooked, dry beans counts as 1 serving (2 ounces of meat).

defects. People who seldom eat dairy products or other rich sources of calcium need a calcium supplement, and people who eat no animal foods need to take a vitamin B_{12} supplement. Sometimes vitamins or minerals are prescribed for meeting nutrient needs or for therapeutic purposes. Supplements of some nutrients, such as vitamin A and selenium, can be harmful if taken in large amounts.

♣ **It's A Fact!!**
Adolescents have an especially high need for calcium, but most people need to eat plenty of good sources of calcium for healthy bones throughout life. When selecting dairy products to get enough calcium, choose those that are low in fat or fat-free to avoid getting too much saturated fat. Young children, teenage girls, and women of childbearing age need enough good sources of iron, such as lean meats and cereals with added nutrients, to keep up their iron stores.

Why Eat Fruits And Vegetables?

Different fruits and vegetables are rich in different nutrients. Some fruits and vegetables are excellent sources of carotenoids, including those which form vitamin A, while others may be rich in vitamin C, folate, or potassium. Fruits and vegetables, especially dry beans and peas, also contain fiber and other substances that are associated with good health. Dark-green leafy vegetables, deeply colored fruits, and dry beans and peas are especially rich in many nutrients. Most fruits and vegetables are naturally low in fat and calories and are filling. Some are high in fiber, and many are quick to prepare and easy to eat. Choose whole or cut-up fruits and vegetables rather than juices most often. Juices contain little or no fiber.

Try serving fruits and vegetables in new ways:

- Try raw vegetables with a low- or reduced-fat dip.

- Enjoy vegetables stir-fried in a small amount of vegetable oil.

- Fruits or vegetables can be mixed with other foods in salads, casseroles, soups, and sauces (for example, add shredded vegetables when making meatloaf).

- Keep ready-to-eat raw vegetables handy in a clear container in the front of your refrigerator for snacks or meals-on-the-go.

Table 36.2. Which Fruits And Vegetables Provide The Most Nutrients?

Sources of vitamin A (carotenoids)
- Orange vegetables like carrots, sweet potatoes, pumpkin
- Dark-green leafy vegetables such as spinach, collards, turnip greens
- Orange fruits like mango, cantaloupe, apricots
- Tomatoes

Sources of vitamin C
- Citrus fruits and juices, kiwi fruit, strawberries, cantaloupe
- Broccoli, peppers, tomatoes, cabbage, potatoes
- Leafy greens such as romaine lettuce, turnip greens, spinach

Sources of folate
- Cooked dry beans and peas, peanuts
- Oranges, orange juice
- Dark-green leafy vegetables like spinach and mustard greens, romaine lettuce
- Green peas

Sources of potassium
- Baked white or sweet potato, cooked greens (such as spinach), winter (orange) squash
- Bananas, plantains, dried fruits such as apricots and prunes, orange juice
- Cooked dry beans (such as baked beans) and lentils

- Keep a day's supply of fresh or dried fruit handy on the table or counter.

- Enjoy fruits as a naturally sweet end to a meal.

- When eating out, choose a variety of vegetables at a salad bar.

♣ It's A Fact!!

Older children and teen girls need about 2,200 calories a day. Teen boys need about 2,800 calories.

Chapter 37

Sports Nutrition: Fueling Your Performance

What diet is best for athletes?

It's important that an athlete's diet provide the right amount of energy, the 50-plus nutrients the body needs, and adequate water. No single food or supplement can do this. A variety of foods are needed every day. But, just as there is more than one way to achieve a goal, there is more than one way to follow a nutritious diet.

Do the nutritional needs of athletes differ from non-athletes?

Competitive athletes, sedentary individuals, and people who exercise for health and fitness all need the same nutrients. However, because of the intensity of their sport or training program, some athletes have higher calorie and fluid requirements. Eating a variety of foods to meet increased calorie needs helps to ensure that the athlete's diet contains appropriate amounts of carbohydrate, protein, vitamins, and minerals.

About This Chapter: This chapter includes information from "Questions Most Frequently Asked About Sports Nutrition" and "Fast Facts About Sports Nutrition," undated fact sheets prepared by the President's Council on Physical Fitness and Sports (www.fitness.gov) with additional information from "U R What U Eat," BAM! (Body And Mind), Centers for Disease Control and Prevention, reviewed April 2002; online at www.bam.gov.

Are there certain dietary guidelines athletes should follow?

Health and nutrition professionals recommend that 55–60% of the calo-ries in our diet come from carbohydrate, no more than 30% from fat and the remaining 10–15% from protein. While the exact percentages may vary slightly for some athletes based on their sport or training program, these guidelines will promote health and serve as the basis for a diet that will maximize performance.

✔ **Quick Tip**

Whether you hit the court, the field, the track, the rink, or your back yard to get some physical activity, you'll need some fuel to keep you going. And no matter what type of physical activity you do, you should always be sure to drink plenty of water—before you start, during the activity, and after you're done, even if you don't feel thirsty.

Here are some great snacks to munch on to keep your body moving and your stomach silent:

- Fresh veggies like carrots and celery sticks

- Snack-sized boxes of raisins

- Pretzels

- Low-fat yogurt

- Crackers—try graham crackers, animal crackers, or saltines

- Bagels

- Fig bars

- Fruit juice boxes (make sure you choose 100% pure fruit juice, or for an added boost, try orange juice with added calcium)

- Small packages of trail mix

- Fresh fruits such as bananas, oranges, grapes (try freezing your grapes for a new taste sensation), and berries

How many calories do I need a day?

This depends on your age, body size, sport and training program. For example, a 250-pound weight lifter needs more calories than a 98-pound gymnast. Exercise or training may increase calorie needs by as much as 1,000 to 1,500 calories a day. The best way to determine if you're getting too few or too many calories is to monitor your weight. If you're keeping within your ideal weight range, you're probably getting the right amount of calories.

Which is better for replacing fluids—water or sports drinks?

Depending on how muscular you are, 55–70% of your body weight is water. Being "hydrated" means maintaining your body's fluid level. When you sweat, you lose water which must be replaced if you want to perform your best. You need to drink fluids before, during, and after all workouts and events.

Whether you drink water or a sports drink is a matter of choice. However, if your workout or event lasts for more than 90 minutes, you may benefit from the carbohydrates provided by sports drinks. A sports drink that contains 15–18 grams of carbohydrate in every 8 ounces of fluid should be used. Drinks with a higher carbohydrate content will delay the absorption of water and may cause dehydration, cramps, nausea, or diarrhea. There are a variety of sports drinks on the market. Be sure to experiment with sports drinks during practice instead of trying them for the first time the day of an event.

What are electrolytes?

Electrolytes are nutrients that affect fluid balance in the body and are necessary for our nerves and muscles to function. Sodium and potassium are the two electrolytes most often added to sports drinks. Generally, electrolyte replacement is not needed during short bursts of exercise since sweat is approximately 99% water and less than 1% electrolytes. Water, in combination with a well- balanced diet, will restore normal fluid and electrolyte levels in the body. However, replacing electrolytes may be beneficial during continuous activity of longer than 2 hours, especially in a hot environment.

What do muscles use for energy during exercise?

Most activities use a combination of fat and carbohydrate as energy sources. How hard and how long you work out, your level of fitness and your diet will affect the type of fuel your body uses. For short-term, high-intensity activities like sprinting, athletes rely mostly on carbohydrate for energy. During low-intensity exercises like walking, the body uses more fat for energy.

What are carbohydrates?

Carbohydrates are sugars and starches found in foods like breads, cereals, fruits, vegetables, pasta, milk, honey, syrups, and table sugar. Carbohydrates are the preferred source of energy for your body. Regardless of origin, your body breaks down carbohydrates into glucose that your blood carries to cells to be used for energy. Carbohydrates provide 4 calories per gram, while fat provides 9 calories per gram. Your body cannot differentiate between glucose that comes from starches or sugars. Glucose from either source provides energy for working muscles.

Is it true that athletes should eat a lot of carbohydrates?

When you are training or competing, your muscles need energy to perform. One source of energy for working muscles is glycogen which is made from carbohydrates and stored in your muscles. Every time you work out, you use some of your glycogen. If you don't consume enough carbohydrates, your glycogen stores become depleted, which can result in fatigue. Both sugars and starches are effective in replenishing glycogen stores.

When and what should I eat before I compete?

Performance depends largely on the foods consumed during the days and weeks leading up to an event. If you regularly eat a varied, carbohydrate-rich diet you are in good standing and probably have ample glycogen stores to fuel activity. The purpose of the pre-competition meal is to prevent hunger and to provide the water and additional energy the athlete will need during competition. Most athletes eat two to four hours before their event. However, some athletes perform their best if they eat a small amount 30 minutes before competing, while others eat nothing for six hours beforehand. For many athletes, carbohydrate-rich foods serve as the basis of the meal. However, there is no magic pre-event diet. Simply choose foods and beverages that you enjoy and that don't bother your stomach. Experiment during the weeks before an event to see which foods work best for you.

Will eating sugary foods before an event hurt my performance?

In the past, athletes were warned that eating sugary foods before exercise could hurt performance by causing a drop in blood glucose levels. Recent studies, however, have shown that consuming sugar up to 30 minutes before an event does not diminish performance. In fact, evidence suggests that a sugar-containing pre-competition beverage or snack may improve performance during endurance workouts and events.

What is carbohydrate loading?

Carbohydrate loading is a technique used to increase the amount of glycogen in muscles. For five to seven days before an event, the athlete eats 10–12 grams of carbohydrate per kilogram body weight and gradually reduces the intensity of the workouts. (To find out how much you weigh in kilograms, simply divide your weight in pounds by 2.2.) The day before the event, the athlete rests and eats the same high-carbohydrate diet. Although carbohydrate loading may be beneficial for athletes participating in endurance sports which require 90 minutes or more of non-stop effort, most athletes needn't worry about carbohydrate loading. Simply eating a diet that derives more than half of its calories from carbohydrates will do.

As an athlete, do I need to take extra vitamins and minerals?

Athletes need to eat about 1,800 calories a day to get the vitamins and minerals they need for good health and optimal performance. Since most athletes eat more than this amount, vitamin and mineral supplements are needed only in special situations. Athletes who follow vegetarian diets or who avoid an entire group of foods (for example, never drink milk) may need a supplement to make up for the vitamins and minerals not being supplied by food. A multivitamin-mineral pill that supplies 100% of the Recommended Dietary Allowance (RDA) will provide the nutrients needed. An athlete who frequently cuts back on calories, especially below the 1,800 calorie level, is not only at risk for inadequate vitamin and mineral intake, but also may not be getting enough carbohydrate. Since vitamins and minerals do not provide energy, they cannot replace the energy provided by carbohydrates.

Will extra protein help build muscle mass?

Many athletes, especially those on strength-training programs or who participate in power sports, are told that eating a ton of protein or taking protein supplements will help them gain muscle weight. However, the true secret to building muscle is training hard and consuming enough calories. While some extra protein is needed to build muscle, most American diets provide more than enough protein. Between 1.0 and 1.5 grams of protein per kilogram body weight per day is sufficient if your calorie intake is adequate and you're eating a variety of foods. For a 150-pound athlete, that represents 68–102 grams of protein a day.

> ♣ **It's A Fact!!**
> It is a myth that eating lots of protein and/or taking protein supplements and exercising vigorously will turn you into a big, muscular person. Building muscle depends on your genes, how hard you train, and whether you get enough calories. The average American diet has more than enough protein for muscle building. Extra protein is eliminated from the body or stored as fat.

Why is iron so important?

Hemoglobin, which contains iron, is the part of red blood cells that carries oxygen from the lungs to all parts of the body, including muscles. Since your muscles need oxygen to produce energy, if you have low iron levels in your blood, you may tire quickly. Symptoms of iron deficiency include fatigue, irritability, dizziness, headaches, and lack of appetite. Many times, however; there are no symptoms at all. A blood test is the best way to find out if your iron level is low. It is recommended that athletes have their hemoglobin levels checked once a year.

The RDA for iron is 15 milligrams a day for women and 10 milligrams a day for men. Red meat is the richest source of iron, but fish and poultry also are good sources. Fortified breakfast cereals, beans, and green leafy vegetables also contain iron. Our bodies absorb the iron found in animal products best.

Should I take an iron supplement?

Taking iron supplements will not improve performance unless an athlete is truly iron deficient. Too much iron can cause constipation, diarrhea, and nausea and may interfere with the absorption of other nutrients such as copper and zinc. Therefore, iron supplements should not be taken without proper medical supervision.

Why is calcium so important?

Calcium is needed for strong bones and proper muscle function. Dairy foods are the best source of calcium. However, studies show that many female athletes who are trying to lose weight cut back on dairy products. Female athletes who don't get enough calcium may be at risk for stress fractures and, when they're older, osteoporosis. Young women between the ages of 11 and 24 need about 1,200 milligrams of calcium a day. After age 25, the recommended intake is 800 milligrams. Low-fat dairy products are a rich source of calcium and also are low in fat and calories.

✔ **Quick Tip**

Make sure you get enough calcium for strong bones and proper muscle function. The best sources of calcium are dairy products, but many other foods such as salmon with bones, sardines, collard greens, and okra also contain calcium. Additionally, some brands of bread, tofu, and orange juice are fortified with calcium.

What is the most important nutrient?

Water is the most important nutrient for active people. When you sweat, you lose water, which must be replaced. Drink fluids before, during, and after workouts. Water is a fine choice for most workouts; however; during continuous workouts of greater than 90 minutes, your body may benefit from a sports drink.

✔ **Quick Tip**

Make sure you pack lunches and snacks safely. Did you know germs that grow on food can make lots more germs in a little over two hours? Without smart packing, some of your sandwiches and snacks could end up making you sick. You can make sure your food gives you the energy you need — not a bellyache you don't need — with these simple tips.

Some food is good to go all the time:

• Fruits

• Vegetables

• Bread

• Crackers

• Peanut butter

• Jelly

• Pickles

• Nuts

• Pretzels

• Graham crackers

• Trail mix

• Fruit cups

Super Storage

Those puffy, insulated lunch boxes or bags keep cold food cold and hot food hot, so germs can't multiply like crazy. Regular lunch boxes and paper bags are okay too, but you have to help them keep stuff the right temperature.

Chapter 38

Sports Supplements

If you're a competitive athlete or a fitness buff, improving your sports performance is probably on your mind. Spending tons of time in the gym or at practice may offer results (along with a pile of sweaty laundry), but it's no shortcut, and teens with busy lives may be looking for fast, effective results.

Some people think that taking drugs known as sports supplements could improve their performance without so much hard work. But do sports supplements really work? And are they safe?

What Are Sports Supplements?

Sports supplements (also referred to as ergogenic aids) are products used to enhance athletic performance. They come in different forms, including vitamins, synthetic (manmade) drugs, and hormones, most of which are available over the counter without a prescription.

Some people think that supplements help them develop more muscle mass, increase strength, and build stamina. Other people use sports supplements to lose weight. If you're thinking about using sports supplements,

About This Chapter: "Sports Supplements," reviewed by Eric Small, MD. This information was provided by TeensHealth, one of the largest resources online for medically reviewed health information written for parents, kids, and teens. For more articles like this one, visit www.TeensHealth.org, or www.KidsHealth.org. © 2003 The Nemours Center for Children's Health Media, a division of The Nemours Foundation.

you're not alone. Many teens who see sports medicine doctors when they want to improve their performance have questions about how supplements work and whether they're safe.

Most of the foods you see on the shelves of your local grocery store and the drugs your doctor prescribes for you are regulated by a government agency called the Food and Drug Administration (FDA). The FDA ensures that many foods, beverages, and drugs adhere to certain safety standards. But sports supplements aren't regulated by the FDA, and no sports supplements have been tested on kids and teens. That means that scientists and doctors don't know whether supplements are safe or effective for teens to use.

♣ **It's A Fact!!**
Lots of sports organizations have developed policies on sports supplements. The National Football League (NFL), the National Collegiate Athletic Association (NCAA), and the International Olympic Committee (IOC) have banned the use of steroids, creatine, ephedra, and androstenedione by their athletes, and competitors who use them face fines, ineligibility, and suspension from their sports.

Common Supplements And How They Affect The Body

Whether you hear about sports supplements from your teammates in the locker room or the sales clerk at your local vitamin store, chances are you're not getting the whole story about how supplements work and the risks you take by using them.

Anabolic steroids are hormones that help the body build muscle tissue and increase muscle mass. Steroids, also known as roids or juice, are similar to the male hormone testosterone, which is produced naturally in larger amounts in guys' bodies and smaller amounts in girls' bodies. When a person takes steroids, the body's muscle tissue is stimulated to grow, producing larger and stronger muscles.

But steroids can have some unwelcome, serious side effects—such as high blood pressure and heart disease, liver damage and cancer, urinary and bowel problems, strokes and blood clots, and sleep problems. A person who takes steroids may develop bigger muscles, but he or she is also at risk for baldness and severe acne. Guys who take juice can suffer from infertility, breast and nipple enlargement, and problems having an erection. Girls may find themselves with deeper voices, smaller breasts, menstrual problems, and an increase in facial and body hair.

Steroids can also have emotional effects on the user, such as severe mood swings, aggressive behavior, irritability, and depressive or suicidal thoughts. Teens who inject steroids with infected needles are also at risk for HIV or hepatitis.

Androstenedione, more commonly known as andro, is another popular nutritional supplement. When a person takes andro, the body may convert it to testosterone, which is necessary for muscle development. When it's taken in large doses, andro is said to increase muscle mass, although studies haven't shown that andro is particularly effective. Scientists don't know exactly how much andro the body absorbs, and the long-term effects of andro use haven't been determined. What is known is that andro can cause hormone imbalances in people who use it. Andro use may have the same effects as taking anabolic steroids and may lead to such dangerous side effects as testicular cancer, infertility, stroke, and an increased risk of heart disease.

Another sports supplement you may have heard about is human growth hormone (hGH). Doctors may prescribe growth hormone for some teens who have certain hormone or growth problems to help them develop normally. But growth hormone can also be abused by athletes who want to build muscle mass. Many athletes still use growth hormone even though several sports organizations (such as the NCAA) have banned it. Teen athletes who abuse growth hormone may have impaired development and altered hormone levels.

In a recent survey of high school senior athletes, about 44% said they had tried or currently used creatine to enhance athletic performance. Creatine is already manufactured by the body in the liver, kidneys, and pancreas, and it occurs naturally in foods such as meat and fish. If a person takes creatine supplements, the extra creatine is stored in the muscles, and some people think that it gives them an energy boost during workouts or competitions.

Available over the counter in pill, powder, or gel form, creatine is one of the most popular nutritional supplements, and teens make up a large portion of the supplement's users. Teens who take creatine usually take it to improve strength, but the long-term and short-term effects of creatine use haven't been studied in teens and kids. Research has not shown that creatine can increase endurance or improve aerobic performance—but it may leave teens prone to muscle cramps and tears. And there have been several reports of creatine use leading to seizures or kidney failure.

Fat burners (sometimes known as thermogenics) are a recent addition to the sports supplement market. Fat burners are often made with an herb called ephedra, also known as ephedrine or ma huang. Ephedra is a stimulant found in over-the-counter pills such as Metabolife, Ripped Fuel, and Yellow Jacket, and it speeds up the nervous system and increases metabolism. Some teens use fat burners to lose weight or to increase energy—but using products containing ephedrine is a bad idea for anyone. Ephedra-based products can be one of the most dangerous supplements. They can cause an irregular heart-beat (known as an arrhythmia), dehydration, fainting, and occasionally even death.

Many products containing ephedrine have been taken off the shelves be-cause of their dangerous effects on health, but many fat burners still contain ephedra. The NCAA and the IOC have banned the use of ephedrine.

Will Supplements Make Me A Better Athlete?

Sports supplements haven't been tested on teens and kids. But studies on adults show that the claims of many supplements are weak at best. Most won't make you any stronger, and none will make you any faster or more skillful.

Many factors go into your abilities as an athlete—including your diet, how much sleep you get, genetics and heredity, and your training program—but the fact is that using sports supplements may put you at risk for serious health conditions. So instead of turning to supplements to improve your performance, concentrate on eating the best nutrition and following a seri-ous weight-training and aerobic-conditioning program.

Tips For Dealing With Athletic Pressure And Competition

Advertisements for sports supplements often use persuasive before and after pictures that make it look easy to get a muscular, toned body. But remember—the goal of supplement advertisers is to make money by selling more supplements. Because sports supplements are not regulated by the FDA, sellers are not required to provide information about their dangerous side effects. Teens and kids may seem like an easy sell on supplements because they may feel dissatisfied or uncomfortable with their still-developing bodies, and many supplement companies try to convince teens like you that supplements are an easy solution.

Don't waste your hard-earned allowance or pay from your after-school job on expensive and dangerous supplements. Instead, try these tips for getting better game:

- Make down time a priority. Some studies show that teens need more than 8 hours of sleep a night—are you getting enough? If you come home from practice to a load of homework, try doing as much homework as possible on the weekend to free up your nights for sleep. If you have an after-school job that's interfering with your ZZZs, consider cutting back on your hours during your sports season.

- Try to R-E-L-A-X. Your school, work, and sports schedules may have you sprinting from one activity to the next, but taking a few minutes to relax can be helpful. Meditating or visualizing your success during the next game may improve your performance; sitting quietly and focusing on your breathing can give you a brief break and prepare you for your next activity.

- Chow down on good eats. Fried, fat-laden, or sugary foods will interfere with your performance in a major way. Instead, focus on eating foods such as lean meats, whole grains, vegetables, fruits, and low-fat dairy products. Celebrating with the team at the local pizza place after a big game is fine once in a while, but for most meals and snacks choose healthy foods to keep your body weight in a healthy range and your performance at its best.

- Eat often. Sometimes teens skip breakfast or have an early lunch and then try to play a late afternoon game. But they quickly wear out because they haven't had enough food to fuel their activity. Not eating enough may place teens at risk for injury or muscle fatigue. So make sure to eat lunch on practice and game days. If you feel hungry before the game, pack easy-to-carry, healthy snacks in your bag, such as fruit, bagels, or string cheese.

- Avoid harmful substances. Drinking, smoking, or doing drugs are all-around bad ideas for athletes. Smoking will diminish your lung capacity and ability to breathe, alcohol will make you sluggish and tired, and drugs will impair your hand-eye coordination and reduce your alertness. And you can kiss your team good-bye if you get caught using these substances—many schools have a no-tolerance policy for athletes.

- Train harder and smarter. If you get out of breath easily during your basketball game and you want to increase your endurance, improving your cardiovascular conditioning is key. If you think that more leg strength will help you excel on the soccer field, consider weight training to increase your muscle strength. Before changing your program, though, get advice from your doctor. You can't expect results overnight, but improving your strength and endurance with hard work will be a lot safer for your body in the long run.

- Consult a professional. If you're concerned about your weight or whether your diet is helping your performance, talk to your doctor or a registered dietitian who can evaluate your nutrition and steer you in the right direction. Coaches can help you too, by helping you focus on weak spots during practice. And if you're still convinced that supplements will help you, talk to your doctor or a sports medicine specialist. The doc will be able to offer alternatives to supplements based on your body and sport.

Chapter 39

Hydration

It's a warm Saturday afternoon and you've been chasing a soccer ball around the field for what seems like weeks. You're tired, thirsty, and sweaty. As practice wraps up, you have just enough time to duck into the rest room, change your shirt, and slather on a fresh layer of deodorant before heading off to meet your friends for a 4:00 P.M. movie.

So what's wrong with this picture? You didn't take the time to rehydrate. After all that exercise, your body has lost some fluid and you might be a little dehydrated. Dehydration is a condition that occurs when a person loses more fluids (such as urine or sweat) than he takes in.

To feel your best, you need to replace that fluid. Dehydration is nowhere near as serious a problem for teens as it can be for babies or young children, but if you ignore your thirst, dehydration can slow you down.

Heed That Thirst

When someone gets dehydrated, it means the amount of water in his body has dropped below the proper level (our bodies are about two-thirds

About This Chapter: From "The Dangers of Dehydration," provided by TeensHealth, one of the largest resources online for medically reviewed health information written for parents, kids, and teens. For more articles like this one, visit www.TeensHealth.org, or www.KidsHealth.org. © 2001 The Nemours Center for Children's Health Media, a division of The Nemours Foundation.

water). Small decreases don't cause problems, and in most cases, they go completely unnoticed. There are three levels of dehydration:

- mild (where you can lose 3% to 5% of your body weight)

- moderate (6% to 9%)

- severe (10% or more)

The most common cause of dehydration in teens is gastrointestinal illness, sometimes called the "stomach flu." When you're flattened by the stomach flu, you may lose fluid through vomit and diarrhea. (Gastrointestinal illness is a major cause of dehydration, but anything—food poisoning or an alcohol overload, for example—that makes you throw up several times in a short period of time can dehydrate you.) And if you're spending that much time getting acquainted with the toilet, you probably won't feel like eating or drinking anything.

You can also become dehydrated from lots of physical activity if you don't replace fluid as you go, although it's rare to reach a level of even moderate dehydration during sports or other normal outdoor activity.

Dieting can sap your reserves of water as well because you're changing the balance of what you eat and drink. Beware of diets that emphasize shedding "water weight" as a quick way to lose weight.

♣ It's A Fact!!

Ever wonder what really happens inside your body to make you sweat? Picture this…when your temperature rises, tiny blood vessels close to your skin open up. This allows your blood to carry the heat in your body away from your hard-working muscles to get closer to the skin. Then, water (sweat) escapes through your sweat glands and onto your skin. When air blows over your wet skin, the sweat evaporates (dries up) and cools your body down. But, on really hot, humid days, there is so much moisture in the air that it can't absorb the sweat from your body. So, to keep your body cool, drink plenty of water, use a fan, or take a dip in the pool.

Source: BAM! (Body And Mind), Centers for Disease Control and Prevention (CDC), November 2002.

Some teen athletes actually dehydrate themselves on purpose to drop weight quickly before a big game or event by sweating in saunas or using laxatives (like Correctol or Ex-Lax) or diuretics (such as Diurex), which make you urinate more. But that only hurts their performance and can lead to more serious problems, like abnormalities in the salt and potassium levels in the body. Such changes can lead to problems in the heart's rhythm.

Dealing With Dehydration

To counter dehydration, you need to restore the proper balance of water in your body. First, though, you have to recognize the problem. Thirst is the best, and earliest, indicator of potential dehydration.

If you ignore your thirst, after a while you could begin to experience the following symptoms:

- feeling dizzy and light-headed

- dry mouth and nose

- producing less urine when you go to the bathroom

As the condition progresses, you could experience deep, rapid breathing and notice that your eyes are sunken and dry. If a person goes without water for several days, he will grow cold and sweaty, his blood pressure may drop, and his muscles will cramp. Kidney problems can set in, and he might become confused.

The easiest way to avoid dehydration is to drink lots of water each day. This might mean as many as six to eight cups a day of water for some people, depending on factors like how much water they're getting from foods and other liquids—and how much they're sweating from physical exertion. Remember that although you may not need eight cups, drinking water adds no calories to your diet and can be great for your health.

When you're sick to your stomach, putting anything in your mouth is probably the farthest thing from your mind, but remember that you still need to drink. Take lots of tiny sips of water, or if you feel up to it, sports drinks, which also replace salts your body has lost.

Stay away from teas, sodas, and coffee, which all usually have caffeine. Caffeine is a diuretic (it makes you urinate more frequently than you usually need to), so it undoes all your hard work. Soda alone is not a good replacement for salts lost due to excessive sweating or illness.

When you're going to be running around outside on a warm day, dress appropriately for the activity. Wear loose-fitting clothes and a hat if you can. That will keep you cooler and cut down on sweating. If you do find yourself feeling parched or dizzy, take a break for a few minutes. Sit in the shade or someplace cool and drink water.

✔ Quick Tip

H2O—Guzzle, Gulp, And Chug

Drinking water before, during, and after physical activity is one way to keep your body's air conditioner working. Keep these tips in mind to help your body stay cool:

- Top off your tank a few hours before you hit the court, the field, or your own backyard by drinking about two cups of cold water.

- Keep a water bottle handy to guzzle during water breaks, half-time, or time outs. Try to drink about 10 ounces—that's about 10 large gulps from your water bottle—every 15–20 minutes.

- Even after the game ends, the chugging shouldn't—the more you sweat, the more water you need. Drink bottled water, water flavored with lemon or lime juice, or water right from your own sink.

- Eating fruit and other cool snacks is another way to keep your body cool. Pack peaches, oranges, watermelon, and grapes in your cooler—they taste great and re-hydrate.

Source: BAM! (Body And Mind), Centers for Disease Control and Prevention (CDC), November 2002.

When To See A Doctor

Dehydration can usually be treated by resting and drinking fluids. But if you faint or you feel faint every time you stand up (even after a couple of hours) or if you have very little urine output, you should tell an adult and visit your doctor. The doctor will probably just have you drink more fluids, but if you're more dehydrated than you realized, you may need to receive fluids through an IV to speed up the rehydration process. An IV is an intravenous tube that goes directly into a vein.

Every so often, dehydration might be a sign of something more serious, such as diabetes, so your doctor may run tests to rule out any other potential problems.

In general, though, dehydration is rarely any trouble, so relax. And remember to keep guzzling that H2O for healthy hydration.

Chapter 40

Mental Wellness

Introduction

Mental health. It's the way your thoughts, feelings, and behaviors affect your life. Good mental health leads to positive self-image and in turn, satisfying relationships with friends and others. Having good mental health helps you make good decisions and deal with life's challenges at home, work, or school.

It is not uncommon for teenagers to develop problems with their mental health. National statistics indicate that one in every five teens has some type of mental health problem in any given year. The problems range from mild to severe. Sadly, suicide is the third leading cause of death among teens.

Unfortunately, most young people with mental health problems don't get any treatment for them. Research shows that effective treatments are available that can help members of all racial, ethnic, and cultural groups.

If you broke your leg or came down with pneumonia, you wouldn't let it go untreated. Often however, young people ignore mental health problems thinking they will "snap out of it," or that they are something to be ashamed of. That kind of thinking prevents people from getting the help they need. Sometimes getting help is a matter of changing your mind.

Learning From Your Peers

The pain and emotional discomfort that people experience when they have mental health problems are real. Fortunately, there's a good chance that an individual will improve by getting appropriate treatment. The following success stories reflect what can happen when young people with mental health problems choose to seek help.

Carmen's Story: Dealing With Panic

Carmen was 14 when she started having panic attacks. Suddenly, her heart would start racing, she couldn't catch her breath, and she felt dizzy. Experiences like eating out in a restaurant seemed to trigger an attack. Carmen began thinking about all the different situations where the attacks might happen, and she avoided those places. In many ways, fear was controlling her life.

She was reluctant at first, but Carmen eventually told her mother about her panic attacks. Carmen was surprised to learn that other family members had dealt with the same problem.

Since Carmen's mother knew something about panic attacks and their treatment, her mother convinced Carmen that she should work with a psychologist to help reduce her fear and relieve her emotional pain.

Through psychotherapy, or talk therapy, Carmen learned relaxation and other techniques for dealing with her intense anxiety. She also learned how her thoughts could influence her panic attacks.

As Carmen practiced her new skills, her attacks occurred less often, and she gradually became more comfortable in situations that had scared her so much.

Emily's Problem: Finding Help For Problem Eating

Early in high school, Emily began to diet occasionally and watch her weight. But by her senior year, she focused constantly on her weight and cut way back on the amount she ate. Emily exercised as much as possible. Despite her scary appearance to others, Emily believed she still needed to lose more weight.

When her family and friends expressed concern to Emily about her weight loss, she withdrew from them. Emily tried to keep her refusal to eat hidden from others. During meals with her family, Emily would move food around her plate instead of eating it.

Emily began to develop medical problems as a result of her eating behavior. During an office visit, her family physician noticed that Emily's weight had dropped and asked questions about her eating habits. The doctor helped Emily realize that her eating problems, if left untreated, eventually could threaten her life.

Emily's physician helped convince her to get the mental health treatment she needed. Through psychotherapy, Emily learned how her feelings influenced her eating. With help, she was able to improve her self-image as well as her eating habits. By getting treatment, Emily was able to stabilize her weight and regain her mental and physical health.

Jason's Story: Recovering From Severe Mental Health Problems

The year he turned 19, Jason began having serious problems. He became so exhausted from severe depression, there were many days when he couldn't even get out of bed. There were times when Jason felt certain someone was out to harm him. He became very confused and frightened by his experiences, and he had thoughts of suicide.

Jason's concerned parents took him to the local mental health center. There Jason and his family began meeting with a treatment team to become educated about the problems he was having. They all worked together to develop an effective treatment plan that included psychotherapy and medication. By participating actively in Jason's treatment, his family members learned helpful ways of supporting Jason.

With good mental health treatment and the support of friends and family, Jason finally began to feel hopeful about his future. He eventually returned to school. There was a long time when Jason couldn't imagine getting any better. But he found out that even someone with severe problems like his can get help.

What It Takes To Be Mentally Well

Life presents us with many obstacles. How we handle these obstacles has a lot to do with mental wellness. When we are mentally well, we feel strong, capable, and satisfied. When wellness turns toward illness, we experience negative thoughts, difficult moods, and destructive behaviors.

Thankfully, there are ways to improve and maintain mental wellness, which can make us better able to handle the hassles of everyday life.

Get Connected

- Develop a trusting, supportive relationship with at least one caring adult. It is especially important for children and teens to have a family member, role model, or mentor to help them work through problems, talk about feelings, and develop personal goals.

- Find a place where you can be helpful, respected, and appreciated. Some people find their job or school rewarding. Others join volunteer, religious, or self-help groups to find personal satisfaction.

- Make the most of your heart-to-heart conversations. Listen carefully to what others say. Be sure you really understand them. Repeat and rephrase other people's statements, "You're saying that you feel frustrated..."

- When expressing your emotions use "I" statements. Say, "I feel frustrated." Don't say, "You make me mad." Only you, no one else, controls your thoughts and feelings.

Get Smart

- Move away from relationships or situations that cause problems, worry, and trouble.

- Rely on your common sense. Don't second-guess things. You know what is best for you.

- Believe in yourself and your abilities.

- Don't ignore problems hoping they'll go away. Figure out causes. Think about solutions—try out the ones that make the most sense. If you're really stuck, ask for help.

- Plan ahead. Set goals for yourself and take small, easy steps toward those goals.

- Pursue your natural talents. Simple as it sounds: hobbies are healthy.

- Find creative, positive ways to refuel yourself everyday.

- Learn from your successes and mistakes.

Get Real

- Forget about being a superhero. Learn to say no. You can't be everything to everybody.

- Put first things first. Know your goals and values. Prioritize your obligations accordingly.

- Don't beat yourself up. Stop running through lists of "oughts" and "shoulds." Accept your limits and don't try to live up to unrealistic standards.

- Accentuate the positive and applaud good fortune. Don't overlook finding a good parking space or getting a green light. Celebrate life's little gifts.

- Reinforce positive behavior in others by rewarding it with praise and gratitude.

- Don't let little things eat you up. Let stuff slide off your back.

- Let your sense of humor help you—don't take your troubles too seriously.

Get Healthy

- Exercise regularly and eat a balanced diet.

- Make sure you get enough satisfying, healthy sleep.

- Avoid addictive substances like drugs, alcohol, and tobacco products.

- Take responsibility for your health. Seek effective medical care for illnesses or conditions.

If you feel overwhelmed, reach out for help. Friends, family members, and teachers can help you sort out a situation and come up with a next step. Mental health and wellness centers can also help you solve problems. Sometimes it's best not to go it alone but to ask for help from someone who cares.

Source: This article first appeared as part of the New Hampshire Division of Behavioral Health's *Building Healthy Communities Campaign*. It can be found on the website of Genesis Behavioral Health, a private, non-profit mental health center serving central New Hampshire, www.genesisbh.org.

Triggers And Signs

Changes in feelings such as fear and anger are a normal part of life. In fact, learning about your own mood changes, like what triggers them and when, is important to knowing who you are.

There are many situations, such as a divorce in the family or strained relationships with friends, that can cause emotional stress. Difficult situations may make you feel sad or "blue" for a while. That's different than having a mental health problem like depression. For example, young people suffering from depression often feel an overwhelming sense of helplessness and hopelessness for long periods. This depression may lead to suicidal feelings.

Certain experiences, thoughts, and feelings signal the presence of a variety of mental health problems or the need for help. The following signs are important to recognize:

- finding little or no pleasure in life

- feeling worthless or extremely guilty

- crying a lot for no particular reason

- withdrawing from other people

- experiencing severe anxiety, panic, or fear

> **✔ Quick Tip**
> Learning about your own mood changes is important to knowing who you are.

- having big mood swings

- experiencing a change in eating or sleeping patterns

- having very low energy

- losing interest in hobbies and pleasurable activities

- having too much energy, having trouble concentrating or following through on plans

- feeling easily irritated or angry

- experiencing racing thoughts or agitation

- hearing voices or seeing images that other people do not experience

- believing that others are plotting against you

- wanting to harm yourself or someone else

♣ It's A Fact!!

Good mental health leads to positive self-image and in turn, satisfying relationships with friends and others.

It's not necessarily easy to spot these signs, or to figure out what they mean. Qualified mental health professionals are skilled in making an accurate diagnosis.

As a general rule: the longer the signs last, the more serious they are; and the more they interfere with daily life, the greater the chance that professional treatment is needed.

Help How-To's

Sometimes people don't get the help they need because they don't know where to turn. When you're not feeling well, it can be a struggle to take the necessary steps to help yourself get better.

When dealing with mental health or emotional problems, it's important not to go at it alone. Healing is a combination of helping yourself and letting others help you. Comfort and support, information and advice, and professional treatment are all forms of help.

First Step: Reach Out To People You Trust

Think of all the people you can turn to for support. These are people who are concerned about you and can help comfort you, who will listen to you and encourage you, and who can help arrange for treatment. In other words, find the caring people in your life who can help you.

These people might include:

- friends

- parents and other family members

- someone who seems "like a parent" to you

- other adults whose advice you would value—perhaps a favorite teacher or coach, a member of your church or other place of worship, or a good friend's parent.

✔ Quick Tip

When dealing with mental health or emotional problems, it's important not to go it alone.

Research shows that males are more reluctant to look for help and receive it than females are. While some people may have difficulty reaching out to others they trust, taking this first step in getting help is important for everyone to do.

Some families have health insurance that helps them get the services they need from mental health professionals. Insurance may cover some of the cost of these services. Many insurance companies provide a list of licensed mental health professionals in your area.

Team Mental Health

Health professionals who specialize in helping individuals and their families with mental health problems include psychologists, psychiatrists, social workers, counselors, and psychiatric nurses. Psychotherapy, sometimes known as talk therapy, is often an important part of mental health treatment by qualified professionals. In some situations, physicians may recommend the use of medication for an individual with mental health problems. Health professionals often work together, for example, as members of a treatment team. Family members may also be asked to support an individual in his or her treatment.

Community Resources Can Help Provide Services And Support

- Schools play an important role in connecting students with mental health professionals. For example, school psychologists, counselors, and school nurses help students get services they need either at school or somewhere else in the community. University and college students may have access to health services through college counseling centers.

- Families that are limited in their ability to pay often have access to community-based services such as community mental health centers.

State departments of mental health and local community health centers can help direct families to community resources. Phone listings for state and local mental health departments often appear in the government section of telephone directory white pages.

- There are free self-help and support groups in many communities for dealing with specific mental health problems such as coping with alcohol and drug abuse. Through sharing information and ideas with others, participants realize they are not alone with their problems.

- Most major cities have at least one mental health crisis center which may be located through telephone directory assistance. The centers typically are staffed 24 hours a day, 7 days a week, and can refer a caller to local sources of health care and support.

> ✔ **Quick Tip**
> There are free self-help and support groups in many communities for dealing with specific mental health problems.

Take Action

The More You Know, The Easier It Is

Libraries are an excellent source of information about mental health. Bookstores often have "self-help" or "psychology" sections.

For those with internet access, there are many websites related to health and mental health. Some are better in quality than others. It is important to know if the information on a site comes from sources you can trust. Use caution whenever you're sharing or exchanging information online: there's a chance that it will not be kept private.

Nothing Is Worse Than Nothing

The consequences of not getting help for mental health problems can be serious. Untreated problems often continue and become worse, and new problems may occur. For example, someone with panic attacks might begin drinking too much alcohol with the mistaken hope that it will help relieve his or her emotional pain.

One Final Word: To Be A Good Friend, Never Keep Talk Of Suicide A Secret

Friends often confide in one another about their problems. But if a friend mentions suicide, take it seriously and seek help immediately from a trusted adult or health professional. Never keep talk of suicide a secret, even if a friend asks you to. It's better to risk losing a friendship than to risk losing a friend forever.

For More Information

American Psychological Association

750 First Street, NE
Washington, DC 20002-4242
Toll-Free: 800-374-2721
Websites:
 http://helping.apa.org and
http://www.NoStigma.org

☞ Remember!!
It's All In The Attitude

Sometimes being able to get the help, support, and professional treatment you need is a matter of changing your mind about mental health and changing the way you react to mental health problems.

Here are some important reminders:

• Mental health is as important as physical health. In fact, the two are closely linked.

• Mental health problems are real, and they deserve to be treated.

• It's not a person's fault if he or she has a mental health problem. No one is to blame.

• Mental health problems are not a sign of weakness. They are not something you can "just snap out of" even if you try.

• Whether you're male or female, it's OK to ask for help and get it.

• There's hope. People improve and recover with the help of treatment, and they are able to enjoy happier and healthier lives.

Chapter 41

Sleep And Your Good Health

Introduction

Sleep is a basic drive of nature. Sufficient sleep helps us think more clearly, complete complex tasks better and more consistently, and enjoy everyday life more fully. Although many questions regarding the role of sleep remain unanswered, scientific studies have shown that sleep contributes significantly to several important cognitive, emotional, and performance-related functions.

Sleep is, in essence, food for the brain, and insufficient sleep can be harmful, even life-threatening. When hungry for sleep, the brain becomes relentless in its quest to satisfy its need and will cause feelings of "sleepiness," decreased levels of alertness or concentration, and, in many cases, unanticipated sleep. Excessive sleepiness is also associated with reduced short-term memory and learning ability, negative mood, inconsistent performance, poor productivity, and loss of some forms of behavioral control.

Researchers have identified several changes in sleep patterns, sleep/wake systems and circadian timing systems associated with puberty. These changes contribute to excessive sleepiness that has a negative impact on daytime

About This Chapter: Excerpted and reprinted with permission from *Adolescent Sleep Needs and Patterns: Research Report and Resource Guide*. © 2000 National Sleep Foundation. To view the complete text of this report, visit www.sleepfoundation.org.

functioning in adolescents, including increasing their risk of injury. Findings are similar in North America and in industrialized countries on other continents.

Scientists hypothesize that these sleep-related problems are due largely to conflicts between physiologically driven sleep needs and patterns, and behavioral and psychosocial factors that influence sleep habits.

Key changes in sleep patterns and needs that are associated with puberty include:

Physiological Patterns

- Adolescents require at least as much sleep as they did as pre-adolescents (in general, 8.5 to 9.25 hours each night).

- Daytime sleepiness increases—for some, to pathological levels—even when an adolescent's schedule provides for optimal amounts of sleep.

- Adolescents' sleep patterns undergo a phase delay, that is, a tendency toward later times, for both sleeping and waking. Studies show that the typical high school student's natural time to fall asleep is 11:00 P.M. or later.

Behavioral And Psychosocial Patterns

- Many U.S. adolescents do not get enough sleep, especially during the week. Survey data show that average total sleep time during the school week decreases from 7 hours, 42 minutes in 13 year olds to 7 hours, 4 minutes in 19 year olds. Only 15 percent of adolescents reported sleeping 8.5 or more hours on school nights, and 26 percent of students reported typically sleeping 6.5 hours or less each school night.

- Adolescents have irregular sleep patterns; in particular, their weekend sleep schedules are much different than their weekday schedules, to some extent as a direct consequence of weekday sleep loss. These differences include both the quantity and the timing of sleep. One study of more than 3,000 adolescents showed that the average increase of weekend over weekday sleep across ages 13–19 was one hour and 50 minutes. In 18-year-olds, the average discrepancy was more than two hours. In addition, 91 percent of the surveyed high school students reported going to sleep after 11:00 P.M. on weekends, and 40 percent went to bed after 11:00 P.M. on school nights.

Irregular sleep schedules—including significant discrepancies between weekdays and weekends—can contribute to a shift in sleep phase (i.e., tendency toward morningness or eveningness), trouble falling asleep or awakening, and fragmented (poor quality) sleep.

Consequences Of Poor Sleep In Adolescents

Data on children, teens, and adults confirm that sleep loss and sleep difficulties can have serious detrimental effects. Research specifically on adolescents and young adults is relatively new and limited, but scientists believe that many effects demonstrated in studies and clinical observations of adults are similar in adolescents. Sleep researchers, therefore, believe that insufficient sleep in teens and young adults is linked to:

- Increased risk of unintentional injuries and death. As noted, drowsiness or fatigue has been identified as a principle cause in at least 100,000 traffic crashes each year. In addition, about 1 million, or one-sixth, of traffic crashes in the United States are believed to be attributable to lapses in the driver's attention; sleep loss and fatigue significantly increase the chances of such lapses occurring. A North Carolina state study found that drivers age 25 or younger cause more than one-half (55 percent) of fall-asleep crashes. The same symptoms of sleepiness that contribute to traffic crashes can also play a role in non-traffic injuries, such as those associated with handling hazardous equipment in the workplace or in the home. Furthermore, adolescents who have not received sufficient sleep and who consume even small amounts of alcohol are at greater risk of injury than those who are not lacking sleep because sleep loss has been shown to heighten the effects of alcohol.

- Low grades and poor school performance. High school students who describe themselves as having academic problems and who are earning

C's or below in school report getting less sleep, having later bedtimes, and having more irregular sleep schedules than students reporting higher grades. (Note: A causal relationship has not yet been established.)

- Negative moods (e.g., anger, sadness, and fear), difficulty controlling emotions and behavior problems. In one study, female high school students who went to sleep on the weekend two or more hours later than their typical weeknight bedtime reported feeling more depressed than those who did not stay up late on the weekends.

Studies also suggest that sleep loss may be associated with a decreased ability to control, inhibit or change emotional responses. Some signs

---

✔ **Quick Tip**

Seven Sleep-Smart Tips For Teens

1. Sleep is food for the brain: Get enough of it, and get it when you need it. Even mild sleepiness can hurt your performance—from taking school exams to playing sports or video games. Lack of sleep can make you look tired and feel depressed, irritable, and angry.

2. Keep consistency in mind: Establish a regular bedtime and waketime schedule, and maintain it during weekends and school (or work) vacations. Don't stray from your schedule frequently, and never do so for two or more consecutive nights. If you must go off schedule, avoid delaying your bedtime by more than one hour, awaken the next day within two hours of your regular schedule, and, if you are sleepy during the day, take an early afternoon nap.

3. Learn how much sleep you need to function at your best. You should awaken refreshed, not tired. Most adolescents need between 8.5 and 9.25 hours of sleep each night. Know when you need to get up in the morning, then calculate when you need to go to sleep to get at least 8.5 hours of sleep a night.

of sleepiness, such as inability to stay focused on a task, impulsivity, difficulty "sitting still," and problems completing tasks, resemble behaviors common also in attention deficit hyperactivity disorder (ADHD). In addition, a 1995 study of students in transition from junior high to senior high school found that conduct/aggressive behaviors were highly associated with shorter sleep times and later sleep start time.

• Increased likelihood of stimulant use (including caffeine and nicotine), alcohol and similar substances.

Teens who are heavily involved in school and community activities, their jobs, and other responsibilities appear to be at greater risk for the above

---

4. Get into bright light as soon as possible in the morning, but avoid it in the evening. The light helps to signal to the brain when it should wakeup and when it should prepare to sleep.

5. Understand your circadian rhythm. Then you can try to maximize your schedule throughout the day according to your internal clock. For example, to compensate for your "slump (sleepy) times," participate in stimulating activities or classes that are interactive, and avoid lecture classes or potentially unsafe activities, including driving.

6. After lunch (or after noon), stay away from coffee, colas with caffeine, and nicotine, which are all stimulants. Also avoid alcohol, which disrupts sleep.

7. Relax before going to bed. Avoid heavy reading, studying, and computer games within one hour of going to bed. Don't fall asleep with the television on—flickering light and stimulating content can inhibit restful sleep. If you work during the week, try to avoid working night hours. If you work until 9:30 P.M., for example, you will need to plan time to "chill out" before going to sleep.

Source: "Seven Sleep-Smart Tips for Teens" is reprinted with permission from the National Sleep Foundation, www.sleepfoundation.org. © 2003 National Sleep Foundation.

effects of sleepiness than those who are less involved in activities and who either do not hold jobs or who work fewer hours.

What Can Be Done

The consequences of insufficient sleep among adolescents are particularly important to understand because they appear to be closely tied to key elements of human development. Achieving developmental goals during adolescence is essential for lifelong success and for what psychologists call social competency.

In addition, the transition from childhood to adulthood is a critical time for "seeding" the values and habits that will shape their lives. Therefore, intervention to improve the sleep patterns of adolescents is important.

Influencing Physiological Sleep Patterns

Sleep researchers have established that basic sleep needs within individuals generally remain the same throughout their lifetime. Furthermore, insufficient sleep accumulates into a sleep debt that can ultimately be relieved only through additional sleep.

Circadian timing systems are also very resistant to change. Behavioral methods, such as controlled light exposure and chronotherapy, can sometimes help shift circadian timing to more socially appropriate sleep and wake times. Because the circadian rhythms in teenagers are typically highly sensitive to erratic schedules, to effectively adjust them requires making gradual, persistent and consistent changes. Adapting to an early school schedule following summer or other vacation periods during which very late schedules are typically kept, for example, can take several days to several weeks.

It is important to recognize that excessive sleepiness during the day and other sleep problems can be an indication of an underlying biological sleep disorder. Accurate diagnosis of disorders such as narcolepsy, sleep apnea and periodic limb movement disorder usually requires examination by a qualified sleep specialist and an overnight stay in a sleep laboratory. In most cases, symptoms of sleep disorders can be eliminated or minimized through the use of appropriate behavior modifications, medication or other therapies.

Making New Discoveries

Sleep research has established clear relationships between sleepiness, health, safety, and productivity. However, the sleep research field in general is relatively young, and scientists still have much to learn about the role of sleep and the effects of sleep loss in humans. Additional studies on the neurobiology, genetics, epidemiology, and neurobehavioral and functional consequences of sleepiness are needed. More studies specifically on the adolescent population are also needed, including interdisciplinary research to further examine sleep's role in adolescent development, health, and behavior.

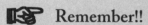 **Remember!!**

Are You Getting Enough Sleep?

Sleep is a critical factor in emotional and physical health. Many people see sleep as a waste of time, but a good nights sleep is critical to our well-being. Many factors contribute to insomnia: anxiety, tension, diet; they can all affect our sleep. A healthy diet and exercise can aid in sleeping well. Many people's diets are full of caffeine and salt, which stimulate the adrenal gland. And we wonder why we can't relax! Without relaxation it is difficult to fall asleep and stay sleeping through the night. One may change their bedtime, find a calming activity such as a walk, bath, or meditation to do before bed in order to aid in relaxation. Exercise and sleep go hand in hand. Our bodies need rest in order to strengthen for the next days' activity and exercise relieves many symptoms of bad sleep.

Anything that interferes with our sleep interferes with our health and well-being. A good night's sleep is important if we want to feel good and avoid illness. So avoiding stimulants and drugs, getting the proper nutrition, finding time to relax, and exercise are all key to assuring a good sleeping pattern.

Source: Reprinted with permission from The National Association for Fitness Certification (NAFC), Pam Germain, Director. ©2003 NAFC. All rights reserved. For additional information, visit www.body-basics.com.

Chapter 42

Locker Room Hygiene

Lurking In The Locker Room

Do you know where nasty things like bacteria and fungi may be hiding? Come into the locker room to see what's lurking under foot and behind closed doors.

Flip-flops: Wear flip-flops to walk around the locker room—those wet floors are popular hangouts for fungi looking for a foot to grab on to.

Sneakers: Air out your sneakers between wears to prevent athlete's foot.

Shorts and t-shirt: Loose-fitting clothes are best for physical activity. If you have acne on your arms, back, or shoulders, keeping it loose cuts down on the amount of friction on your body. Friction can make your acne worse.

Towels: When you're in the gym, using two towels can help to cut down on the spread of bacteria—use one to wipe off the equipment before and after you use it, and one to wipe the sweat from your skin

Washcloth: Wash your face right after you work out to get rid of sweat—keeping your pores clean helps prevent acne.

About This Chapter: "Infection Protection," BAM! (Body And Mind), Centers for Disease Control and Prevention (CDC), reviewed April 30, 2002.

Water Bottle: Clean out your water bottle after each time you use it—this will prevent bacteria from growing inside.

Water Fountain: Drink plenty of water before, during, and after you are physically active to stay hydrated. In addition to keeping your body working right, it can help prevent acne by flushing out your pores.

Additional Notes for Boys

Athletic Supporter: Always wear a clean, dry athletic supporter or pair of underwear when you participate in sports or your regular activity—otherwise, you're at risk for a nasty case of jock itch.

Talc powder: Use an anti-fungal or talc powder on your feet and groin area after you shower to prevent athlete's foot and jock itch.

Showers: Shower immediately and dry off well after you work out—it will remove sweat and fungi from your skin, reducing the risk of getting athlete's foot and jock itch.

Additional Notes for Girls

Sweatband: Sweatbands can trap sweat in your pores and provide a perfect place for bacteria to grow and cause acne, so it's best not to wear them.

Makeup Bag: Be sure to take off your make-up before you work out—it will keep your pores clear and help prevent acne.

Gym bag and clothes in locker: Storing damp or wet workout clothes in your locker or gym bag is an invitation for fungus to grow. Hang your clothes up to dry before cramming them in your locker, and take them home at least once a week to be washed.

Towel (on bench): When sitting in the locker room, sit on a clean towel. Damp benches can be germ-fests of bacteria and fungi that can easily be spread from person to person. If you can, get dressed first, before you sit down.

Part 5

Avoiding Fitness Busters

Chapter 43

Overcoming Barriers To Fitness

Make Activity Easy

Our understanding of fitness has evolved since the fitness craze first took hold. Scientific evidence now clearly indicates that regular moderate-intensity physical activity offers many of the health benefits traditionally associated with more intense exercise.

Moderate-intensity activity includes many of the things you may already be doing during a day or week: walking the dog, raking leaves, playing, even housework (it may not be fun, but chores, such as vacuuming, can be a work-out). For many people, being more active may simply mean taking advantage of or creating opportunities for activity. The point is not to make physical activity an unwelcome chore, but to seize the opportunities you have and make the most of them.

There's really no mystery to fitness. And though there may be barriers, there are also solutions. Once you commit yourself, the barriers to fitness will be easily surmountable, and the rewards of better living will be yours.

About This Chapter: This chapter contains excerpts adapted from "The Nolan Ryan Fitness Guide," President's Council on Physical Fitness and Sports, 1993. Despite the date of this document, the tips are still valid. Also included are excerpts from "Fit for Life," National Women's Health Information Center, a project of the Office on Women's Health in the U.S. Department of Health and Human Services, July 2002.

Common Barriers And Solutions

Can't Find Time

Work exercise into your day:

- Get up a little earlier for a fun physical activity.

- Walk to school. Walk home.

- Use the stairs.

- Play with pets.

- Walk during your lunch break.

- Write physical activity into your calendar, and don't book conflicting appointments.

- Ride a stationary bike while watching television or reading.

Can't Get Motivated

Fitness will never be a priority until you make a commitment to it. Some things that can help:

- Read books and/or magazines on fitness to inspire you.

- Identify people you look up to who are fit, and use them as role models.

- Set specific, short-term goals, and reward yourself when you achieve them.

- Do it for yourself.

- Associate with friends who believe in fitness for mutual support.

Can't Stay Motivated

- Enlist a friend or family member as an exercise partner.

- Choose activities you really enjoy, that are fun and offer a reward, such as hiking for a great view, or walking to a friend's house.

- Make activities into social occasions, such as tennis tournaments among friends.

- Earn one or more Presidential Sports Awards.

It's Boring

Looking for some excitement? Vary your workouts so you don't get bored. You will also reap more of the benefits by training different muscle groups through different kinds of activities. If the idea of jogging or cycling bores you to tears, you might want to try adventure sports, such as:

- Kickboxing
- Snowboarding
- Skateboarding
- Mountain biking
- Surfing
- Sandboarding
- Rock climbing
- Kayaking
- SCUBA diving
- Pilates
- Yoga
- T'ai chi

You will need your parents' permission to invest some time and money in safety equipment and lessons for most of these sports. All of these activities carry risks for serious injury and it is important to learn the proper techniques before trying them out on your own. It's also a good idea to try these sports with a friend, so you can watch out for each other and share new things that you learn.

> ✔ **Quick Tip**
> **Take The First Step**
>
> Most of us need to take a simple approach: do something. The first step is just being more active even if its only a little. Start by walking; it can always be worked into your day. Anyone can do it any time, in almost any place, without any special equipment. The opportunities are plentiful: go for a walk after dinner instead of watching television; walk to school; walk to the store rather than driving; or take the dog or the younger siblings for a walk. A moderately brisk pace is preferable, but build up to it gradually.
>
> Of course, there are lots of other activities besides walking that will give you the benefits of an aerobic workout, and you should pursue as many as you can and want to. Choose the ones you enjoy most, and have a great time while you get in shape. Here are some other suggestions: jogging; swimming; rowing; tennis; cycling; and dancing.

Don't Know Where To Start

- Start by making the most of the activities you do already: increase their frequency, duration, or intensity.

- Ask a friend someone who has the experience and is willing to help you.

- Go to health fairs, sports expositions, clinics; learn from the variety of offerings presented.

- If you've been inactive for a long time, start off slowly. Walk for 10 minutes, or just around the block.

- Match your activity to your fitness level.

- Don't concern yourself with fancy equipment or health club memberships. Just activate.

☞ Remember!!

Now that you know just how easy being more physically active can be, the only thing left is to do it. Just think about all the great things being physically fit will do for you and your health and well-being, and activate yourself. Involve your family, your friends—anyone and everyone that you can. Start incorporating more active pursuits into your lifestyle, and before you know it, activity will be the most natural and enjoyable part of your day. Every single day you do something physically active—even if its just walking home from school— is one day closer to realizing the mental and physical benefits of fitness.

Don't Like Organized Sports

There are lots of ways of being fit that don't involve a gym, organized sports, or activities like jogging or stair climbing. By making your lifestyle naturally active, you ensure that you will stay fit for many years to come. Here are some easy ways to add fitness to your life without ever setting foot in a gym:

- Walk your dog (or a neighbor's dog)
- Play a game of tag with your little brother or sister.
- Take the stairs instead of the elevator
- Walk to school or shopping instead of driving
- Go dancing with your friends
- Help with the gardening or housework
- Wash the car
- Go for a hike
- Mow the law

Avoid Injuries

Nothing is more frustrating than finally getting involved in an activity you enjoy, only to hurt yourself and be forced into a prolonged rehabilitation period. Although some injuries may be unavoidable, proper conditioning and attention to the details of warm-ups, cool-downs, and stretching will help keep you off the disabled list.

An Ounce Of Prevention

Preventing injuries requires both common sense and careful preparation. By following a few basic principles, you can help ensure that your activity wont put you out of commission.

Warm Up: This is the number one tenet of injury prevention, consisting of three to five minutes of low-level activity followed by a few minutes of stretching.

Stay Flexible: Stretching during the warm-up and cool-down phases will help prevent muscle pulls and strains, as well as the general aches and pains that can occur after exercising.

Build Gradually: Start out slowly and build up gradually in intensity and duration of activity. Weekend athletes are famous for trying to do too much, too soon. Don't fall into this trap.

Be Prepared: Use the right equipment for your sport, whether its a good pair of running shoes, or knee pads for inline skating. Be sure its in good condition and is appropriate for your skill level.

Rehydrate: Water is the best sports drink and you should drink plenty of it before, during and after exercise especially in warm weather. Keep drinking it throughout the day.

Avoid Extremes: Try not to exercise outdoors in extreme hot or cold weather, but, if you do, be sure to dress properly. Use caution against heat exhaustion or, at the other extreme, frostbite.

Cool Down: Gradually decrease the intensity of your activity to restore a normal heart rate. Postexercise stretching should not be overlooked.

Chapter 44

Mental Roadblocks

Are You Ready To Exercise?

Studies have shown that seven out of 10 people who start an exercise program drop out within a few months. One problem is that most people jump into exercise without doing any planning up front. They're just not prepared for the commitment involved. Are you ready to make exercise part of your lifestyle? Sherri McMillan, MSc, co-owner of Northwest Personal Training & Fitness Education in Vancouver, Washington, and 1998 IDEA Personal Trainer of the Year has discovered that people who stick with exercise buy into the following four "Laws of Success."

The Law Of Possession

"If it is going to be, it is up to me." Understand that you need to take ultimate responsibility for the success or failure of your exercise program. It may be tempting to blame your family or shift responsibility to your group exercise instructor or personal trainer, but you will be the one who actually exercises. Loved ones can support you and fitness professionals can help educate and guide you, but you must be willing to give up a sedentary lifestyle.

About This Chapter: This chapter includes text from "Are You Ready to Exercise?," "Overcoming the Fear Factor," and "Using Positive Self-Talk," © 2003 IDEA Inc. Reproduced with permission of IDEA Health & Fitness Association, (800) 999-IDEA, www.IDEAfit.com.

The Law Of Effort

"Anything worth achieving is worth working for." Exercise takes discipline, willpower, character, persistence, and a commitment to delayed gratification. Starting and staying with an exercise program requires hard work, but you can do it.

The Law Of Consistency

"I have to stick to the game plan." Researchers have found one characteristic common to those who adhere to exercise: They move toward their goals one step at a time and are committed to constant, never-ending improvement. Consistency and persistence are key to achieving results. If you get off track for a week or so, it's no big deal. However, if you are regularly tempted away from your program, you will not succeed. Regardless of busy work schedules or lack of energy, you must keep exercising. For example, if you want to be 10 pounds lighter 10 years from now, it is not what you do over the next eight weeks that matters; it is what you do over the next 10 years.

The Law Of Self-Efficacy

"If I think I can or I think I can't, I'm probably right." If you immediately start questioning whether you can make the changes required to live an active lifestyle, you are going to have a difficult time. You must believe you can do it. But don't think you have to make the changes alone. Get support from a personal trainer, an exercise instructor, friends and family, and/or online exercise buddies.

Overcoming The Fear Factor

Fear of failure stops many people from exercising or trying new activities. According to David E. Conroy, PhD,

> **☞ Remember!!**
>
> These four principles can help you stay with your fitness program:
>
> - Possession: *You* own the responsibility.
>
> - Effort: *You* have to make the effort.
>
> - Consistency: *You* need to stick with it.
>
> - Self-efficacy: *You* make the necessary changes.

assistant professor of kinesiology and director of the sport psychology lab at Pennsylvania State University, University Park, they may specifically fear the shame and embarrassment that come with failure. They may be afraid that they won't fulfill their ideal self-image. The thought of not doing well at exercise may make them anxious that they are not as competent as they believed and lower their self-esteem. If fear of failure keeps you from exercising, try these motivational tips from Conroy.

Start Small

Usually, those who fear failure are very critical of themselves. Do what you can to cultivate your success. Take group fitness classes or start an exercise program at the level right for you. In addition, don't assume that, just because you excel at one sport, you'll be equally skilled at other sports or fitness activities; give yourself time to make mistakes and learn. If you don't want to go through that learning curve in front of others, hire a personal trainer who can train you in a private location.

Exercise More For Rewards Than To Avoid Punishment

There are two main ways to motivate yourself to exercise. If you're avoidance-oriented, you exercise to avoid punishment such as criticism or embarrassment. If you're approach-oriented, you exercise to receive a reward such as praise or improved fitness. Both orientations can influence the quality of your exercise. An avoidance orientation can make you avoid activities that would leave you feeling unskilled or inadequate, such as fitness classes too advanced for your current level or activities in which others may evaluate the appearance of your body. On the other hand, an avoidance orientation can make you pursue exercise to avoid future health problems. You may also be shamed into exercising out of fear of health consequences of inactivity.

In contrast, an approach orientation can lead you to exercise because you want the physical and psychological benefits of exercise. Although both orientations can motivate, avoidance-oriented motivation is associated with higher levels of fear and anxiety and therefore less likely to motivate you to continue exercising. Approach-oriented motivation is usually associated with greater persistence and therefore more likely to help you keep exercising.

✎ **Weird Words**

Approach-Oriented: Activity undertaken to receive a reward, such as praise or improved fitness.

Avoidance-Oriented: Activity undertaken to avoid punishment, such as criticism or embarrassment.

Develop Your Inner Motivation

Of course, although external, tangible rewards can be quite a motivation to exercise, constantly focusing on them by saying to yourself things such as, "If I go to the gym three times this week, I will buy myself a new outfit" decreases your intrinsic motivation. You begin to exercise not for the enjoyment of the activity itself but only for those rewards, and, once you no longer have them, you become much more likely to stop exercising. Instead of exercising for an external reward such as weight loss, develop you inner motivation to exercise.

Using Positive Self-Talk

Thoughts play a critical role in determining your emotional responses to events. Your thoughts about yourself and your performance and your interpretation of specific situations have a direct impact on your feelings and behavior. Increasing the amount of positive self-talk can improve your exercise program—and your life in general. To enhance your self-talk, use these pointers from IDEA Master Personal Fitness Trainer Daniel Ball, MS, a Seattle-based specialist in occupational fitness consulting and personal wellness coaching.

Understand Self-Talk

Whenever you think about something, you are, in essence, talking to yourself. Self-talk serves as the vehicle for making perceptions and beliefs conscious.

Determine If You Need More Positive Self-Talk

Is your self-talk generally negative? To find out, try this simple exercise: Carry some paper clips in your pocket. Each time you make a negative self-statement, hook two clips together, building a chain. Just seeing the length of the chain at the end of the day may motivate you to make some changes. Keeping a daily record of your self-talk in a workout log can also effectively increase your awareness. Record the situation in which the self-talk occurred; the content of the self-talk; and the consequences, in terms of performance, emotion or both.

Recognize The Benefits

Self-talk can be used to correct bad habits, modify intensity, focus attention, build and maintain self-confidence, and encourage exercise maintenance. Research by E. F. Gauvin reported in *Exploring Sport and Exercise Psychology* found that persistent exercisers use positive self-talk while dropouts and sedentary people use self-defeating, negative self-verbalization, such as, "How many times am I going to make that mistake?" or, "I don't like to exercise." Self-talk can be used in many different situations.

Acquire New Skills

When learning new skills, use self-talk as cue words to focus your attention. For example, you might use simple cues such as "Stretch," "Pull," or "Reach" to focus attention on your movement.

Break Bad Habits

To break old habits and make new responses automatic, you need to decide on the best instructional cues. The greater the change, the more self-instruction you require. For example, if you are a bodybuilder who drops your head while performing squats, you may want to repeat "Head up" throughout the exercise until the correct posture becomes second nature.

Initiate Action

Self-talk can be motivating. A runner can increase speed by using such cue words as "Quick!" or "Kick!" A golfer can improve his form by intentionally verbalizing cues like "Arm straight," "Head down" and "Follow through."

Sustain Effort

Once an exercise or movement has begun, sustaining effort or motivation may be a problem. Positive instructional cues like "Focus," "Keep your feet moving" or "Hang in there," can help you sustain effort when you are fatigued.

Be In The Here And Now

During exercise the mind tends to wander and lose focus. Staying in the present is critically important to foster improvement and prevent injury. Commands like "Focus," "Concentrate," or "Be here now" can bring you back to center. Using a specific set of verbal cues can help you keep your mind sharply focused on relevant tasks.

Chapter 45

When The Weather Turns Too Hot Or Too Cold

When It's Hot Out

How Does Hot Weather Affect The Heart?

Extremely hot weather causes dehydration, heat exhaustion and heat stroke. These risks increase when the humidity is above 70 percent and the temperature is above 70° F. Heat and humidity interfere with the body's natural cooling process.

Exercising outside in hot and humid conditions can be hard on your heart. This is true even for athletes who haven't yet adapted to the heat. The problem is made worse because the heart is trying to deliver blood and oxygen to your working muscles while your body is trying to cool off by sweating. If you sweat too much, you lose fluid. This decreases your total blood volume. That means your heart has to pump even harder to get the smaller volume of blood to your working muscles, skin and the other body parts. When you lose too much fluid, your body temperature rises and your nervous system doesn't work properly. Extreme fluid loss can lead to brain and heart damage.

A good way to monitor your body fluid level is to weigh every morning after using the bathroom. If you weigh two pounds less than normal in the morning, you're probably dehydrated and need to drink more water before doing any vigorous physical activity. (You may have lost weight as water but not as fat.)

If you plan to exercise outside in hot and humid weather, wear very light, comfortable clothing and work out in the early morning or late evening, if

---

Sunscreen Tips   ✔ **Quick Tip**

Sunscreen with SPF 15 or higher, that is. You've gotta have the right stuff.

SPF stands for "sun protection factor"—how well a sunscreen works at keeping the sun's burning rays from roasting your skin. (FYI: SPF 45 and higher protects only a bit more than 30 does…) Make sure your sunscreen blocks both UVA and UVB rays (types of light).

You'll need to get a bottle, shake it, fill up a handful, and slather it all over your body. (Yes, we said "handful." You need that much for good coverage.) Put it on 30 minutes before you go out in the sun…and remember to cover your face, lips, hands, forearms, shoulders, ears, back of your neck, under your chin, and the top of your head. Watch your eyes—it could sting! If you're worried about breaking out, try a gel sunscreen. And if your skin reacts badly to one brand, try another. Not all sunscreens have the same ingredients.

Apply, reapply, and then do it again! Even if the bottle says it's waterproof, sweat proof, or any other "proof," you should reapply. Put more sunscreen on every couple of hours or right after swimming, working up a sweat, or rubbing on your skin with a towel or clothes.

And one more thing…Wearing sunscreen protects you but it doesn't make it okay to stay in the sun longer. Try to stay out of the sun when you can.

Source: Body And Mind (BAM), Centers for Disease Control and Prevention (CDC), November 2002.

possible. Know the symptoms of heat exhaustion and heat stroke. If any symptoms appear, stop exercising and cool down immediately by dousing yourself with cold water. You may need to get medical attention. Heat exhaustion can progress quickly to heat stroke, which can kill you.

What Are The Symptoms Of Heat Exhaustion?

- heavy sweating
- cold, clammy skin
- dizziness or fainting (syncope)
- a weak and rapid pulse
- muscle cramps
- shallow and fast breathing
- nausea, vomiting or both

What Are The Symptoms Of Heat Stroke?

- warm, dry skin with no sweating
- strong and rapid pulse
- confusion and/or unconsciousness
- high fever
- throbbing headaches
- nausea, vomiting or both

♣ It's A Fact!!

Get out and work your body—there are a million things to do! But hang out in the shade whenever you can. The sun is the strongest between 10 in the morning and 4 in the afternoon.

If you're like most people, the sun will do almost all of its damage to your skin before your 18th birthday.

Source: Body And Mind (BAM), Centers for Disease Control and Prevention (CDC), November 2002.

When The Weather Turns Cold

When exercising, your body is much more susceptible to problems in cold weather than in warm weather. Don't let the winter be an excuse not to exercise; instead be prepared for your cold-weather workouts.

What impact does the cold weather have on exercise performance? The answer depends on what activity is being performed and how cold it is outside. Of primary interest is maintaining normal body temperature (98.6 degrees). During exposure to the cold, normal body temperature can be maintained two ways: either by increasing the amount of heat produced and/or reducing the amount of heat that is lost.

Heat production can be increased by the intensity of the exercise or by shivering, caused by involuntary muscle contractions. Heat loss can best be reduced by dressing appropriately for weather conditions.

Although too much body fat is unhealthy, it is your body's natural insulator. Individuals with greater amounts of body fat are better insulated against the cold and lose less heat than their leaner counterparts. It has been theorized that we tend to eat more in the winter because our bodies are trying to store extra fat as a survival mechanism.

Winter winds cause significant heat loss. Always try to head out facing the wind and come back with your back against it. This will help you to avoid exposure to extreme wind chill while wearing sweat-soaked clothing.

The temperature of your muscles, tendons and ligaments are significantly reduced in the cold, making them less pliable and thus less moveable. This is one reason exercise in cold weather feels so much more tiring and difficult. With any cold-weather activity, especially those that rely on speed and power, elevation of muscle temperature is critical.

The colder it is outside, the more important it is for you to warm up, stretch, and cool down before and after exercising. Warming up and cooling down, along with proper stretching, not only will help to elevate muscle temperature, but it will allow you to maintain flexibility in the muscles and joints, making you less prone to injury. An adequate warm-up/cool-down involves a low-intensity 5–10 minute activity, followed by gentle stretching for all the major muscle groups. In severe conditions, it can be difficult to adequately elevate muscle temperature. Then your warm up should be longer and with a bit more intensity.

Ever wonder which outdoor activity burns the most calories? Cross-country skiing comes out on top, with as many as 612 calories burned per hour. In addition, it is one of the best for working every major muscle group. If exercising outdoors isn't your thing or cross-country skiing isn't possible in your area, you can still benefit from using a cross-country skiing machine.

✔ Quick Tip

Gotta shield your eyes from the sun, too, right? Yep. Slip on some shades because the sun's rays can hurt your eyes. Choose some cool wraparound shades that block 100 percent of UVA and UVB.

Source: Body And Mind (BAM!), Centers for Disease Control and Prevention (CDC), November 2002.

Most shoes worn when exercising lose cushioning ability in cold temperatures. For winter activities, try to find shoes with softer compression-molded midsoles; in the summer, choose shoes with firmer polyurethane midsoles.

The American Medical Association recently published a study showing that inactive individuals are up to 30 times more likely to suffer a heart attack when they engage suddenly in an intense activity, such as shoveling snow. If you are unaccustomed to exercise or have any type of medical condition, talk to your doctor about how to stay safe this winter.

No one ever expects to get stranded in freezing weather, but it happens more often than you think, so be prepared. Dress appropriately, put an extra heavy blanket or two in the car and take along an emergency cold-weather kit containing such items as wax candles, matches, a heavy-duty flashlight, flares, food and water.

If you get caught without a kit, start building a "snow cave." Once snow is packed, it is an excellent insulator and has saved many a life protecting against harsh winter winds. Slip a few extra candles and matches in your pocket before heading out on foot; they can provide an amazing amount of heat.

Individuals who spend a lot of time outdoors in the winter often complain of burning in the throat or difficulty breathing. Any type of exercise, especially if it is intense enough to cause aggressive panting, might lead to such symptoms. Winter wind and cold can cause severe bronchial irritation resulting from inhaling very cold air faster that your airway can warm it up. This produces spasms in the muscles of the airway, a burning pain and, in severe cases, even the possibility of coughing up blood.

In addition, mucous production increases, creating wheezing sounds. To avoid this, wear a coat with a large hood, and scarf or other covering for your face. Once inside, if your airways are still irritated, try to rest, stay warm and breathe humidified air.

Chapter 46

Alcohol, Tobacco, And Other Drugs: Impact On Athletic Performance

Drugs In Sports: General Information

What is the background of drug use in sport?

During the past 30 years the use of performance enhancing substances in athletics increased at every level of competition. Student athletes have used different supplements including vitamins and minerals, amino acid supplements, anabolic steroids and other anabolic substances, stimulants, painkillers, and a variety of illegal street drugs.

What are some reasons why student athletes take different kinds of drugs?

Student athletes have used drugs: to cope with academic and athletic stress; to speed up increases in strength and physical size; and to socialize and relax after competition.

Alcohol

What are the physiological and psychological effects of alcohol use?

Alcohol acts on the central nervous system as a depressant. Users of moderate amounts of alcohol experience relief from anxiety and disinhibition.

For example, a 150 lb. male with normal tolerance levels would experience a "relaxing" effect after drinking one to two (3%–5%) beers in one hour. The effects of alcohol on individuals vary and are often unpredictable. One person can become euphoric, friendly, and talkative, while others become aggressive and hostile.

Alcohol interferes with motor activity, reflexes, and coordination. In moderate quantities alcohol increases heart rate and dilates peripheral blood vessels. Alcohol is diffused in the blood stream after ingestion by passing through the gastrointestinal walls. Once alcohol is in the small intestine its absorption is not affected by food. The effect of alcohol on the body depends on the amount of alcohol in the blood (commonly referred to as BAC or blood alcohol level).

The BAC concentration is affected by the presence of food in the stomach, the rate of alcohol consumption, the concentration of alcohol, and the drinker's body composition. One drink is equal to one beer (4% alcohol, 12 oz.) or 1 oz. whisky.

Alcohol can elevate the mood, act as a relaxant, decrease reaction time and fine muscle coordination, impair judgement, impair balance, speech, and vision, create a feeling of euphoria, and result in loss of motor coordination. Depending on individual tolerance levels, severe intoxication can occur with higher BAC levels (0.3%).

♣ It's A Fact!!

Alcohol And Athletics: A Dangerous Mix

Alcohol affects the body by:

- Causing dehydration
- Depleting the body of vital nutrients
- Interfering with sleep patterns
- Depressing the central nervous system
- Increasing fat stores

Alcohol affects performance by:

- Decreasing reaction time, coordination, balance, strength, and endurance
- Increasing fatigue
- Increasing risk of injury
- Impairing ability to recover from injury

Source: Excerpted with permission from *The Effects of Alcohol on Nutrition and Athletic Performance*, a brochure from George Mason University Health Education Services, http://www.gmu.edu/student/health/serv01.htm, and George Mason University Intercollegiate Athletics. © 2001.

Deep coma and death from respiratory failure can occur with 0.5% to 0.6% BAC levels. Psychological and physiological dependence can result from the regular consumption of large amounts of alcohol.

Heavy drinking over a long period of time can result in serious mental disorders and permanent brain damage. Liver disorders are the most common cause of death among alcoholics. Prolonged use of alcohol may cause ulcers, hiatal hernia, and cancers throughout the digestive track. The pancreas is also damaged by heavy alcohol use. High concentrations of alcohol increase the functioning of the hematopoietic system and effect a decrease in red blood cell production and impair the functioning of white cells and platelets, causing problems with clotting and immunity which can lead to infection and bleeding disorders.

Other serious consequences of chronic alcohol abuse include heart disease, malnutrition and vitamin deficiencies, sexual malfunctioning, atrophy of testicles and lowered sperm count. Females can experience menstrual delays, ovarian abnormalities, and infertility. Alcohol abuse also can cause severe kidney damage, urinary tract infections, mental disorders, and brain damage. Fetal alcohol syndrome is a condition that affects children born to alcohol-consuming mothers. It is characterized by facial deformities, mental retardation and growth deficiency.

What are the effects of alcohol use on performance?

Although alcohol has been used by student athletes to cope with anxiety and stress related to competition and academics and to enhance mental status before competition, the use of alcohol decreases reaction time, fine muscle coordination, balance, speech, vision, and hearing. The feeling of disinhibition and reduced anxiety is accompanied by loss of motor coordination, decreased reaction time, lack of balance and coordination and judgment. Alcohol also lowers muscle glycogen.

Tobacco/Nicotine

What is the chemical composition of tobacco?

The burning of tobacco generates approximately 4,000 compounds. The smoke can be separated into gas and particulate phases. The composition of the smoke delivered to the smoker depends on the composition of tobacco and how densely it is packed, the length of the column of tobacco, the characteristics of the filter and the paper, and the temperature at which the tobacco is burned.

Among the gaseous components are carbon monoxide, carbon dioxide, nitrogen oxides, ammonia, volatile nitrosamines, hydrogen cyanide, volatile sulfur-containing compounds, volatile hydrocarbons, alcohols, aldehydes, and ketones. Some of these compounds inhibit ciliary movement in the lungs. Tar is the compound in tobacco that remains after the moisture and nicotine are subtracted and consists of polycyclic aromatic hydrocarbons, which are carcinogens. Non-volatile nitrosamines and aromatic amines play an role in the development of bladder cancer. The actual content of nicotine in tobacco can vary from 0.2% to 5%.

What are the different forms of spit tobacco?

Spit tobacco exists as:

- loose leaf tobacco which is placed in foil pouches and placed between cheek and lower gum where it is sucked and chewed.

- snuff, which is moist or dry powdered tobacco is sold in small round containers. The use of snuff is referred to as "dipping" which involves leaving a pinch of tobacco between the cheek and the lower gum.

Chewing tobacco and snuff are two types of smokeless tobacco products that are commonly referred to as "spit tobacco." Compressed tobacco is used in pieces and each piece is called a "plug." The user bites off a small piece and places in the mouth. Nicotine gum is another form of oral nicotine intake mainly used by individuals who are trying to quit smoking.

How safe are spit tobacco products compared with cigarettes?

Taking a pinch of snuff has the same effects as smoking three or four cigarettes. The possibility of getting oral cancer increases significantly for individuals who use smokeless tobacco on a daily basis for 3.5 years or longer. Continued use of smokeless tobacco can cause cancer of the pharynx and esophagus. Long-term snuff users have a 50% greater risk of developing oral cancer than non-users. Severe inflammation of gum tissue, tooth decay, and tooth loss are also associated with the use of smokeless tobacco. The Comprehensive Smokeless Tobacco Health Education Act of 1986 requires the rotation of three health warnings on smokeless tobacco packages and advertisements and bans smokeless tobacco advertising on broadcasting media.

What is the chemical composition of nicotine?

Nicotine is the most abundant of the volatile alkaloids in the tobacco leaf. Nicotine is a colorless and volatile liquid alkaloid found in smoking and smokeless tobacco which turns brown and acquires the odor of tobacco upon exposure to air. The alkaloid is water-soluble and forms water-soluble salts.

What is the pharmacology of nicotine?

Diverse effects of nicotine occur as a result of both stimulant and depressant actions on various central and peripheral nervous system pathways. This drug can increase the heart rate by excitation of the sympathetic nervous

---

♣ It's A Fact!!

Research has shown that students who participate in interscholastic sports are less likely to be regular and heavy smokers. Students who play at least one sport are 40% less likely to be regular smokers and 50% less likely to be heavy smokers. Regular and heavy smoking decreases substantially with an increase in the number of sports played.

The lower rates of smoking for student athletes may be related to a number of factors:

- Greater self-confidence gained from sports participation.
- Additional counseling from coaching staff about smoking.
- Reduced peer influences about smoking.
- Perceptions about reduced sports performance because of smoking.
- Greater awareness about the health consequences of smoking.

Source: Excerpted from "Facts on Sports and Smoke Free Youth," National Center for Chronic Disease Prevention and Health Promotion, Centers for Disease Control and Prevention, reviewed November 02, 2000.

system or by paralyzing the parasympathetic nervous system. Nicotine affects the medulla in the brain to increase heart rate. Nicotine also causes a discharge of epinephrine from the adrenal medulla, which causes an increase in heart rate and raises blood pressure.

What are the physiological effects of nicotine?

Briefly, nicotine can stimulate the brain at all levels, significantly increase breathing, lower HDL cholesterol (the good fats) levels, increase blood pressure, and constrict peripheral blood vessels.

Some individuals experience nausea and vomiting, decreased urinary flow, and increased free fatty acids. Nicotine increases the oxygen requirements of the heart muscle, but lowers oxygen supply, and this effect may lead to heart attacks. Nicotine initially stimulates the salivary and bronchial secretions and then inhibits them. Cigarette smoke causes the excessive saliva associated with smoking. Nicotine inhibits hunger and also causes a slight increase in blood sugar. It deadens the taste buds. Smokers often report weight gain and appetite increase after quitting smoking.

What are the psychological effects of nicotine?

Nicotine is a highly addictive drug. More than 24 billion packages of cigarettes are purchased annually in the United States, and approximately 400,000 deaths every year are attributed to cigarette smoking. Nicotine is so addictive that approximately 70% of smokers who want to quit smoking cannot, and about 83% of smokers smoke every day. Smokers report that cigarettes help them to relax. Nicotine is a cholinergic agonist and stimulates the brain. Smokers experience withdrawal symptoms when trying to quit smoking.

What is the relationship between tobacco use and chronic illnesses?

A dose response relationship exists between the number of cigarettes smoked per day and particular illnesses. Men who smoke two packs of cigarettes per day have a four time higher risk of developing chronic bronchitis or emphysema than do nonsmokers. In the long run, lung tissue is damaged leading to emphysema.

Cigarette smoking also increases the risk of cardiovascular disease, and smoking is a major risk factor for heart attacks. The probability of heart attack is related to the amount smoked, which can be intensified when combined with other risk factors such as obesity. Smoking is a major risk factor for arteriosclerotic disease and aneurysm.

A direct relationship (in men and women) has been found between amount of cigarettes smoked and the development of lung cancer. The risk for developing lung cancer increases:

* with the amount smoked

* duration of smoking

* age at which person started to smoke

* degree of inhalation

* tar and nicotine levels of the cigarettes

A relationship also exists between smoking and cancers of the oral cavity, esophagus, urinary bladder, kidneys, and pancreas. Cigarette smoking is the leading cause of bronchopulmonary disease. Respiratory infections are also more prevalent and more severe among smokers than nonsmokers. Lower birth weight and survival rate of infants born to women who smoke during pregnancy is a major concern. Infants born to mothers who smoke are more likely to die from sudden infant death syndrome (SIDS). Long term effects been observed in their physical growth, mental development, and behavioral characteristics.

♣ It's A Fact!!

* Smoking hurts young people's physical fitness in terms of both performance and endurance—even among young people trained in competitive running.

* Smoking among youth can hamper the rate of lung growth and the level of maximum lung function.

* The resting heart rates of young adult smokers are two to three beats per minute faster than those of nonsmokers.

Source: Excerpted from "Facts On Youth Smoking, Health, And Performance," National Center For Chronic Disease Prevention and Health Promotion, Centers for Disease Control and Prevention, reviewed November 2000.

What are the effects of nicotine on athletic performance?

Athletes participating in a 2001 National Collegiate Athletic Association (NCAA) survey reported using spit tobacco for recreational or social purposes, to deal with the stresses of college athletics, and to feel good. About 53% of the athletes who use spit tobacco reported using it 1–5 times daily.

The use of nicotine in high doses is toxic and can cause nicotine poisoning. Signs of nicotine poisoning are vomiting, sweating, mental confusion, diminished pulse rate, headache, breathing difficulty, respiratory failure caused by muscle paralysis, and death. Nicotine poisoning can also cause impaired oxygen transport secondary to increases in carboxyhemoglobin. In many cases smoking will increase breathing rate during submaximal exercise, and this will reduce athletic performance.

Caffeine And Other Xanthines

What is the chemistry of caffeine and other xanthines?

Caffeine is one member of the group called xanthines. The other xanthines are theophylline and theobromine. Caffeine is found in 63 species of plants. Caffeine, theophylline, and theobromine are all called methylated xanthines and are usually referred to as xanthine derivatives, methylxanthines, or xanthines.

What are the effects of caffeine and other xanthines on the central nervous system?

Xanthines stimulate the central nervous system. Traditionally caffeine was considered the most potent methylxanthine; however, theophylline produces a more profound central nervous system stimulation action than caffeine. Caffeine effects the central nervous system in doses ranging from 85 to 250 mg.; the amount contained in 1 to 3 cups of coffee. Many individuals use caffeine to reduce drowsiness and fatigue, improve mood, alertness, and productivity. Caffeine increases capacity for sustained intellectual effort with clearer flow of thought. Doses above 250 mg. methylxanthines produce nervousness, insomnia, restlessness, and tremors. At higher doses focal and generalized convulsions have been observed.

What are the adverse effects associated with the use of caffeine and other xanthines?

Student athletes who use large amounts of caffeine may experience nervousness, irritability, insomnia, increased heart beat, hypertension, gastric distress, peptic ulcer, delirium, seizures, coma, and increased serum cholesterol.

What are the effects of caffeine on athletic performance?

Some studies have reported that long-term endurance exercise has been shown to be positively enhanced by caffein. Caffeine has been found to have no significant effect on high intensity, short-term work. Reports on caffeine's effect on VO2 max are inconsistent. The delay in the onset of fatigue is attributed to the sparing of muscle glycogen and to caffeine's lipolytic effect, or ability of the body to release more fat for energy. Coordination and other fine motor skills are not enhanced or diminished following caffeine ingestion. The NCAA limit for caffeine in a urine specimen is 15 micrograms per ml. Two cups of black coffee will yield urine levels of approximately 3 to 6 micrograms per ml.

Marijuana

What is the chemistry of marijuana?

Marijuana is derived from the plant *Cannabis sativa* which grows in many parts of the world. Most researchers agree that there is only one species (*sativa*) and all the variants belong to that species. Others believe that the variants are three distinct species. India is considered to have the most potent resin. Climate, soil, and selective plant breeding all have a large influence on the potency of marijuana.

There are more than 400 different chemicals in the cannabis plant. Delta-9-tetrahydrocannabinol or THC is the primary psychoactive agent in marijuana. THC is mostly concentrated in the flowering tops and upper leaves of the female plant. When the plant is crushed or eaten the flowering tops produce resin in which THC is found. In cultivated marijuana male plants are removed from the fields so that they can not pollinate the female plants. Lack of pollination increases the potency of female plants. This method produces a type of marijuana known as "Sinsemilla," which means "without seeds" in Spanish. It is one of the most potent varieties of marijuana available. The average concentration of THC is 7.5% and can reach as high as 24%. The amount of THC found in "street" sold marijuana ranges from 0.5% to 11%. Hashish is another cannabis derivative that contains the purest form resin.

Another derivative of the cannabis plant is "ganja" which consists of the dried tops of female plants. The weakest from of marijuana is known as "bhang," popularly called "ditch weed." It is made from parts of the cannabis plant that contain the least amount of THC. Marijuana is also mixed into drinks, teas, and cookie or brownie batter.

What are the behavioral effects of marijuana use?

A general analysis of the pharmacology of marijuana is difficult due to the variations in dosage, presence of contaminants, and the many additives and adulterants (such as PCP) added to marijuana products. Marijuana produces both central nervous system excitation and depression. These effects are expressed both behaviorally and neurophysiologically. In most individuals low to moderate doses of marijuana produce euphoria and relaxation. After a few minutes of holding the smoke in the lungs most people experience the "high." During this state the individual experiences a dry mouth, increased heart rate, loss of coordination and balance, and slower reaction times; however, the state of euphoria is usually short lived. A typical high from one marijuana cigarette may last from two to three hours. Impaired memory and impaired physical coordination are often side effects of use.

✎ **Weird Words**

Tolerance and Dependence: Tolerance to a drug means that the drug effect becomes less intense with repeated use. Frequent use of marijuana can produce tolerance, which means that higher doses are needed to obtain the same effects. Frequent use of high doses of marijuana in some cases can lead to physical and psychological dependence.

What are the physiological effects of marijuana use?

Marijuana affects the central nervous system (CNS). The effects of marijuana on the CNS can vary depending on the route of administration, the dosage, the setting and previous use. Marijuana users report a sense of altered perceptions associated with hunger. High doses can cause hallucinations, delusions, paranoia, and anxiety. Long-term users show a decreased interest in goals, decreased concentration, lessened ability to make appropriate decisions, and memory loss. Marijuana use can also cause serious damage to the lungs and impair respiratory function. Cannabis produces more tar than an equivalent weight of tobacco. Blood vessels of the eyes expand due to vasodilation causing a reddening of the eye. Some users experience high blood pressure. These effects can become intensified with the use of other drugs such as LSD and psychedelic "mushrooms."

Marijuana use may interfere with sexual function and reproduction. Marijuana increases vasodilatation in the genitals delaying ejaculation. High doses over a period of time lead to depression and a loss of libido and impotence. The total number of sperm per unit volume is decreased during ejaculation. These effects can be associated with lower fertility and a higher chance of producing abnormal embryo.

What are the effects of marijuana use on athletic performance?

Marijuana use can cause changes in personality and induce hallucinations, delusions, and symptoms of psychosis. The primary effects of marijuana produced on the CNS can impair short-term memory and perception. Other effects associated with marijuana use are tachycardia, bronchodilation, increased blood flow to the limbs, and decreased maximal work capacity.

Cocaine

What is the chemistry of cocaine?

Cocaine is an alkaloid extracted from the leaf of the coca plant, *Erythroxylon coca*. Free base cocaine is produced by the extraction of cocaine hydrochloride by using a base and a solvent. "Crack," which is free-based cocaine, is pure cocaine and is made by preparing an aqueous solution of cocaine hydrochloride and adding ammonia to alkalinize the solution and precipitate the cocaine in its alkaloid form. The free-based cocaine and crack are transformed when heated, and inhaled as smoke.

What is the pharmacology of cocaine?

Cocaine has two main pharmacological actions. This drug is a strong CNS stimulant and an effective vasoconstrictor when used as a local anesthetic. "Snorted" cocaine can produce its maximum CNS effects (in doses of 25 to 100 mg.) after 15 to 30 minutes. The effects included euphoria, a perceived increase in self control, greater work capacity, perceived long-lasting mental or physical work without fatigue, and perceived ability to forego food and sleep. These effects have also been referred to as the "perfect illusion." Cocaine affects the brain by stimulating the release of dopamine and norepinephrine, while also blocking their reuptake. In this way, more catecholamines stimulate the brain to the point of euphoria.

The main effects of intravenous cocaine last about 20 minutes. When cocaine is smoked or injected very high plasma concentrations of cocaine are achieved leading to the development of tolerance and physical dependence or addiction to the drug. Intravenous injection of cocaine effects can be seen within 30 seconds and wear off within 30 minutes. Abrupt termination of cocaine use can lead to psychological withdrawal.

What are the adverse effects associated with the use of cocaine?

Cocaine is a highly addictive drug. Individuals who use cocaine experience psychotic symptoms and euphoria, paranoid psychosis, delirium and confusion, seizures, and strokes caused by rupture of cerebral vascular vessels.

What are the effects of cocaine on athletic performance?

South American natives used cocaine for centuries to increase physical endurance and work efficiency. Early studies showed that cocaine had no positive effect on running times within a dose range of 0.1–20 mg/kg body weight.

What are the side effects of cocaine use specific to student athletes and the general population?

Cocaine related deaths from heart failure of Len Bias and Don Rogers in 1986 increased public attention to the harmful effects of cocaine use and abuse among athletes and the general population.

Heavy alcohol abuse combined with cocaine increases cocaine's cardiotoxicity by the production of "cocaethylene" as a metabolite. Cardiovascular side effects such as ventricular arrhythmia, angina pectoris, myocardial infarction, and cerebrovascular complications such as cerebral infarction. Cerebral hemorrhage can also result from cocaine use. Individuals differ in their ability to metabolize cocaine, and some experience seizures, headaches, optic neuropathy, insomnia, delirium, confusion, paranoia, hallucinations, psychosis, anorexia, sexual dysfunction, liver toxicity, and loss of smell.

Amphetamines

What are the various forms of amphetamine?

A variety of compounds contain amphetamine substances such as dextroamphetamine (Dexedrine) and methamphetamine (Desoxyn). Other similar drugs are phenmetrazine (Preludin) and methylphenidate (Ritalin). Illegal forms of amphetamine appears as crystals, chunks, and fine to coarse powders, off-white to yellow in color, and supplied loose (in plastic or foil bags) or in capsules or tablets of various sizes and colors. The drug may be sniffed, smoked, injected, or taken orally in tablet or capsule form.

Amphetamines are sometimes used in combination with other drugs such as barbiturates, benzodiazepines, alcohol, and heroin. Amphetamine misuse has declined dramatically since the near epidemic between 1950 and 1970. However, there has been a marked increase in the use of such other stimulants as cocaine and "designer" amphetamines that mimic the psychoactive effects of amphetamines—such as methcathinone (CAT) and MDMA (Ecstasy).

♣ It's A Fact!!

Common street names for amphetamines include:

• crystal	• speed	• meth	• bennies
• dexies	• uppers	• pep pills	• diet pills
• jolly bean	• copilots	• hearts	• footballs
• crosstops	• ice		

What are the general effects of amphetamines?

The effects depend on:

- the amount taken at one time
- the user's past drug experience
- the manner in which the drug is taken
- the circumstances under which the drug is taken
- the setting in which the drug is taken
- the user's psychological and emotional stability
- the simultaneous use of alcohol or other drugs

Amphetamine limits appetite, increases plasma free fatty acid levels and body temperature, and has effects on the cardiovascular and respiratory functions.

Amphetamines increase alertness and arousal; however, an extended level of arousal may change to anxiety or panic. Amphetamines cause feelings of intense pleasure when taken intravenously. Chronic use can lead to a condition generally called "behavioral stereotypy"—or getting "hung up." The individual will get caught up in the meaningless repetition of a single activity such as repeatedly cleaning the same object or taking objects apart.

What are the effects of amphetamines on athletic performance?

Athletes have used amphetamines to increase alertness and increase excitement for an upcoming event. One study (Goldberg, 1981) showed no correlation between subjective feelings of increased alertness in athletes taking amphetamine, or lethargy in subjects who were randomly given a tranquilizer, with any change in reaction time or manipulative skills. None of the athletes knew which drug they were taking. Chandleer and Blair (1980) reported improved athletic performance in knee extension strength, but reported no effect on overall sprint speed. Athletes taking amphetamines may sweat less than normal and be unaware of fatigue. This may lead to heat stroke during an athletic event.

Why would student athletes want to use amphetamines?

Student athletes have taken amphetamines to improve mood states, improve confidence, increase alertness and concentration, and increase endurance.

What are some of the unwanted side effects of amphetamines on athletic performance?

Amphetamine causes blood to flow away from the skin and increase the risk of heat stroke. In 1967 British cyclist Tommy Simpson died from complications from using amphetamine during the Tour de France. The Danish cyclist Knut Jensen died of heat stroke and cardiac arrest during the Olympic Games.

What are some of the main effects of amphetamines on the body?

Amphetamines increase heart rate and blood pressure, decrease appetite and increase weight loss, increase respiration, increase inability to sleep, increase dry mouth, and lead to headache and dizziness, heat intolerance, and lead to increased risk for kidney damage, cerebral hemorrhage, and seizures. Regular amphetamine use may lead to dependency, irritability, fearfulness (in some cases paranoia), apprehension, hallucination, and even psychosis. Heavy users of amphetamines may be prone to sudden, violent, and irrational acts, self-centeredness, distortions of perception, and paranoid delusions.

Peptide Hormones and Analogues

Human Growth Hormone (HGH)

The NCAA bans this hormones and its analogues.

What are the sources of HGH?

HGH is a naturally occurring polypeptide hormone produced by the anterior pituitary gland and secreted into the general circulation. HGH is released from the somatotroph cells of the anterior pituitary, which is under the control of the hypothalamic hormones.

What are the actions/effects of HGH?

HGH is one of the major hormones influencing growth and development in humans. A major function of HGH is the maintenance of normal linear growth from birth to adulthood. The metabolic action of HGH is also important in the regulation of energy production and storage.

Why would some student athletes want to use HGH?

Some individuals use HGH because they perceive that it is as effective as anabolic steroids with fewer side effects, and is not detectable in a drug test. Therefore, they may also choose to use HGH as a steroid substitute to prevent loss of muscle after discontinuing the use of steroids.

What are the effects of HGH on performance?

According to some controlled scientific studies HGH does not increase muscle strength. Most reports on HGH efficacies are either anecdotal or based on animal studies.

What are the side effects of HGH use?

The side effects of using HGH may lead to life-threatening health conditions, especially since some estimates report that athletes who use HGH to enhance performance are taking 10 times the therapeutic dosage. Some reported side effects of HGH are:

- developing irreversible acromegaly (abnormal growth of bones of the hands and feet and face) high blood pressure
- heart damage
- premature aging and death
- soft tissue swelling
- thickening of the skin, abnormal hair growth
- colonic polyps
- liver damage and glucose intolerance
- muscle weakness
- enlargement of the internal organs
- arthritis
- impotence

Adrenocorticotropic Hormone (ACTH)

The NCAA bans this hormone and its analogues.

Why would a student athlete be interested in using ACTH?

A student athlete might perceive that this substance would enhance muscular development.

What are the actions/effects of ACTH?

ACTH is secreted by the anterior pituitary and stimulates the adrenal cortex to produce and secrete adrenocortical hormones. Increased levels of corticosteroid levels in the plasma suppress ACTH secretion. Heavy use of anti-inflammatory corticosteroid-like drugs will decrease ACTH stores and negatively affect the pituitary gland. In the absence of ACTH stimulation the adrenal cortex may shrink.

What are some of the adverse reactions associated with the use of ACTH?

ACTH may mask signs of infection. Diabetics may have increased requirements for insulin or oral hypoglycemics. ACTH can also cause fluid and electrolyte disturbances, muscle weakness and loss of muscle mass, ulcerative esophagitis and peptic ulcer, impaired wound healing, headache and vertigo, increased intracranial pressure, menstrual irregularities, suppression of growth in children, and ophthalmic, metabolic and allergic reactions.

Other Ergogenic Aids

Erythropoietin (EPO)

The NCAA bans EPO.

What are the actions/effects of erythropoietin (EPO)?

EPO is a glycoprotein that stimulates red blood cell production.

Why would some student athletes want to use EPO?

The use of EPO is believed to increase oxygen absorption, reduce fatigue, and improve endurance by increasing the rate of red cell production. Promoters of EPO claim that this drug increases the metabolism and the healing process of muscles because the extra red cells carry more oxygen and nutrients.

What are the adverse effects associated with using EPO?

EPO causes an increase in the total number of circulating red bloods cells. This can lead to increased thickening (blood viscosity) of the blood. Added to the dehydration that frequently occurs in endurance sports, excess thickening of the blood takes place. The risk for coronary and cerebral artery blockages increases when the hematocrit (percentage of red blood cells in the blood) level exceeds 55%.

Diuretics

The NCAA bans use of diuretics.

What are the therapeutic uses of diuretics?

Diuretics are drugs that increase urination. These drugs are used medically used to control hypertension (high blood pressure), reduce edema, and to treat congestive heart failure.

Why would some student athletes want to use diuretics?

Diuretics have been used by athletes to achieve rapid weight loss, to reduce the concentration of drugs in the urine through rapid diuresis, and to reduce the likelihood of detection of banned drugs in a urine test. Athletes involved in weight-category sports have used a combination of heat exposure, exercise, food, and water restriction, self-induced vomiting, laxatives, and diuretics to lose weight. Diuretics have also been used by female athletes in conjugation with strict dieting which could lead to anorexia. Diuretics have also been used to manage premenstrual fluid retention.

What are some potential adverse effects associated with using diuretics?

Some individuals may experience dehydration, muscle cramps, dizziness, high potassium levels, high calcium levels, low blood sugar levels, headache, nausea, vomiting, drowsiness.

Chapter 47

Are Steroids Worth The Risk?

Dominic had baseball on the brain. Just being a good player wasn't enough—he wanted to be the best. He dreamed of playing pro ball someday, but he worried about the intense competition for positions on major league teams. His girlfriend, Deborah, was also a highly competitive athlete. Deborah's appearance and her performance were very important to her. She wanted to stand out and to have what she thought was the ideal body. Because of the pressure they felt to excel, Dominic and Deborah wondered whether steroids would work for them. They'd heard rumors about the bad side effects of using steroids, but they didn't have many facts. Here's the scoop on steroids.

What Are Steroids?

Steroids, sometimes referred to as roids, juice, hype, weight trainers, gym candy, or pumpers, are the same as, or similar to, certain hormones in the body. The body produces steroids naturally to support such functions as fighting stress and promoting growth and pubertal development.

About This Chapter: "Are Steroids Worth the Risk?" reviewed by Steven Dowshen, MD, July 2003. This information was provided by TeensHealth, one of the largest resources online for medically reviewed health information written for parents, kids, and teens. For more articles like this one, visit www.TeensHealth.org, or www.KidsHealth.org. © 2003 The Nemours Center for Children's Health Media, a division of The Nemours Foundation.

✎ Weird Words

Anabolic: Related to the building up in the body of complex chemical compounds from smaller simpler compounds (for example, proteins from amino acids), usually with the use of energy.

Anabolic Steroids: A steroid compound with the capacity to increase muscle mass; compounds with androgenic properties which increase muscle mass and are used in the treatment of emaciation. Sometimes used by athletes in an effort to increase muscle size, strength, and endurance. Examples include methyltestosterone, nandrolone, methandrostenolone, and stanozolol.

Androgen: A generic term for an agent, usually a hormone (for example, androsterone or testosterone), that stimulates activity of the accessory male sex organs and encourages development of male sex characteristics.

Steroids: A large family of chemical substances, comprising many hormones, body constituents, and drugs. There are eight principal classes of steroids.

Testosterone: A male hormone; the most potent naturally occurring androgen, formed in greatest quantities by the interstitial cells of the testicles.

Source: From *Stedman's Medical Dictionary, 27th Edition*, Copyright © 2000 Lippincott Williams & Wilkins. All rights reserved.

Anabolic steroids are artificially produced hormones that are the same as, or similar to, androgens, the male-type sex hormones in the body. The most powerful androgen is testosterone (pronounced: teh-stoss-tuh-rone). Although testosterone is mainly a mature male hormone, girls' bodies produce smaller amounts of it as well. Testosterone promotes masculine traits that guys develop during puberty, such as deepening of the voice and the growth of body hair. Testosterone levels also can affect how aggressive a person is and how much sex drive he or she has. Athletes sometimes take anabolic steroids because of their testosterone-like effects, such as increasing muscle mass and strength. Steroids can be taken in the form of pills, powders, or injections.

Another group of anabolic steroids, sometimes called steroidal supplements, contain dehydroepiandrosterone (DHEA) and/or androstenedione (also known as andro). Steroidal supplements are often sold at health food stores or gyms. The effects of steroidal supplements aren't well known, but it's thought that, when taken in large doses, they cause effects similar to stronger anabolic steroids like testosterone. Here's what is known: companies that manufacture steroidal supplements often make claims that are false and very little is known about the long-term effects on the body of some of these substances.

The term "steroids" is also used to describe some types of non-anabolic steroids, such as cortisone, which have other medical uses and are available by prescription to treat medical problems like asthma or arthritis. These steroid medications do not have the male hormone effects of androgens.

How Do Anabolic Steroids Work?

Anabolic steroids stimulate muscle tissue to grow and "bulk up" in response to training by mimicking the effect of naturally produced testosterone on the body. Steroids have become popular because they may improve endurance, strength, and muscle mass. But research has not shown that they improve skill, agility, or performance.

Dangers Of Steroids

Anabolic steroids cause many different types of problems. Less serious side effects include acne, oily hair, purple or red spots on the body, swelling of the legs and feet, and persistent bad breath. Some of the more serious or long-lasting side effects are:

- premature balding

- dizziness

- mood swings, including anger, aggression, and depression

- seeing or hearing things that aren't there (hallucinations)

- extreme feelings of mistrust or fear (paranoia)

- problems sleeping

- nausea

- vomiting

- trembling

- high blood pressure that can damage the heart or blood vessels over time

- aching joints

- greater chance of injuring muscles and tendons

- jaundice or yellowing of the skin; liver damage

- urinary problems

- shortening of final adult height

- increased risk of developing heart disease, stroke, and some types of cancer

Specific risks for girls associated with anabolic steroids include:

- increased facial hair growth

- development of masculine traits, such as deepening of the voice, and loss of feminine body characteristics, such as shrinking of the breasts

- menstrual cycle changes

Specific risks for guys include:

- testicular shrinkage

- pain when urinating

- breast development

- impotence (inability to get an erection)

- sterility (inability to have children)

Steroids can also have serious psychological side effects. Some users become aggressive or combative, developing "roid rage"—extreme, uncontrolled bouts of anger caused by long-term steroid use.

Steroid users who inject the drugs with a needle are at risk for contracting HIV (human immunodeficiency virus), the virus that causes AIDS, if they share needles with other users. People who use dirty needles are also at greater risk for contracting hepatitis, a disease of the liver, or bacterial endocarditis, an infection of the inner lining of the heart. It can be impossible to tell if your friend or an athlete on your team is sick. It's not enough to take their word for it; they may not know. Sharing needles is never safe.

Some people combine or "stack" anabolic steroids with other drugs. Other steroid users may "pyramid" or "cycle" their steroid doses, starting with a low dose of stacked drugs and then periodically increasing and decreasing the dosage of the steroid, which users believe helps their bodies recuperate from the drugs. Because it is difficult to understand how the drugs interact, there is the possibility of taking a deadly combination. As with medications that should not be taken together, anabolic steroids have the potential for negative interactions. Emergency departments have reported cases of vomiting, tremors, dizziness, and even coma (unconsciousness) when patients were admitted after taking combinations of steroids.

A lot of people tell themselves they'll only use steroids for a season or a school year. Unfortunately, steroids can be addictive, making it hard to stop taking them when you want to. Steroid users may spend lots of time and money trying to get the drugs. And once users stop taking steroids, they're at risk of developing irritability, paranoia, and severe depression, which may lead to suicidal thoughts or attempted suicide. Teens who use steroids may also be at greater risk for using other drugs, such as alcohol or cocaine.

Some of the long-term effects of steroids may not show up for many years. Lyle Alzado, a former Los Angeles Raiders defensive lineman, believed his prolonged use of steroids and growth hormones caused the rare form of brain cancer that affected his central nervous system before he died.

 Remember!!
Alternatives To Steroids

Anabolic steroids are controversial in the sports world because of all the health risks associated with them. Most are illegal and are banned by professional sports organizations and medical associations. As we know too well from the high-profile cases, if an athlete is caught using steroids, his or her career can be destroyed.

When it comes right down to it, harming your body or getting disqualified aren't smart ways to try to improve your athletic performance. Being a star athlete means training the healthy way: eating the right foods, practicing, and strength training without the use of drugs.

Chapter 48

Questionable Exercises

Introduction

Any activity selected for an exercise program should have something to offer that is a benefit (such as to improve flexibility, strength, or cardiovascular fitness). However, there are exercises that also can have elements that make them harmful. An exercise practiced by extremely physically fit individuals can be appropriate because the quality of movement they display in doing it meets the objectives for which the exercise was designed. If the same exercise were done by individuals with poor physical fitness (such as by people who lack flexibility or have weak abdominal muscles), their performance of the exercise could be deemed totally inappropriate (something they shouldn't be doing at all) because their quality of movement is poor.

Understanding The Spine

The spinal column (your "backbone") is made of vertebrae: 7 cervical (neck) vertebrae, 12 thoracic (chest) vertebrae, 5 lumbar (lower back), and 5 fused-sacral (pelvic) vertebrae. The sacral vertebrae (sacrum) transfer the weight of all structures above it to the other bones of the pelvis.

About This Chapter: Text in this chapter was excerpted and adapted from "Questionable Exercises," *Research Digest*, December 1999, President's Council on Physical Fitness and Sports. The full text, including references, is available online at http://fitness.gov/activity/activity2/digest_dec1999/digest_dec1999.html.

There are disks between all of the vertebrae. The outer fibers of each disc (called the *annulus fibrosis*) and its top and bottom (called the *vertebral end-plates*) enclose the disk's fluid center (which is called the *nucleus pulposus*). These intervertebral disks act as spacers and shock absorbers for the spinal column. The disks also permit movement between vertebrae. Any grouping of two vertebrae and the disk between them are called a "motion segment" of the spinal column. A motion segment is the smallest functional unit of the spine.

Spinal Movements

Neck (Cervical) Area: The cervical spine has an exceptional amount of movement. Cervical vertebrae can bend or extend about 145 degrees (from up to down), tilt about 90 degrees from side to side (about 45 degrees to each side) and turn about 180 degrees from left to right. The greatest amount of rotation occurs between the top two cervical vertebrae (which are called C1 and C2).

Trunk Area: The trunk has a more limited range of motion. In essence, bending the lower back is just a removal of the lordotic curve (the curved area of the lower back); people really do not flex their lumbar spines. If range of motion movement exceeds a person's ability, forward and back or side to side, there could be (a) compression damage to disks, nerves, and blood vessels on the side of the bending and (b) stretching of ligaments and other soft tissues on the opposite side. If range of motion ability in rotation is exceeded, the outer fibers of disks could be torn. The damage may be only small and seem insignificant at the beginning. The first few times the normal range of motion of a joint is exceeded, perhaps only a

♣ **It's A Fact!!**

If you are having difficulty imagining the structure of an intervertebral disk (the "shock absorber" between the vertebrae that up your spine), just think of it as a thin jelly donut. The donut part would represent the *annulus fibrosis* and *vertebral end plates*; the jelly would represent the *nucleus pulposus*. Some neck and low back problems relate to movement of the nuclear "jelly" material from its normal confines and into contact with pain receptors in the annulus fibrosis or adjacent tissues.

few bands of collagen (a protein that makes up the connective tissue in liga-ments, disks, and in other soft-tissue structures) is damaged. However, re-petitive microtrauma can eventually lead to serious damage of tissues.

Pelvic Area: The muscles crossing the hip joint can be viewed as "guy wires" that control pelvic positioning; if any of these guy wires are too tight, a person will have difficulty controlling pelvic position with the trunk muscles. The pelvis includes the five fused sacral vertebrae (that is, the sacrum and ilia). Because these joints (the sacroiliac) permit so little movement, the pel-vis in essence becomes the foundation of the spinal column. Therefore, tight-ness in any muscle crossing the hip joint can affect the biomechanics of the spine. It is for this reason that range of motion at the hip joint is often measured, and exercise programs try to improve it.

The normal range of motion for the hip joint in forward and backward bending is 135 degrees; this includes 10 degrees of hip extension and 125 degrees of hip flexion. Hip joint extension can be limited by tightness of the hip flexor muscles. When the knee-joint is extended, hip-joint flexion can be limited by the hamstring muscle group that crosses both hip and knee joints. Although other hip-joint muscles are also important, the flexors and extensors of the hip joint have greater roles in exercise considerations than do the other muscles.

Exercises Of Concern For The Spine

Cervical Spine Range Of Motion

The yoga plough is done by lying down on your back and extending your legs overhead and backwards behind your head and neck; this movement involves transferring body weight over the cervical spine. The purpose of this exercise is to stretch the lower back; however, the extreme amount of flexion of the neck that occurs in doing the exercise can be a problem. This exercise would be particularly inappropriate for individuals with either arthritis or osteoporosis of the spine, or in women or girls whose menstrual periods have stopped. This exercise may not pose a problem for healthy youngsters.

Exercises involving neck hyperextension (for example, as seen in neck circles) are considered potentially dangerous if done forcefully and quickly.

This type of exercise is inappropriate because it may result in the compression of nerve structures and blood vessels at the base of the skull, and potentially damage disks and other soft tissue structures. Obviously neck hyperextension can be dangerous for individuals with degenerative joint disease, osteoporosis, or those who have suffered whiplash injuries. Hyperextension movements can be considered safe if done slowly and with controlled movement in the normal range of motion.

One neck exercise with great risk is bridging, as done by wrestlers and football players to strengthen the neck. Bridging is inappropriate for almost everyone because of the extreme pressure it places on cervical disks.

✎ Weird Words

Ballistic Movement: Sudden (jerky) movement; a movement initiated by forceful muscle contraction followed by an inertial or coasting movement of the body part.

Ballistic Rotation: Ballistic rotation movements of the spine are quick, with little control; they have been cited as being a major cause of neck and low back problems because of the stress they place on disks and other structures of the spine. This movement is truly inappropriate.

Movement Quality: Typically individuals who are physically fit and have good body awareness, can do an exercise precisely as it should be done; thus, their quality of movement is usually good. However, individuals lacking in these variables may attempt the same exercise and produce such incorrect movements that for them the exercise is inappropriate.

Movement Tempo: If some exercise activities are done too quickly and without good body control, the momentum of the body part being moved may be so great that the movement exceeds the physiologic limits of a joint. This would be an example of a ballistic movement.

Repetitive Microtrauma: Also called repetitive motion injury. If you bend a paper clip a couple of times, it is still strong but its molecular makeup has been changed forever. With continued bending it will eventually break. This is similar to what happens in a repetitive microtrauma injury to soft tissue structures such as ligaments and intervertebral discs. The minor damage is not noted initially; however, by the time it becomes painful the injury has become serious.

Hip-Joint Flexion Range Of Motion

The movements inherent in both the fingertips-to-floor (touch your toes) and the sit-and-reach (sitting, reach toward your toes) exercises and tests have been questioned with respect to spinal dangers. If either activity is done repeatedly, and if the exerciser has tight hamstrings, the limited movement at the hip joint can transfer the stress to the connective-tissue structures of the spine. If the exerciser has good hip-joint flexibility, the activity is more apt to achieve what it is intended to do—namely stretch the hamstrings. If the tempo of the activity were increased markedly by someone with tight hamstrings, the torso would have greater momentum that is more ballistic in nature (sudden, quick, or bouncy), and there would be a greater chance of back injury.

An important point to remember in the fingertips-to-floor or sit-and-reach exercises is that the quality of the movement may be more important than the number of centimeters reached. A person who fails to reach 80 degrees of movement at the hip joint is more apt to stress in the connective tissue structures of the spine rather than stretch the hamstrings. Ideally the spine should make a smooth arc; there should neither be a flattening or an excessive curve in any area.

Hip-Joint/Trunk (Extension Strength)

In the previous discussion on spine extension range of motion, we mentioned that the movement is often done without active contraction of the muscles of the spine; therefore hyperextension movements are appropriate as long as they are done slowly and under total control (that is, not done ballistically). On the other hand, if strengthening the lower back muscles is the objective, the rules change. If there is active contraction of these muscles, you should not hyperextend the spine.

Trunk/Hip-Joint (Flexion Strength)

As mentioned earlier, the amount of lower back flexion is in essence limited to the removal of the lordotic curve and any subsequent flexion occurs at the hip. Because the abdominal muscles do not cross the hip joint, they obviously cannot produce flexion at this joint. However, individuals with weak abdominal muscles often do full-sit-up-type exercises entirely with their hip flexors; the role of the hip flexors in this type of sit-up becomes even more dominant if the feet are held.

The full sit-up (either with legs bent or straight) has been criticized for a number of years, and some researchers believe that this exercise can cause low-back injury. Some studies indicate that either the straight-leg or bent-leg sit-up can place extremely high compressive forces on intervertebral discs. The tempo of timed sit-ups can add to their drawbacks. For example, too much flexion may occur at the neck if the hands are placed behind the head. If done too quickly, movement quality dimin-

♣ **It's A Fact!!**

Too often we forget that while physical activity has many benefits, when done improperly it can have negative consequences. Some exercises, especially those designed to produce flexibility and muscle fitness, can cause harm.

ishes. An individual with strong abdominal muscles may be able to do this exercise at a speed of 20 repetitions per minute with good movement quality, but a person with weak abdominal muscles might be at risk for injury if they tried to maintain the same speed. A "crunch-type" exercise may be a safer alternative.

The Knee

Besides being the largest joint in the body, the knee joint is very complex. The knee is particularly susceptible to injury because of the high forces it sustains due to its location between the leg bones (femur and tibia). Poor technique or uncontrolled movement during exercises increases the risk of injury to the knee.

Exercises Of Concern For The Knee

Structures of the knee can be put at risk for injury when individuals perform flexibility exercises in which the hip is incorrectly moved outward during the stretch (such as the standing quadricep/hip-flexor stretch). In doing this stretch, the leg should be pulled straight back rather than back and to the side. A simple way to avoid the stress of pulling the leg to the side is to hold the ankle with the opposite hand.

The hurdler stretch is unique because it can be used for either stretching the hamstrings or quadriceps, dependent upon whether the body leans forward or backward. When used for stretching the hamstrings, the individual leans forward. In this position a considerable stress is placed on the bent leg; strain or discomfort in the hip and groin area may also occur because the femur of the bent leg is placed in extreme rotation. A safer alternative is to bend the knee in front of the body rather than to the side. When used for stretching quadriceps, the individual leans backward. This movement also has its drawbacks because the position of the bent leg does not allow the pelvis to rotate as the trunk is brought backward. This results in stress being placed on the lumbar spine. Furthermore, the leg rotation may damage the soft tissue structures of the knee.

> ### ✔ Quick Tip
>
> "When choosing an exercise, be sure that it is appropriate for you—that means doing it will help you achieve a fitness goal and that you can do the exercise in a safe manner. The microtrauma that can occur from repeatedly doing exercises that are unsafe for you can have long-term health and injury consequences." —Wendell Liemohn, Ph.D. Professor, Exercise Science University of Tennessee, Knoxville.

Exercises that involve knee hyperflexion (for example, 120 degrees or more) are also questionable. The supportive structures of the knee are placed in a vulnerable position in activities involving deep squatting or that are performed with added weight. They should be avoided by individuals who have a history of knee injury. Sports such as weight or power lifting, ballet, and gymnastics sometimes require movements that place the knee in a hyperflexed position of more than 90 degrees. Although elite athletes in these sports may be capable of performing knee hyperflexion exercises without any problem, other types of individuals may benefit less from them because of the risks of injury.

In general, high impact exercises are common causes of injury to the hip, knee, ankle, and foot. Particularly questionable are jumping or bouncing type movements in which the exerciser lands on one foot. High impact aerobic dance movements that require bouncing in the same spot can increase the risk of shin pain, compartment syndrome, and stress fractures of the tibia and fibula. A resilient exercise surface would lessen the chances of injuries.

> **☞ Remember!!**
>
> All questionable exercises have not been covered in this brief discussion. The main point is that certain exercises that are appropriate for some individuals may be totally inappropriate for others. The quality of the exerciser's movements is a most critical variable when evaluating exercises for inclusion in a conditioning program.

Chapter 49

Muscle Soreness

Maybe you just started playing basketball or you've added weight training to your workout. You felt fine yesterday, but you woke up this morning and—ouch! Suddenly, muscles you didn't even know you had are sore. Washing your hair feels like torture and your legs ache when you go down the stairs. This isn't what you bargained for—or is it?

Why do I get sore after I exercise?

Getting stiff and sore a day or two after exercising is natural, especially when you're trying something new. Even the most highly trained athletes get sore after intense exercise. It's called delayed onset muscle soreness (DOMS) because it kicks in about 24 to 48 hours after you exercise harder than usual. Your muscles feel like they're screaming because they're not used to the extra work yet.

When you exercise, your muscles get small tears that fill up with fluid. But don't freak out. Your muscles will repair those tears all by themselves. And every time your muscles "tear and repair," they get a little stronger. That means the more you do when you work out, the less likely you are to get sore.

♣ It's A Fact!!

Have you ever heard fitness gurus or coaches use the expression "go for the burn"? What are they talking about? Well, that "burn" is a sensation you get from something called lactic acid building up in your muscles. It's that warm feeling in your legs when you're sprinting hard or in your arms when you are doing a bunch of chin-ups.

Lactic acid is a by-product that your body creates when you do high-intensity anaerobic exercise. Unlike cardiorespiratory exercise, which is fueled by fat and carbohydrates (sometimes called glucose), anaerobic exercise burns carbohydrates. That's OK. It just means that your muscles work differently when you do anaerobic exercise. Add a few minutes of stretching to your workout to help your body eliminate the lactic acid and reduce muscle soreness.

Lactic acid is a natural part of your metabolic system. It may cause your muscles to "burn" and get tired quickly, but lactic acid isn't harmful or dangerous. In fact, the more anaerobic exercise you do, the better your body gets at clearing out the lactic acid that builds up in your muscles. That's why strength training seems to get easier as you get stronger. It's a sign that you're getting fit.

Source: This information is excerpted with permission from www.iEmily.com. © 2000 iEmily.com. All rights reserved. Complete information about iEmily.com is included at the end of this chapter.

How can I ease my sore muscles?

Sore muscles are your body's way of letting you know it has been working hard and could use a little TLC. Here are some soothing tips to try:

- Soak in a warm bath to help your muscles relax. Add some yummy-smelling bath oil, close your eyes, and think about the great workout you had.

- Stretch gently after your workout to help get rid of the lactic acid that has built up in your muscles and made them sore.

- Moving may be the last thing you want to do right now, but a brisk walk or swim followed by some stretching will help loosen up your body and keep you from getting stiff.

- Resting, icing your sore muscles, wrapping sore joints with an ACE bandage for support, and propping up tired limbs will help ease the pain.

How can I prevent getting sore?

Sore muscles aren't fun, but that mild discomfort (not pain) is a sign that you're doing something good for your body. Here are some tips that can help reduce muscle soreness:

- Rest for a day between workouts so your body has a chance to recover.

- Dehydrated muscles get sore and tired faster than well-watered muscles.

- Don't overtrain. Too much exercise too soon can lead to injuries. And you're more likely to burn out and give up on exercise if you overdo it.

Of course, if you feel more than mild discomfort, check with your health professional to make sure that your pain is not something more serious.

About iEmily

iEmily.com is a health website that provides teen girls with respectful, in-depth information about physical health and emotional well-being. The site includes articles reviewed by physicians, psychologists, and educators on nutrition, physical fitness, sexual health, emotional and psychological concerns, and other topics. iEmily.com also offers links to websites for additional information, as well as a list of hotlines for immediate help.

Chapter 50

Sports Injuries

Sport and other physical activities are fun and a great way to keep fit and feel good. When you enjoy sport and physical activity, the last thing you want is to miss out on sport because of injury. The good news is that, by following a few simple rules and using some plain common sense, many sporting injuries can be prevented.

Common Sports/Exercise Related Injuries

Sporting injuries usually fall into two separate groups. These are 'traumatic' or acute injuries and injuries caused by over use.

Traumatic Or Acute Injuries

Traumatic injuries are caused by a specific incident or trauma. Some examples of traumatic injuries are:

- twisting an ankle while running
- wrenching a knee by landing awkwardly
- strains, sprains, and broken bones
- cuts, grazes, and bruises

- head injuries

- injuries caused by being hit by a ball or other equipment used in your sport, falls, or contact with another competitor or participant.

Over Use Injuries

As the name suggests, over use injuries are injuries that happen more gradually and are caused by over using or over working a particular body part or muscle group.

Examples of overuse injuries are:

- a baseball pitcher over-using his arm for a whole season

- one incident of over use (the same pitcher pitching too long in one game)

- a ballet dancer over-using the feet, ankles, legs, and back

- a weight lifter using the same muscles over and over

- tennis elbow

✎ Weird Words

Strain: A 'strain' is the word used to describe an injury that happens when a muscle is damaged by being 'over stretched'. You have probably heard of football players who miss games because of 'hamstring' or 'groin' injuries. These are usually 'strain' injuries caused by a movement or action that stretched a particular muscle further than it was able to go without being damaged.

Sprain: The word 'sprain' is used to describe an injury to the muscles, tendons and ligaments surrounding a 'joint' such as an ankle or wrist. This type of injury can be caused by an awkward fall or landing, where the joint is 'forced' past its usual range of movement.

Fracture (broken bone): Broken bones are usually the result of some kind of impact. This could include being hit or kicked by an opponent, or be caused by a combination of momentum (the force caused by movement) and your own body weight during a fall. The term 'broken bones' is used to describe cracks in bone, clean breaks where the bone 'snaps', and 'compound fractures' where the broken bone actually pokes out of the flesh and skin.

Stress fracture: Stress fractures are tiny cracks or weak spots usually in the bones in the feet or lower legs. Stress fractures are also most common in people who perform 'high impact' sporting activities that involve a lot of running or jumping on hard surfaces. Your muscles usually absorb 'shock' when you move, like shock absorbers on a car. If you run, jump or exercise for too long or too often, your muscles become tired and are unable to absorb as much impact. This exposes the bones to increased stress, and fine cracks begin to appear in the surface of the bone.

Prevention Of Common Sport/Exercise Injuries

All of the injuries mentioned above can be very painful. They can mess up your sporting fun and your daily life. A serious injury to your wrist or shoulder could stop you being able to do basic things like dressing and undressing yourself, or washing your own hair in the shower. If your leg or another body part is in plaster, even having a shower can turn into a three act circus.

Fortunately, there are some basic steps you can take to reduce your chances of becoming injured during your exercise routine or your favorite sport.

Here are some guidelines that you can follow in preventing traumatic injury.

1. Warm up and cool down correctly before and after physical activity.

2. Use the proper safety equipment.

3. Drink plenty of fluids while exercising.

Use The Proper Safety Equipment

If any kind of safety equipment is recommended for your sport or activity, make sure you use it. Sport 'safety' equipment is important because certain types of injuries are common in certain activities. Safety equipment should be used during training as well as during the actual game or activity. Using the proper safety equipment will reduce your risk of injuries. Table 50.1 gives some ideas around sports and safety gear you should use.

Footwear

Whatever sport or physical activity you choose, make sure that you wear good quality, well fitting footwear. (It doesn't have to be the most expensive brand, good quality shoes can be less expensive because some companies don't spend as much on advertising.) Suitable shoes will support your feet and ankles, and help absorb high impacts like jumping and running. This is especially important in games like football and basketball where knee and ankle injuries are very common.

Drinks

It is important to have lots of drinks before, during and after sport and physical activity. This is to help avoid heat related injury. Getting too hot can lead to dehydration, heat exhaustion and heat stroke. This can be fatal.

Here are some more tips to avoid heat related injury.

- If it's a hot day, avoid outdoor exercise, especially in the hottest part of the day between about 10–11 A.M. and 3–4 P.M. If it's really hot, it can be best to consider canceling the event.

Table 50.1. Safety Equipment

Sport	Safety Gear
Skateboarding/Inline skating	Helmet, elbow pads, knee pads
Soccer	Shin pads
Horse riding	Helmet, proper boots
Cricket	Pads, gloves, helmet, and a "cup" (for males)
Cycling/Motor cycling	Helmet. Motor cycle riders should also wear thick protective clothing and gloves.
Football	Protective pads over the body
Baseball/Softball	Batters wear a helmet when batting. Catchers wear a helmet, facemask, and chest protector. Males should wear a "cup." Gloves.
Contact ball sports like rugby or hockey	Mouth guard

- For sport on hot/warm days a grassy shaded area is better than an open sunny area, especially if a sunny area has a hot surface. Even better, is an indoor, air-conditioned venue.

- Games or sport that are run over a long time, like long distance running, build up more heat in your body than quicker events like a 100 meter hurdle race. Keep this in mind.

- Make sure you drink lots of water.

- If you have put on weight since you last played sport, or if you aren't fit, you are at increased risk of a heat related injury. Take it easy. Build up your fitness slowly but surely. Have a medical check before starting a fitness program or sport.

- Wear a shady wide brimmed hat—and sunscreen.

- Avoid alcohol. Alcohol dehydrates your body.

Although this text gives some practical suggestions and information about health, it is important to see your doctor or health professional for information specific to a health concern you may have about yourself.

Cross Training

Cross training means doing a variety of exercises/sports as part of your exercise program. People who spend all of their time training for and playing one kind of sport may find that they are over using some muscle groups and joints, and basically ignoring others. For example, keen cyclists will build strength and muscle in their legs and lower body and improve their 'aerobic' fitness, but may be quite weak in their upper body. These people could benefit from activities such as rowing or resistance training to build up upper body strength.

Another good reason for cross training is to make sure that 'oppositional' muscle groups are developed evenly. Runners, joggers, and walkers usually have strong hamstrings (muscles at the back of the thighs), but these activities don't put as much strain on the quadriceps, an opposing muscle group at the front of the thighs. This means that the hamstrings are much stronger than the quadriceps. These two muscle groups are designed to work together but if one is stronger than the other, this can cause instability of the knee joints that can result in serious knee injuries. By alternating running or walking with another activity such as cycling or weight training, you can ensure that all of the muscles in your legs are getting an even work out.

Gradually building up strength and flexibility in all muscle groups will increase the muscle's ability to support joints and to absorb impact and protect the bones, all of which will greatly reduce the likelihood of injury.

Treatment Of Sporting Injuries

Any injury should be treated properly to prevent any further injury. This means looking after the injury by the "RICE" (rest, ice, compression, elevation) method immediately the injury happens. It also means letting the injury completely heal before returning to play. Use the "MSA" (movement, strength, alternate activities) method to help you with this.

It is important to treat any injury as soon as possible. If it is obvious that a bone is broken, if the injured area swells rapidly, or if the area below the injury goes white, cold, or numb, you need to seek medical treatment immediately.

Less severe injuries including minor sprains and strains should be treated straight away, using the R.I.C.E. method of treatment.

R: REST. Rest from activity. You might have to take the weight off your foot or leg or support your arm or shoulder in a sling, depending on the injury. Keep the weight off the injured joint for at least 24–48 hours.

I: ICE. Apply ice or a cold pack to the site of the injury as soon as possible. This will help reduce swelling. Keep the ice on the injury for about 10 minutes, and reapply every hour for the first 72 hours. Do not apply heat to a fresh injury. This will increase swelling and make an injury worse.

C: COMPRESSION. Firmly wrap the injured area, using an elastic bandage if possible. This will support the joint and also help to reduce any swelling. Don't wrap the bandage too tight. This will make the swelling worse. Don't try to use the injured area just because it is bandaged. The injury will need complete rest for 1–2 days.

E: ELEVATION. Try to keep the injured area elevated above the level of the heart when ever you are sitting or lying down.

If an injury is still painful after a couple of days of this treatment at home, you should see a doctor to make sure that the injury is not more serious than you first thought. Your doctor may need to prescribe anti-inflammatory' medication, or want to send you for x-rays to find out the extent of the damage.

After a joint or muscle group has had time to heal, you need to help it recover fully by introducing M.S.A.

M: Movement. After 1–2 days of rest, begin moving the injured joint (without putting weight on it). If the movement hurts, the joint will require more rest. Moving the joint will prevent internal scar tissue from restricting the joint's range of movement in the future.

S: Strength. Once the injury has healed and a full range of motion is possible, you may need to do some special exercises to strengthen the muscles that have been weakened by the injury. Your doctor, trainer or coach should be able to advise you about what is needed.

A: Alternate activities. Having an injury doesn't mean an end to your exercise program. It is possible to work 'around' an injury so that you can maintain overall fitness while still allowing the injury time to heal. For example, if you have injured a knee or ankle, you could do upper body work in the gym, or even swimming. If you have injured an arm or shoulder, you could still ride an exercise bike, walk, or weight training for the lower body.

Here are some more tips to avoid injury.

1. Have regular and thorough physical examinations, especially before beginning training or a sporting season.

2. Choose sporting clubs and venues carefully.

    • Choose venues that have equipment to deal with injury at the sporting site.

    • Choose clubs that have coaches who care for the physical health of individuals.

• Choose venues that use umpires who won't accept foul pay and rough play.

Warning

In some sports, someone may encourage you to try steroids to help your injury heal faster. Steroids are dangerous and can cause heart failure and damage to other organs. Many types of steroids are designed for treating farm animals and not for use by human beings. The methods described above are the best ways of healing an injury. Do not allow anyone to talk you into using steroids for any reason.

 Remember!!

Warming Up And Cooling Down

One of the most important things you can do to reduce the risk of serious injury is to warm up before strenuous activity, and to take the time to cool down' afterwards.

1. Walk around or pedal an exercise bike for 10 minutes. This will warm up the muscles, get the heart pumping and the blood flowing through the body. It will get the muscles ready to work well while playing sport or working out. These same exercises can be used to cool down afterwards.

2. Gently stretch muscle areas, holding each stretch for 10–20 seconds. Stretching your muscles before and after sport or exercise will make your muscles more flexible and reduce risk of injuries such as muscle strain. It is important to remember not to 'bounce' or use jerky movements when stretching. Try for a slow even stretch, stopping when you feel muscle resistance (and before you feel any pain). Hold the stretch for about 20 seconds, then slowly return to your starting position. Regular stretching exercises will help your body perform better during sport or exercise as well as other daily activities.

3. Your cool down routine should be similar and should include some gentle exercise that allows your body to cool down as well as some stretches. Cooling down properly means less stiffness and muscle soreness the next day.

Chapter 51

Preventing Foot Problems

Your Podiatric Physician Talks About Foot Health

The human foot is a biological masterpiece. Its strong, flexible, and functional design enables it to do its job well and without complaint—if you take care of it and don't take it for granted.

The foot can be compared to a finely tuned race car, or a space shuttle, vehicles whose function dictates their design and structure. And like them, the human foot is complex, containing within its relatively small size 26 bones (the two feet contain a quarter of all the bones in the body), 33 joints, and a network of more than 100 tendons, muscles, and ligaments, to say nothing of blood vessels and nerves.

Tons Of Pressure

The components of your feet work together, sharing the tremendous pressures of daily living. An average day of walking, for example, brings a force equal to several hundred tons to bear on the feet. This helps explain why your feet are more subject to injury than any other part of your body.

About This Chapter: Reprinted with permission from, "Your Podiatric Physician Talks about Foot Health," a brochure produced by the American Podiatric Medical Association, www.apma.org. © 2003 APMA. Reprinted by permission. "Shoes for Athletics" is excerpted with permission from, "Your Podiatric Physician Talks about Footwear," a brochure produced by the American Podiatric Medical Association, www.apma.org. © 2003 APMA. Reprinted by permission.

Shoe Buying Tips

- Have your feet measured while you're standing.

- Always try on both shoes, and walk around the store.

- Always buy for the larger foot; feet are seldom precisely the same size.

- Don't buy shoes that need a "break-in" period; shoes should be comfortable immediately.

- Don't rely on the size of your last pair of shoes. Your feet do get larger, and lasts (shoemakers' sizing molds) also vary.

- Shop for shoes later in the day; feet tend to swell during the day, and it's best to be fitted while they are in that state.

- Be sure that shoes fit well—front, back, and sides—to distribute weight. It sounds elementary, but be sure the widest part of your foot corresponds to the widest part of the shoe.

- Select a shoe with a leather upper, stiff heel counter, appropriate cushioning, and flexibility at the ball of the foot.

- Buy shoes that don't pinch your toes, either at the tips, or across the toe box.

- Try on shoes while you're wearing the same type of socks or stockings you expect to wear with the shoes.

- If you wear prescription orthotics—biomechanical inserts prescribed by a podiatric physician—you should take them along to shoe fittings.

Source: Excerpted with permission from, "Your Podiatric Physician Talks about Footwear," a brochure produced by the American Podiatric Medical Association, www.apma.org. © 2003 APMA. Reprinted by permission.

Foot ailments are among the most common of our health problems. Although some can be traced to heredity, many stem from the cumulative impact of a lifetime of abuse and neglect. Studies show that 75 percent of Americans experience foot problems of a greater or lesser degree of seriousness at some time in their lives; nowhere near that many seek medical treatment, apparently because they mistakenly believe that discomfort and pain are normal and expectable.

There are a number of systemic diseases that are sometimes first detected in the feet, such as diabetes, circulatory disorders, anemia, and kidney problems. Arthritis, including gout, often attacks foot joints first.

Specialized Care

Your feet, like other specialized structures, require specialized care. A doctor of podiatric medicine can make an important contribution to your total health, whether it is regular preventive care or surgery to correct a deformity.

In order to keep your feet healthy, you should be familiar with the most common ills that affect them. Remember, though, that self treatment can often turn a minor problem into a major one, and is generally not advisable. You should see a podiatric physician when any of the following conditions occur or persist.

Athlete's foot is a skin disease, usually starting between the toes or on the bottom of the feet, which can spread to other parts of the body. It is caused by a fungus that commonly attacks the feet, because the wearing of shoes and hosiery fosters fungus growth. The signs of athlete's foot are dry scaly skin, itching, inflammation, and blisters. You can help prevent infection by washing your feet daily with soap and warm water; drying carefully, especially between the toes; and changing shoes and hose regularly to decrease moisture. Athlete's foot is not the only infection, fungal and otherwise, which afflicts the foot, and other dry skin/dermatitis conditions can be good reasons to see a doctor of podiatric medicine if a suspicious condition persists.

Blisters are caused by skin friction. Don't pop them. Apply moleskin or an adhesive bandage over a blister, and leave it on until it falls off naturally in the bath or shower. Keep your feet dry and always wear socks as a cushion between your feet and shoes. If a blister breaks on its own, wash the area, apply an antiseptic, and cover with a sterile bandage.

Bunions are misaligned big toe joints which can become swollen and tender. The deformity causes the first joint of the big toe to slant outward, and the big toe to angle toward the other toes. Bunions tend to run in families, but the tendency can be aggravated by shoes that are too narrow in the forefoot and toe. There are conservative and preventive steps that can minimize the discomfort of a bunion, but surgery is frequently recommended to correct the problem.

Corns and calluses are protective layers of compacted, dead skin cells. They are caused by repeated friction and pressure from skin rubbing against bony areas or against an irregularity in a shoe. Corns ordinarily form on the toes and calluses on the soles of the feet. The friction and pressure can burn or otherwise be painful and may be relieved by moleskin or padding on the affected areas. Never cut corns or calluses with any instrument, and never apply home remedies, except under a podiatrist's instructions.

Foot odor results from excessive perspiration from the more than 250,000 sweat glands in the foot. Daily hygiene is essential. Change your shoes daily to let each pair air out, and change your socks, perhaps even more frequently than daily. Foot powders and antiperspirants, and soaking in vinegar and water, can help lessen odor.

Hammertoe is a condition in which any of the toes are bent in a claw-like position. It occurs most frequently with the second toe, often when a bunion slants the big toe toward and under it, but any of the other three smaller toes can be affected. Although the condition usually stems from muscle imbalance, it is often aggravated by ill-fitting shoes or socks that cramp the toes. Avoid pressure on the toes as much as possible. Surgery may be necessary to realign the toes to their proper position.

Heel pain can generally be traced to faulty biomechanics which place too much stress on the heel bone, ligaments, or nerves in the area. Stress could result while walking or jumping on hard surfaces, or from poorly made footwear. Overweight is also a major contributing factor. Some general health conditions—arthritis, gout, and circulatory problems, for example—also cause heel pain.

Heel spurs are growths of bone on the underside of the heel bone. They can occur without pain; pain may result when inflammation develops at the point where the spur forms. Both heel pain and heel spurs are often associated with plantar fasciitis, an inflammation of the long band of connective tissue running from the heel to the ball of the foot. Treatments may range from exercise and custom-made orthotics to anti-inflammatory medication or cortisone injections.

Ingrown nails are nails whose corners or sides dig painfully into the skin, often causing infection. They are frequently caused by improper nail trimming, but also by shoe pressure, injury, fungus infection, heredity, and poor foot structure. Toenails should be trimmed straight across, slightly longer than the end of the toe, with toenail clippers. If painful or infected, your podiatric physician may remove the ingrown portion of the nail; if the condition reoccurs frequently, your podiatrist may permanently remove the nail.

Neuromas are enlarged, benign growths of nerves, most commonly between the third and fourth toes. They are caused by bones and other tissue rubbing against and irritating the nerves. Abnormal bone structure or pressure from ill-fitting shoes also can create the condition, which can result in pain, burning, tingling, or numbness between the toes and in the ball of the foot. Conservative treatment can include padding, taping, orthotic devices, and cortisone injections, but surgical removal of the growth is sometimes necessary.

Warts are caused by a virus, which enters the skin through small cuts and infects the skin. Children, especially teenagers, tend to be more susceptible to warts than adults. Most warts are harmless and benign, even though painful and unsightly. Warts often come from walking barefooted on dirty surfaces or littered ground. There are several simple procedures which your podiatric physician might use to remove warts.

Shoes For Athletics

Different sports activities call for specific footwear to protect feet and ankles. Sports-specific athletic shoes are a wise investment for serious athletes, though perhaps a less critical consideration for the weekend or occasional athlete; nevertheless, it's a good idea to use the correct shoe for each sport. Probably a more important consideration is the condition of the shoe—don't wear any sport or other shoes beyond their useful life.

Athletic footwear should be fitted to hold the foot in the position that's most natural to the movement involved.

For example, a running shoe is built to accommodate impact, while a tennis shoe is made to give relatively more support, and permit sudden stops and turns. For sports, "cross trainers" are fine for a general athletic shoe, such as for physical education classes. But if a child is involved more heavily in any single sport, he or she should have a shoe specifically designed for that sport.

Shoe Care

For longer service, keep shoes clean and in good repair. Avoid excessive wear on heels and soles. Give your shoes a chance to breathe—don't wear the same pair two days in a row (you prolong the life of shoes by rotating their use). Never wear hand-me-down shoes (this is especially important for children).

Chapter 52

Compulsive Exercise

Rachel, head cheerleader, and her team practiced three to five times a week. They worked hard to keep their weight down so they could be lifted into the air during games. Always battling to keep those pounds off, Rachel began to add extra workouts before and after practice. Even though the team drills left her exhausted, Rachel felt she couldn't control her weight without extra workouts every day. Soon, her body was worn out and she couldn't even make it through a regular team practice.

You may think you can't get too much of a good thing, but in the case of exercise, sometimes a healthy activity can turn into an unhealthy compulsion. Rachel is a good example of how an overemphasis on physical fitness or weight control can become unhealthy. Read on to find out more about compulsive exercise and its effects.

Too Much Of A Good Thing?

We all know the benefits of exercise, and it seems that everywhere we turn, we hear that we should exercise more. Studies report that high-school

About This Chapter: Text is from "Compulsive Exercise," reviewed by Kim Rutherford, MD, August 2001. This information was provided by TeensHealth, one of the largest resources online for medically reviewed health information written for parents, kids, and teens. For more articles like this one, visit www.TeensHealth.org, or www.KidsHealth.org. © 2001 The Nemours Center for Children's Health Media, a division of The Nemours Foundation.

gym classes are being reduced and teens are finding it easier than ever to avoid exercising. Sitting in front of the TV or computer has become a way of life for many teens.

Exercise can do many things for your body and soul: it can strengthen your heart and muscles, lower your body fat, and reduce your risk of many diseases. Many teens who play sports have higher self-esteem than their less active pals.

Exercise is a refreshing stress-buster and can help keep the blues at bay with an endorphin rush. Endorphins are naturally produced chemicals that affect your sensory perception. These chemicals are released in your body during and after a workout and they go a long way in helping to control stress. So how can something with so many benefits have the potential to be harmful to you?

> ♣ **It's A Fact!!**
> Exercise can become a compulsive habit when it is done for the wrong reasons.

Signs Of Larger Problems

Changes in activity of any kind—eating or sleeping, for example—can often be a sign of something else that's wrong in your life. Many teens start working out because it's fun or makes them feel good, but exercise can become a compulsive habit when it is done for the wrong reasons. Some teens start exercising with weight loss as the main goal.

Although exercise is part of the safe and healthy way to control weight, these teens may have unrealistic expectations. We are bombarded with images from advertisers of the ideal body: young and thin for women; strong and muscular for men. To try to reach these unreasonable body ideals, teens may turn to diets, which can develop into eating disorders such as anorexia and bulimia. If they are frustrated with the results from diets alone, compulsive exercise may be added to speed up weight loss.

A teen athlete may also think that repeated exercise will help her to win an important game. Some teens add extra workouts to those regularly scheduled with their teams without consulting their coaches or trainers. The pressure to succeed may be causing these teens to exercise more than is healthy. Your body needs activity but it also needs rest. Overuse will cause injuries, things like fractures and muscle strains.

Fitness experts recommend exercising three times a week for at least 30 minutes to achieve better health. Most people exercise much less and some—such as professional athletes—do much more, but working out more than once a day is often a warning sign of compulsive exercise.

Am I A Healthy Exerciser?

How do you know if your fitness routine is out of control? The main difference between a healthy exercise habit and people who are exercise-dependent is how activity fits into your life. If you put workouts ahead of your classes, friends, and other responsibilities, you may be developing a dependence on exercise.

Rachel goes to the gym when she has a cold and runs in the pouring rain. She turns down dates and lies to her best friend rather than miss a workout. If she goes on vacation with her family, she worries about how she will be able to exercise. If she eats a large meal, she increases the amount of exercise she does that day. She also gets upset if she does a minute less exercise today than yesterday. These are all signs of compulsive exercise.

If you are concerned about your own or your friend's exercise habits, ask yourself the following questions. Do you or your friend:

- force yourself to exercise, even if you don't feel well?

- prefer to exercise rather than to be with friends?

- become very upset if you miss a workout?

- base the amount you exercise on how much you eat?

- have trouble sitting still because you think you're not burning calories?

- worry that you'll gain weight if you skip exercising for a day?

If you answer yes to any of these questions, you or your friend may have a problem. What should you do?

How To Get Help

The first thing you should do if you suspect that you or a friend is a compulsive exerciser is get help. Talk to your parents, a teacher or counselor, a coach, or another trusted adult. Compulsive exercise, especially when it is combined with an eating disorder, can cause serious and permanent health problems, and in extreme cases, death.

Because compulsive exercise is closely related to eating disorders, help can be found at community agencies specifically set up to deal with these issues. Your school's physical education department may have healthy body-image programs and nutrition advice available. Ask your teacher, coach, or counselor to recommend local organizations that may be able to help. They'll be able to direct you to help within your community.

Make A Positive Change

There are things you can do to help yourself as well. Compulsive exercising is part of a distorted body image and low self-esteem. You may see yourself as overweight or out of shape even when you are a healthy

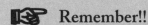 **Remember!!**

Exercise and sports are supposed to be fun and keep you healthy. Working out in moderation will do both.

weight. The first thing you can do to help is work on changing your daily self-talk. When you look in the mirror, make sure you find at least one good thing to say about yourself. Be more aware of your positive attributes. When you exercise, focus on the positive mood-boosting qualities. And try giving yourself a break! Listen to your body and give yourself a day of rest after a hard workout. Control your weight by exercising and eating moderate portions of healthy foods. Don't try to change your body into an unrealistically lean shape. Talk with your doctor, dietitian, coach, athletic trainer, or other adult about what a healthy body weight is for you, and how to develop healthy eating and exercise habits.

Chapter 53

The Female Athlete Triad: Amenorrhea, Osteoporosis, and Disordered Eating

With dreams of Olympic trials and college scholarships in her mind, Hannah joined the track team her freshman year and trained hard to become a lean, strong sprinter. When her coach told her losing a few pounds would improve her performance, she didn't hesitate to start counting calories and increasing the duration of her workouts. She was too busy with practices and meets to notice that her period had stopped—she was more worried about the stress fracture in her ankle slowing her down.

Although Hannah thinks her intense training and disciplined diet are helping her performance, they may actually be hurting her—and her health.

What Is Female Athlete Triad?

There's no doubt about it—playing sports and exercise are part of a balanced, healthy lifestyle. Girls who play sports are healthier; get better grades; are less likely to experience depression; and use alcohol, cigarettes, and drugs

About This Chapter: "Female Athlete Triad" was provided by TeensHealth, one of the largest resources online for medically reviewed health information written for parents, kids, and teens. For more articles like this one, visit www.TeensHealth.org, or www.KidsHealth.org. © 2003 The Nemours Center for Children's Health Media, a division of The Nemours Foundation.

less frequently. But for some girls, not balancing the needs of their bodies and their sports can have major consequences.

Some girls who play sports or exercise are at risk for a problem called female athlete triad. Female athlete triad—also known as female athletic triad—is a combination of three conditions: disordered eating, amenorrhea (pronounced: ay-meh-nuh-ree-uh, which means loss of a girl's period), and osteoporosis (a weakening of the bones). A female athlete can have one, two, or all three parts of the triad.

Triad Factor #1: Disordered Eating

Girls who have the disordered eating that accompanies female athlete triad often have many of the signs and symptoms of anorexia nervosa or bulimia nervosa, such as low body weight for their height and age and episodes of binge eating and purging. But girls with female athlete triad try to lose weight primarily to improve their athletic performance. Sometimes the disordered eating that accompanies this condition isn't technically an eating disorder. Many girls with female athlete triad are simply trying to become better at their chosen sports. But like teens with eating disorders, girls with female athlete triad may use behaviors such as calorie restriction, purging, and exercise to lose weight.

> **♣ It's A Fact!!**
> The condition female athlete triad was first recognized by the American College of Sports Medicine in 1992. Before then, doctors considered disordered eating separately from a girl's athletic participation, but health pros now know that athletic participation and the disordered eating in girls with female athlete triad are interrelated.

Triad Factor #2: Amenorrhea

Because a girl with female athlete triad is simultaneously exercising intensely and reducing her weight, she may experience decreases in estrogen, the hormone that helps to regulate the menstrual cycle. As a result, a girl's periods may become irregular or stop altogether. (In many cases, of course, a missed period indicates another medical condition—pregnancy. If you have missed a period and you are sexually active, you should talk to your doctor.)

Some girls who participate intensively in sports may never even get their first period because they've been training so hard—this is called primary amenorrhea. Other girls may have had periods, but once they increase their training and change their eating habits, their periods may stop—this is called secondary amenorrhea.

Triad Factor #3: Osteoporosis

Low estrogen levels and poor nutrition can also lead to osteoporosis, the third aspect of the triad. Osteoporosis is a weakening of the bones due to the loss of bone density and improper bone formation. This condition can ruin a female athlete's career because it may lead to stress fractures and other injuries due to weakened bones. Because of poor nutrition, a girl's body may not be able to repair the injuries efficiently.

Usually, the teen years are a time when girls should be building up their bone mass to their highest levels—called peak bone mass. Female athlete triad can lead to a lower level of peak bone mass and a lot of time on the sidelines. After she becomes an adult, a girl may also develop health problems related to osteoporosis at an earlier age than she would have otherwise.

Who Gets Female Athlete Triad?

Most girls have concerns about the size and shape of their bodies, but girls who develop female athlete triad have certain risk factors that set them apart. Being a highly competitive athlete and participating in a sport that requires you to train extra hard is a risk factor. Girls with female athlete triad often care so much about their sports that they would do almost anything to improve their performances. Martial arts and rowing are examples of sports that classify athletes by weight class, so focusing on weight becomes an important part of the training program and can put a girl at risk for disordered eating.

Participation in sports where a thin appearance is valued can also put a girl at risk for female athlete triad. Sports such as gymnastics, figure skating, diving, and ballet are examples of sports that value a thin, lean body shape. Some girls may even be told by coaches or judges that losing weight would improve their scores.

Even in sports where body size and shape aren't as important for judging purposes, such as distance running and cross-country skiing, girls may be pressured by teammates, parents, partners, and coaches who mistakenly believe that "losing just a few pounds" would improve their performance. Losing those few pounds generally doesn't improve performance at all—people who are fit and active enough to compete in sports generally have more muscle than fat, so it's the muscle that gets starved when a girl cuts back on food. Plus, if a girl loses weight when she doesn't need to, it interferes with healthy body processes such as menstruation and bone development.

In addition, for some competitive female athletes, problems such as low self-esteem, a tendency toward perfectionism, and family stress place them at risk for disordered eating.

What Are The Signs And Symptoms?

If a girl has risk factors for female athlete triad, she may already be experiencing some symptoms and signs of the disorder, such as:

- weight loss
- no periods or irregular periods
- fatigue and decreased ability to concentrate
- stress fractures (fractures that occur even if a person hasn't had a significant injury)
- muscle injuries

Girls with female athlete triad often have signs and symptoms of eating disorders, such as:

- eating alone
- preoccupation with food and weight
- continuous drinking of water and diet soda
- frequent trips to the bathroom during and after meals
- using laxatives
- presence of lanugo hair (fine, soft hair that grows on the body)
- tooth enamel that's worn away from frequent vomiting

- anemia (fewer red blood cells in the blood than normal)

- sensitivity to cold

- heart irregularities and chest pain

What Do Doctors Do?

It may be easy for girls with female athlete triad to keep their symptoms a secret because information about their periods and any damage done to bones usually isn't visible to friends and family. And lots of girls become very skilled at hiding their disordered eating habits.

A doctor may recognize that a girl has female athlete triad during a regular exam. An extensive physical examination is a crucial part of diagnosing the triad. A doctor who suspects a girl has female athlete triad will probably ask questions about her periods, her nutrition and exercise habits, any medications she takes, and her feelings about her body. Because poor nutrition can affect the body in many ways, a doctor might also test for blood problems and nutritional imbalances. Because osteoporosis can put a girl at higher risk for bone fractures, a doctor who suspects female athlete triad may also request tests to measure bone density.

Doctors don't work alone to help a girl with female athlete triad—coaches, parents, physical therapists, pediatricians and adolescent medicine specialists, nutritionists and dietitians, and mental health specialists all work together to treat the physical and emotional problems that a girl with female athlete triad faces.

It might be tempting for a girl with female athlete triad to shrug off several months of missed periods, but getting help right away is important. In the short term, a girl with female athlete triad may have muscle weakness, stress fractures, and reduced physical performance. Over the long term, a girl with female athlete triad may suffer from bone weakness, damage to her reproductive system, and heart problems.

A girl who is recovering from female athlete triad may work with a dietitian to help get to and maintain a healthy weight and ensure she's eating enough nutrients for health and good athletic performance. Depending on how much the girl is exercising, she may have to reduce the length of her workouts. Talking to a psychologist or therapist can help a girl deal with depression, pressure from coaches or family members, or low self-esteem and can help her find ways to deal with her problems other than restricting her food intake or exercising excessively.

Some girls with female athlete triad may need to take hormones to supply their bodies with estrogen so they can get their periods started again. In such cases, birth control pills are often used to regulate a girl's menstrual cycle. Calcium and vitamin D supplementation is also common for a girl who has suffered bone loss as the result of female athlete triad.

What If I Think Someone I Know Has Female Athlete Triad?

A girl with female athlete triad can't just ignore the disorder and hope it goes away—she needs to get help from a doctor and other health professionals. If your friend, sister, or teammate has signs and symptoms of female athlete triad, discuss your concerns with her and encourage her to seek treatment. If she refuses to seek treatment, you may need to mention your concern to her parent, coach, teacher, or school nurse.

Looking for ways to be supportive to your friend with female athlete triad? You may worry about being nosy, but don't: Your concern is a sign that you're a caring friend. Lending an ear may be just what your friend needs.

Tips For Female Athletes

Here are a few tips to help teen athletes stay on top of their physical condition:

- **Keep track of your periods.** It's easy to forget when you had your last visit from Aunt Flo, so keep a little calendar in your gym bag and mark down when your period starts and stops and if the bleeding is particularly heavy or light. That way, if you start missing periods, you'll know right away and you'll have accurate information to give to your doctor.

- **Don't skip meals or snacks.** You're constantly on the go between school, practice, and competitions, so it may be tempting to skip meals and snacks to save time. But eating now will improve your performance later, so stock your locker or bag with quick and easy favorites such as bagels, string cheese, unsalted nuts and seeds, raw vegetables, energy bars, and fruit.

- **Visit a dietitian or nutritionist who works with teen athletes.** He or she can help you get your dietary game plan into gear and can help you determine if you're getting enough key nutrients such as iron, calcium, and protein. And, if you need supplements, a nutritionist can recommend the best choices.

- **Do it for you.** Pressure from teammates, parents, or coaches can turn an activity you took up for fun into a nightmare. If you're not enjoying your sport, make a change.

☞ **Remember!!**

It's your body and your life. Any damage you do to your body now, you—not your coach or teammates—will have to live with later.

Part 6

Resources For Additional Help And Information

Chapter 54

The President's Challenge Sports Awards

Keeping America Fit

The President's Council on Physical Fitness and Sports (PCPFS) strives to make the health and fitness of all Americans a top national priority.

The President appoints 20 of America's most distinguished citizens to the Council. They hail from all walks of life: athletes, civic leaders, educators, business people, and health experts. Together they serve as a shining example, inspiring millions to live more active lives.

The PCPFS promotes the benefits of fitness everywhere it can by partnering with organizations across the country—including schools, boys and girls clubs, corporations, and more.

The Council's latest initiative is the new and improved President's Challenge for Americans age 6 and up. It's a series of programs designed to take fitness beyond the gym, and make it a lifestyle. Because everyone can benefit from staying active.

About This Chapter: This chapter includes excerpts from "The Fun Start's Here: Let's Go!" 2003–2004; reprinted with permission from The President's Challenge, the physical activity and fitness awards program of the President's Council on Physical Fitness and Sports. For additional information visit www.presidentschallenge.org.

The Active Lifestyle Program

The Active Lifestyle program is designed to help you make a commitment to staying active and sticking to it. It helps adults get active at least 30 minutes a day/5 days per week (or at least 60 minutes a day for youths under 18). All it takes is a few simple steps.

1. Choose An Activity: You can take the Challenge by yourself, or together with friends and family. Choose activities that you enjoy and make you feel good. For example, it could be walking, taking an exercise class, playing a sport, or doing chores around the house.

2. Get Active: You need to meet your daily activity goal (30 minutes a day for adults/60 minutes a day for youths under 18) at least 5 days per week, for a total of 6 weeks. You can take up to 8 weeks to complete the program.

3. Track Your Activity: Our online activity log makes it easy for you to track the time you spend on activities. You can log your time as often as you want, in increments as short as 5 minutes (visit www.presidentschallenge.org). You can also keep track of your progress on paper with an activity log form (contact The President's Challenge at 800-258-8146 to obtain a copy). Keep in mind, however, that using a log form on paper means an online record of the activity points you earn—which could apply to other programs in the President's Challenge—will not be available.

4. Earn Your Award: Whenever you reach a goal, the Active Lifestyle program recognizes your accomplishment with special awards. Awards are available online, by mail, fax, or phone. You can then continue earning awards in the Active Lifestyle program or move on to the next challenge: the Presidential Champions program.

The Presidential Champions Program

The Presidential Champions program is for adults who are active more than 30 minutes a day/5 days per week (or more than 60 minutes a day for youths under 18). There's even a special track for athletes and others who train at more advanced levels. You can only join the Presidential Champions program online at www.presidentschallenge.org. Taking part in the program takes just a few simple steps:

1. Choose An Activity: Select activities that you enjoy and make you feel good. For example, you could go running, walk the dog, or participate in martial arts. You can take the Challenge by yourself, or together with friends and family.

2. Get Active: Your goal is to see how many points you can earn by being active. You'll earn points for every activity you log. Points are based on the amount of energy each activity burns. So the more active you are, the more points you'll get.

3. Track Your Activity: Our online activity log makes it easy for you to track the time you spend on activities. You can log your time as often as you want, in amounts as short as 5 minutes. Although you can't log time for activities you haven't done yet, you can go back up to 7 days to enter past activities.

4. Earn Your Award: The Presidential Champions program recognizes your accomplishments with special awards. The first goal to aim for is a Bronze award. Then you can keep going for a Silver or Gold. Awards are available online, by mail, phone or fax. You'll find all the program details—including how many points are needed for each award level—online at www.presidentschallenge.org. The only thing left to do is to log on and sign up.

The Physical Fitness Program

The Physical Fitness Program includes five events that measure muscular strength/endurance, cardiorespiratory endurance, speed, agility and flexibility. The program offers three different awards:

The Presidential Physical Fitness Award: This award recognizes youths who achieve an outstanding level of physical fitness. Boys and girls who score at or above the 85th percentile (based on the 1985 School Population Fitness Survey) on all five events are eligible for this award.

The National Physical Fitness Award: This award is for those who score at or above the 50th percentile on all five events—but fall below the 85th percentile in one or more of the events. This demonstrates a basic, yet challenging, level of physical fitness.

The Participant Physical Fitness Award: Those whose scores fall below the 50th percentile on one or more events receive this award for taking part in the Physical Fitness Test.

The Health Fitness Program

This program recognizes students who achieve a healthy level of fitness. It also offers schools an alternative to the traditional Physical Fitness Program.

Youths can earn this award by meeting the qualifying standards in each of five events: partial curl-ups, one-mile run/walk, V-sit or sit and reach, right angle push-ups or pull-ups, and Body Mass Index (BMI). A BMI calculator can be found on the President's Challenge website at www.presidents challenge.org/tools_to_help/bmi-aspx.

Stay Connected

To learn more about these programs, how to perform and score the tests, or to receive information about accommodating students with disabilities visit www.presidentschallenge.org or call toll-free at 800-258-8146.

You can ask for helpful information (like the *Get Fit!* handbook and PCPFS *Research Digest*), sign up for the *Fitness Is Fun* newsletter, or find answers to your questions.

The President's Challenge
501 N. Morton, Suite 104
Bloomington, IN 47404
Toll-Free: 800-258-8146
Website: http://www.presidentschallenge.org
E-mail: preschal@indiana.edu

The President's Council on Physical Fitness and Sports
Hubert Humphrey Building
200 Independence Avenue SW, Rm. 738H
Washington, DC 20201-0004
Phone: 202-690-9000
Website: http://www.fitness.gov

Chapter 55

Fitness Organizations

General Sports and Fitness Organizations

Aerobics and Fitness Association of America
15250 Ventura Blvd., Suite 200
Sherman Oaks, CA 91403
Toll-Free: 877-YOURBODY
(877-968-7263)
Phone: 818-9050040
Fax: 818-990-5468
Website: http://www.afaa.com
E-mail: contactAFAA@afaa.com

Amateur Athletic Union
National Headquarters
1910 Hotel Plaza Blvd.
P.O. Box 22409
Lake Buena Vista, FL 32830
Toll-Free: 800-AAU-4USA
Phone: 407-934-7200
Fax: 407-934-7242
Website: http://www.aausports.org

American Alliance for Health, Physical Education, Recreation and Dance
1900 Association Dr.
Reston, VA 20191-1598
Toll-Free: 800-213-7193
Website: http://www.aahperd.org

American College of Sports Medicine (ACSM)
P.O. Box 1440
Indianapolis, IN 46206-1440
Phone: 317-637-9200
Fax: 317-634-7817
Website: http://www.acsm.org
E-mail: publicinfo@acsm.org

About This Chapter: The list of organizations in this chapter was compiled from many sources deemed accurate. Inclusion does not constitute endorsement. All contact information was verified in February 2004.

American Council on Exercise
4851 Paramount Drive
San Diego, CA 92123
Toll-Free: 800-825-3636
Phone: 858-279-8227
Fax: 858-279-8064
Website: http://www.acefitness.org
E-mail: support@acefitness.org

BAM! (Body And Mind)
Centers for Disease Control and
Prevention (CDC)
1600 Clifton Road, MS C-04
Atlanta, GA 30333
Website: http://www.bam.gov
E-mail: bam@cdc.gov

Idea, Inc.
10455 Pacific Center Court
San Diego, CA 92121-4339
Toll-Free: 800-999-4332
Phone: 858-535-8979
Fax: 858-535-8234
Website: http://www.ideafit.com

iEmily.com
136 West Street, Suite 201
Northampton, MA 01060
Phone: 413-587-0244
Website: http://www.iemily.com
E-mail:
iemily@healthcommunities.com

National Association for Fitness Certification
Bodybasics Fitness Training
Sierra Vista, AZ 85635
Toll-Free: 800-324-8315
Phone: 520-452-8712
Website: http://www.body-basics.com

National Collegiate Athletic Association
700 W. Washington Street
P.O. Box 6222
Indianapolis, Indiana 46206-6222
Phone: 317-917-6222
Fax: 317-917-6888
Website: http://www.ncaa.org

National High School Athletic Coaches Association
P.O. Box 4342
Hamden, CT 06514
Phone: 203-288-7473
Fax: 203-288-8224
Website: http://www.hscoaches.org
E-mail: office@hscoaches.org

President's Challenge
501 N. Morton, Suite 104
Bloomington, IN 47404
Toll-Free: 800-258-8146
Fax: 812-855-8999
Website: http://
www.presidentschallenge.org
E-mail: preschal@indiana.edu

President's Council on Physical Fitness and Sports

200 Independence Ave. SW, Rm. 738H
Washington, DC 20201-0004
Phone: 202-690-9000
Fax: 202-690-5211
Website: http://www.fitness.gov
E-mail: pcpfs@osophs.dhhs.gov

Shape Up America!

c/o WebFront Solutions Corporation
15009 Native Dancer Road
N. Potomac, MD 20787
Phone: 240-631-6533
Fax: 240-632-1075
Website: http://www.shapeup.org
E-mail: customer-care@shapeup.org

Special Olympics

1325 G Street, NW, Suite 500
Washington, DC 20005
Phone: 202-628-3630
Fax: 202-824-0200
Website: http://
www.specialolympics.org
E-mail: info@specdialolympics.org

Women's Sports Foundation

Eisenhower Park
East Meadow, NY 11554
Toll-Free: 800-227-3988
Phone: 516-542-4700
Fax: 516-542-4716
Website: http://
www.womenssportsfoundation.org
E-mail: wosport@aol.com

Nutrition Information

American Dietetic Association

120 S. Riverside Plaza, Suite 2000
Chicago, IL 60606-6995
Toll-Free: 800-366-1655
Website: http://www.eatright.org

International Food Information Council Foundation

1100 Connecticut Ave. NW, Suite 430
Washington, DC 20036
Phone: 202-296-6540
Fax: 202-296-6547
Website: http://www.ific.org
E-mail: foodinfo@ific.org

National Eating Disorders Association

603 Stewart St., Suite 803
Seattle, WA 98101
Toll-Free: 800-931-2237
Phone: 206-382-3587
Website: http://
www.nationaleatingdisorders.org
E-mail:
info@nationaleatingdisorders.org

Weight-control Information Network

1 Win Way
Bethesda, MD 20892-3665
Toll-Free: 877-946-4627
Phone: 202-828-1025
Fax: 202-828-1028
Website: http://www.niddk.nih.gov/
health/nutrit/win.htm
E-mail: win@info.niddk.nih.gov

Sports-Specific Organizations

Baseball and Softball

Amateur Softball Association of America
2801 NE 50th Street
Oklahoma City, OK 73111
Toll-Free: 800-654-8337
Phone: 405-424-5266
Website: http://
www.asasoftball.com

Little League Baseball International
P.O. Box 3485
Williamsport, PA 17701
Phone: 570-326-1921
Fax: 570-322-2376
Website: http://www.littleleague.org

National Softball Association (NSA)
P.O. Box 7
Nicholasville, KY 40340
Phone: 859-887-4114
Fax: 859-887-4874
Website: http://www.playnsa.com
E-mail: nsahdqtrs@aol.com

PONY Baseball and Softball
International Headquarters
P.O. Box 225
Washington, PA 15301-0225
Phone: 724-225-1060
Fax: 724-225-9852
Website: http://www.pony.org
E-mail: pony@pony.org

USA Baseball Headquarters
P.O. Box 1131
Durham, NC 27702
Phone: 919-474-8721
Fax: 919-474-8822
Website: http://www.usabaseball.com
E-mail: info@usabaseball.com

Basketball

Jr. NBA and Jr. WNBA
P.O. Box 8066
Wausau, WI 54402
Toll-Free: 800-NBA-0548
Phone: 715-261-9390
Fax: 715-261-9560
Website: http://www.nba.com/jrnba
E-mail: fanrelations@NBA.com

Mid-America Youth Basketball
216 N. Main
P.O. Box 348
Newton, KS 67114
Phone: 316-284-0354
Fax: 316-284-0294
Website: http://www.mayb.com
E-mail: mayb@mayb.com

National Junior Basketball
555 N. Parkcenter Dr., Suite 130
Santa Ana, CA 92705
Phone: 714-541-4450
Fax: 714-541-5145
Website: http://www.njbl.org
E-mail: info@njbl.org

Youth Basketball of America
10325 Orangewood Blvd.
Orlando, FL 32821
Phone: 407-363-9262
Fax: 407-363-0599
Website: http://www.yboa.org

Boating and Watercraft

American Canoe Association
7432 Alban Station Blvd.
Suite B-232
Springfield, VA 22150
Phone: 703-451-0141
Website: http://www.acanet.org

National Safe Boating Council
P.O. Box 509
Bristow, VA 20136
Phone: 703-361-4294
Fax: 703-361-5294
Website: http://
www.safeboatingcouncil.org
E-mail:
NSBCdirect@safeboatingcouncil.org

USA Canoe/Kayak
230 South Tryon Street, Suite 220
Charlotte, NC 28202
Phone: 704-348-4330
Fax: 704-348-4418
Website: http://
www.usacanoekayak.org
info@usack.org

Bicycling

Bicycle Helmet Safety Institute
4611 Seventh Street South
Arlington, VA 22204-1419
Phone/Fax: 703-486-0100
Website: http://www.bhsi.org
E-mail: info@helmets.org

USA Cycling
1 Olympic Plaza
Colorado Springs, CO 80909
Phone: 719-866-4581
Fax: 719-866-4528
Website: http://www.usacycling.org
E-mail: membership@usaccling.org

Cheerleading

American Cheerleading
Lifestyle Media, Inc.
110 William Street, 23rd Floor
New York, NY 10038
Phone: 646-459-4800
Fax: 646-459-4900
Website: http://
www.americancheerleader.com

Pop Warner Little Scholars, Inc.
586 Middletown Blvd., Suite C-100
Langhorne, PA 19047
Phone: 215-752-2691
Fax: 215-752-2879
Website: http://www.popwarner.com

Varsity.com
6745 Lenox Center Court
Memphis, TN 38115
Toll-Free: 800-238-0286
Phone: 901-387-4306
Fax: 901-387-4357
Website: http://www.varsity.com

Equestrian Activities

National Barrel Horse Association
P.O. Box 1988
Augusta, GA 30901
Phone: 706-722-7223
Fax: 706-722-9575
Website: http://www.nbha.com
E-mail: nbha@nbha.com

United States Dressage Foundation
220 Lexington Green Circle, Suite 510
Lexington, KY 40503
Phone: 859-971-2277
Fax: 859-971-7722
Website: http://www.usdf.org
E-mail: events@usdf.org

United States Equestrian Federation
4047 Iron Works Parkway
Lexington, KY 40511
Phone: 859-258-2472
Fax: 859-231-6662
Website: http://www.usef.org

United States Pony Clubs, Inc.
4041 Iron Works Parkway
Lexington, KY 40511
Phone: 859-254-7669
Fax: 859-233-4652
Website: http://www.ponyclub.org
E-mail: activities@ponyclub.org

US Equestrian Team (USET)
Pottersville Road, P.O. Box 355
Gladstone, NJ 07934
Phone: 908-234-1251
Fax: 908-234-9417
Website: http://www.uset.org

Football

NFL for Kids
280 Park Avenue
New York, NY 10017
Website: http://www.playfootball.com

Pop Warner Little Scholars, Inc.
586 Middletown Blvd., Suite C-100
Langhorne, PA 19047
Phone: 215-752-2691
Fax: 215-752-2879
Website: http://www.popwarner.com

Golf

Hook A Kid On Golf
2050 Vista Parkway
West Palm Beach, FL 33411
Toll-Free: 800-729-2057
Fax: 561-712-9887
Website: http://
www.hookakidongolf.org
E-mail: info@hookakidongolf.org

Junior Links
USGA Foundation
Copper Building
1631 Mesa Ave.
Colorado Springs, CO 80906
Phone: 719-471-4810
Website: http://www.juniorlinks.com
E-mail: juniorlinks@usga.org

Kids Golf

P.O. Box 30098
Palm Beach Gardens, FL 33420
Phone: 561-691-1700
Website: http://www.kidsgolf.com
E-mail: WorldKidsGolf@aol.com

U.S. Kids Golf

3040 Northwoods Parkway
Norcross, GA 30071
Toll-Free: 888-3-US KIDS (888-387-5437)
Phone: 770-441-3077
Fax: 770-448-3069
Website: http://www.uskidsgolf.com
E-mail: customerservice@uskidsgolf.com

Gymnastics

International GYMNAST Magazine

P.O. Box 721020
Norman, OK 73070
Phone: 405-447-9988
Fax: 405-447-5810
Website: http://www.intlgymnast.com
E-mail: customerservice@intlgymnast.com

USA Gymnastics

Pan Am Plaza, Suite 300
201 S. Capitol Avenue
Indianapolis, IN 46225
Toll-Free: 800-345-4719
Phone: 317-237-5050
Fax: 317-237-5069
Website: http://www.usa-gymnastics.org

Hockey

USA Hockey

1775 Bob Johnson Drive
Colorado Springs, CO 80906
Phone: 719-576-USAH (8724)
Fax: 719-538-1160
Website: http://www.usahockey.com
E-mail: comments@usahockey.com

United States Field Hockey

1 Olympic Plaza
Colorado Springs, CO 80909-5773
Phone: 719-866-4567
Fax: 719-632-0979
Website: http://www.usfieldhockey.com
E-mail: usfha@usfieldhockey.com

Racquet Sports

College and Junior Tennis

100 Harbor Road
Port Washington, NY 11050
Phone: 516-883-6601
Fax: 516-796-2854
Website: http://www.clgandjrtennis.com
E-mail: info@collegeandjuniortennis.com

U.S. Racquetball Association

P.O. Box 983
Wilbraham, MA 01095-0983
Phone: 413-539-0399
Website: http://www.usra.org

U.S. Tennis Association
70 West Red Oak Lane
White Plains, NY 10604
Phone: 914-696-7000
Website: http://www.usta.com
E-mail: feedback@usta.com

Skating and Skateboarding

Aggressive Skaters Association
13468 Beach Avenue
Marina del Rey, CA 90292
Phone: 310-823-1865
Fax: 310-823-4146
Website: http://www.asaskate.com
E-mail: info@asaskate.com

International Inline Skating Association
7210 Trailmark Dr.
Wilmington, NC 28405
Phone: 718-874-2424
Website: http://www.iisa.org
E-mail: director@iisa.org

United Skateboarding Association (USA)
P.O. Box 986
New Brunswick, NJ 08903
Phone: 732-432-5400 ext. 2168 or
ext. 2169
Fax: 732-432-5410
Website: http://
www.unitedskate.com
info@unitedskate.com

U.S. Figure Skating
20 First Street
Colorado Springs, CO 80906
Phone: 719-635-5200
Fax: 719-635-9548
Website: http://www.usfsa.org
E-mail: info@usfigureskating.org

Soccer

American Youth Soccer Organization
12501 S. Isis Ave.
Hawthorne, CA 90250
Toll-Free: 800-872-2976
Website: http://soccer.org

CC United
P.O. Box 62
Cedar Park, TX 78613
Phone: 512-331-0180
Fax: 800-742-0065
Website: http://www.ccunited.com
E-mail: info@ccunited.com

Major League Soccer
110 East 42nd Street, 10th Floor
New York, NY 10017
Phone: 212-450-1200
Fax: 212-450-1300
Website: http://www.mlsnet.com

US Youth Soccer
1717 Firman Drive, Suite 900
Richardson, TX 75081
Toll-Free: 800-4SOCCER
Fax: 972-235-4480
Website: http://usysa.org
E-mail:
nationaloffice@usyouthsoccer.org

Swimming and Other Water Sports

Aquatic Exercise Association
3439 Technology Drive, Suite 6
North Venice, FL 34275-3627
Toll-Free: 888-AEA-WAVE
Phone: 941-486-8600
Fax: 941-486-8820
Website: http://www.aeawave.com
E-mail: info@aeawave.com

National Scholastic Surfing Association
P.O. Box 495
Huntington Beach, CA 92648
Phone: 714-536-0445
Fax: 714-960-4380
Website: http://www.nssa.org

Surfrider Foundation
P.O. Box 6010
San Clemente, CA 92674-6010
Toll-Free: 800-743-SURF
Phone: 949-492-8170
Fax: 949-492-8142
Website: http://surfrider.org

United States Diving, Inc.
201 S. Capitol Ave., Suite 430
Indianapolis, IN 46225
Phone: 317-237-5252
Fax: 317-237-5257
Website: http://www.usadiving.org
E-mail: usdiving@usdiving.org

United States Surfing Federation
P.O. Box 1070
Virginia Beach, VA 23451
Toll-Free: 888-9US-SURF
Website: http://www.ussurf.org

United States Synchronized Swimming
201 S. Capitol Ave., Suite 901
Indianapolis, IN 46225
Phone: 317-237-5700
Fax: 317-237-5705
Website: http://www.usasynchro.org

U.S. Swimming
One Olympic Plaza
Colorado Springs, CO 80909
Phone: 719-866-4578
Website: http://www.usswim.org

U.S. Water Polo
1531 Mesa Ave., Suite A-1
Colorado Springs, CO 80904
Phone: 719-634-0699
Fax: 719-634-0866
Website: http://www.usawaterpolo.org

U.S.A. Water Ski
1251 Holy Cow Road
Polk City, FL 33868
Phone: 863-324-4341
Fax: 863-325-8259
Website: http://usawaterski.org
E-mail:
usawaterski@usawaterski.org

Volleyball

Starlings Volleyball Clubs, USA
P.O. Box 232416
Encinitas, CA 92023-2416
Phone: 760-230-1870
Fax: 760-230-1871
Website: http://www.starlings.org

United States Youth Volleyball League
12501 South Isis Avenue
Hawthorne, CA 90250
Toll-Free: 888-988-7985
Phone: 310-643-8398
Fax: 310-643-8396
Website: http://www.volleyball.org
E-mail: USYVL@aol.com

USA Volleyball
715 South Circle Drive
Colorado Springs, CO 80910
Phone: 719-228-6800
Fax: 719-228-6899
Website: http://www.usavolleyball.org
E-mail: postmaster@usav.org

Walking, Running, and Jumping

American Hiking Society
1422 Fenwick Lane
Silver Spring MD 20910
Phone: 301-565-6704
Fax: 301-565-6714
Website: http://
www.americanhiking.org
E-mail: info@americanhiking.org

American Running Association
4405 East West Highway, Suite 405
Bethesda, MD 20814
Toll-Free: 800-776-2732
Phone: 301-913-9517
Website: http://
www.americanrunning.org
E-mail: run@americanrunning.org

North American Race Walking Foundation
P. O. Box 50312
Pasadena, CA 91115-0312
Phone: 626-441-5459
Fax: 626-799-5106
Website: http://
www.members.aol.com/rwnarf
E-mail: NARWF@aol.com

U.S. Amateur Jump Rope Federation
P.O. Box 569
Huntsville, TX 77342-0569
Toll-Free: 800-225-8820
Phone: 936-295-3332
Fax: 936-295-3309
Website: http://www.usajrf.org

Weight Training and Wrestling

National Strength and Conditioning Association (NSCA)
1885 Bob Johnson Dr.
Colorado Springs, CO 80906
Toll-Free: 800-815-6862
Phone: 719-632-6722
Fax: 719-632-6367
Toll-Free: 800-815-6826
Website: http://www.nsca-lift.org
E-mail: nsca@nsca-lift.org

United States Girls Wrestling Association
3105 Hickory Ridge Lane
Ortonville, MI 48462
Phone: 248-627-8066
Fax: 248-627-8197
Website: http://www.usgwa.com

USA Wrestling
6155 Lehman Dr.
Colorado Springs, CO 80918
Phone: 719-598-8181
Fax: 719-598-9440
Website: http://www.themat.com

Winter Sports

SkiHealth
520 S Eagle Road, Suite 1205
Meridian, ID 83642
Phone: 208-884-8300
Fax: 208-884-3903
Website: http://
www.SkiHealth.com
E-mail: info@skihealth.com

United States Ski and Snowboard Association
Box 100
Park City, Utah 84060
Phone: 435-649-9090
Website: http://www.ussa.org
E-mail: webmaster@ussa.org

U.S. Ski Team
PO Box 97254
Washington, DC 20077-7684
Toll-Free: 800-809-SNOW
Website: http://
www.usskiteam.com

Chapter 56
Suggested Additional Reading

Books

Alvin Ailey Dance Moves: A Dance-Based Approach to Movement and Exercise
By Lise Friedman
Published by Stewart, Tabori & Chang, Inc., 2003
ISBN: 158479285X

Aqua Fit: Water Workouts for Total Fitness
By Jane Katz
Published by Broadway Books, 2003
ISBN: 0767914821

Be Healthy! It's a Girl Thing: Food, Fitness, and Feeling Great
By Mavis Jukes and Lillian Wai-Yin Cheung
Published by Alfred A. Knopf, Inc., 2003
ISBN: 0679990291

Bodypride: An Action Plan for Teens Seeking Self-Esteem and Building Better Bodies
Edited by Cynthia Stamper Graff
Published by Griffin Publishing, 1997
ISBN: 188213081X

Diet Information For Teens
Edited by Karen Bellenir
Published by Omnigraphics, Inc., 2001
ISBN: 0780804414

About This Chapter: The books, articles, webpages, magazines, and newsletters in this chapter were selected from a wide variety of sources deemed accurate. Inclusion does not constitute endorsement. To make topics readily apparent, they are listed alphabetically by title within each category.

Fitness and Exercise Sourcebook, Second Edition
Edited by Kristen Gledhill
Published by Omnigraphics, Inc., 2001
ISBN: 0780803345

Healthy Teens: Facing the Challenges of Young Lives
By Alice R. McCarthy
Published by: Bridge Communications, Inc., 2000
ISBN: 0962164550

No Body's Perfect
By Kimberly Kirberger
Published by Scholastic, Inc., 2003
ISBN: 0439426383

Sports Injuries Information For Teens
Edited by Joyce Brennfleck Shannon
Published by Omnigraphics, Inc., 2003
ISBN: 0780804473

Strength and Power for Young Athletes
By Avery D. Faigenbaum and Wayne Westcott
Published by Human Kinetics Publishers, 2000
ISBN: 0736002189

The Teenage Body Book
By Kathy McCoy and Charles Wibbelsman
Published by Perigee Trade, 1999
ISBN: 0399525351

Toning for Teens: The 20-Minute Workout That Makes You Look Good and Feel Great!
By Joyce L. Vedral
Published by Warner Books, Inc., 2002
ISBN: 0446678155

Trim Kids: The Proven 12-Week Plan That Has Helped Thousands of Children Achieve a Healthier Weight
By Melinda S. Sothern, Heidi Schumacher, T. Kristian von Almen, and Alexis Seabrook
Published by HarperCollins Publishers, 2003
ISBN: 0060934174

Ultimate Fitness: The Quest for Truth about Exercise and Health
By Gina Kolata
Published by Farrar, Straus and Giroux, 2003
ISBN: 0374204772

Yoga for Teens: How to Improve Your Fitness, Confidence, Appearance and Health and Have Fun Doing It
By Thia Luby
Published by Clear Light Publishers, 1999
ISBN: 157416032X

Articles

"After Hours: Nutritional Strategies to Help You Get the Most from Your Workouts," by Paul Ward, *Muscle & Fitness*, vol. 62, no. 12, (December 2001), p. 106–110.

"Body Image," by Kathiann M. Kowalski, *Current Health 2*, vol. 29, no. 7 (Mar. 2003), p. 6–12.

"Fit or FAT," *American Fitness*, vol. 19, no. 4 (July 2001) p.10.

"Helping Kids Get Fit," by Peg Tyre and Julie Scelfo, *Newsweek*, vol. 142, no. 12 (September 22, 2003), p. 60–2.

"How Fit Are You?" by Carolyn Gard, *Current Health 2*, vol. 30, no. 1, (September 2003). p. 13–16.

"Specialized Bodybuilding Advice for Teens," by Frank Claps, *Muscle & Fitness*, vol. 63, no. 6 (June 2002), p. 158–60.

"Sports-Supplement Dangers," *Consumer Reports*, vol. 66, no. 6 (June 2001), p. 40–2.

"S-t-r-e-t-c-h Your Way to Fitness Success," *Jet*, vol. 103, no. 17 (April 21, 2003), p.20–1.

"Strong Start: Strength and Resistance Training Guidelines for Children and Adolescents," by Scott O. Roberts. *American Fitness*, vol. 20, no. 1 (January–February 2002), p. 34–38.

"Total Package (a group of articles about exercises for specific muscle groups)," *Muscle & Fitness/Hers*, vol. 3, no. 7 (December 2002).

"Training for Perfection," by Kathiann M. Kowalski, *Current Health 2*, vol. 28, no. 5 (January 2002), p. 6–12.

"Waiting to Inhale: Don't let asthma slow down your exercise regimen," by Carey Rossi Walker, *Muscle & Fitness*, vol. 62, no. 12 (December 2001), p. 102–104.

"We Exercise Every Day—And So Can You! by Betsy Dru Tecco, *Current Health 2*, vol. 30, no. 5 (January 2004), p. 30–3.

"Why Diet Drugs Can Be Diet Dangers," by Dee Murphy, *Current Health 2*, vol. 27, no. 4 (Dec. 2000), p. 18–21.

Internet Pages, Magazines, And Newsletters

ADOL: Adolescent Directory On-Line
http://education.indiana.edu/cas/adol/adol.html

American Medical Association: Adolescent Health Information
http://www.ama-assn.org/ama/pub/category/1947.html

Aquademics
http://www.aquademics.com

Bicycling Magazine
http://www.bicycling.com

Black Belt Magazine
http://w3.blackbeltmag.com

Eat Smart Play Hard
http://www.fns.usda.gov/eatsmartplayhard

Fitness for Youth
http://Fitnessforyouth.umich.edu

GirlPower!
http://www.girlpower.gov

HealthierUS
http://www.healthierus.gov

Healthy People 2010
http://www.healthypeople.gov

Legends of Gymnastics
http://www.intlgymnast.com/legends

Nutrition.gov
http://www.nutrition.gov

PaddleNews (Kayaking and Canoeing)
http://www.paddling.com

Runner's World for Kids
http://www.kidsrunning.com

Sports Illustrated for Kids
http://www.sikids.com

Swimming World
http://www.swiminfo.com

TeensHealth
http://www.teenshealth.org

Tennis Magazine
http://www.tennis.com

VERB
http://www.verbnow.com

Water Ski Magazine
http://www.waterskimag.com

Index

Index

Page numbers that appear in *Italics* refer to illustrations. Page numbers that have a small 'n' after the page number refer to information shown as Notes at the beginning of each chapter. Page numbers that appear in **Bold** refer to information contained in boxes on that page (except Notes information at the beginning of each chapter).